The DREAMers

The DREAMers

How the Undocumented Youth Movement Transformed the Immigrant Rights Debate

Walter J. Nicholls

Stanford University Press

Stanford, California

Stanford University Press
Stanford, California

Printed in the United States of America on acid-free, archival-quality paper.

Library of Congress Cataloging-in-Publication Data

Nicholls, Walter, author.
  The DREAMers : how the undocumented youth movement transformed the immigrant rights debate / Walter J. Nicholls.
     pages cm
  Includes bibliographical references and index.
  ISBN 978-0-8047-8703-1 (cloth : alk. paper)
  ISBN 978-0-8047-8884-7 (pbk. : alk. paper)
  1. Immigrant youth—Political activity—United States. 2. Illegal aliens—Political activity—United States. 3. Immigrant youth—Civil rights—United States. 4. Immigrants—Civil rights—United States. 5. Youth protest movements—United States. I. Title.
JV6477.N53 2013
325.73—dc23

                                                                    2013011191

  ISBN 978-0-8047-8869-4 (electronic)

To Marie

Contents

Figures

Acknowledgments

This book is the result of a web of personal and professional relations stretching across many years. While it would be impossible to pinpoint the precise contribution of each person who has given to this project, I would like to acknowledge the importance of some people who made this book possible in one way or another.

I began to study immigrant rights campaigns as a graduate student at the University of California, Los Angeles. Edward Soja provided important support for my early research on immigrant and labor campaigns in Los Angeles. My first colleagues at California State University, Long Beach, especially Norma Chinchilla, Gary Hytrek, and Christine Zentgraf, reinforced my interests in immigration politics in Southern California.

In 2006 much of my attention shifted to the struggles of undocumented immigrants in France. This research showed how families struggled to assert rights claims in a country that was becoming more inhospitable by the day. With almost no resources, immigrants came out of the shadows, occupied public places, faced off against aggressive police and political adversaries, and slowly cobbled together a network of supportive allies. Through my conversations with many activists, I learned that in spite of severe challenges, there was still room for extremely marginalized immigrants to build broad support among the public and leverage this support to win concessions from a hostile government. I extend my deepest gratitude to all those activists and advocates in France who spent hours teaching me the lessons of their struggles. This was the most important educational experience of my life. It provided me with the intellectual foundations needed to study the undocumented youth movement in the United States.

After moving to the University of Amsterdam in 2009, I continued to study immigrant mobilizations in France, but my attention also turned to the struggles of undocumented youth in the United States. As I took the first steps in this direction, certain people played crucial roles in introducing me to the vibrant world of immigrant youth activists. Pablo Alvarado of the National Day Laborer Organizing Network and Victor Narro and Kent Wong of the UCLA Labor Center played important roles in orienting me and introducing me to several key actors in the field.

This project could not have been done without the participation of youth activists who have worked tirelessly to advance the rights of immigrants in the United States. Youth activists affiliated with the California Dream Network and the California Immigrant Youth Justice Alliance were critical in providing information and insight into this movement. In addition to being extraordinary activists, they are also rigorous analysts of immigration politics and the mechanics of the struggle. They displayed enormous patience in teaching me the histories, trials, and complexities of the movement. I must give a special thanks to Dream Team Los Angeles. This organization welcomed two of my Dutch graduate students, Tara Fiorito and Dirk Eisema, to observe and participate in their activities during a five-month period. The members of Dream Team Los Angeles taught Tara and Dirk the ins and outs of grassroots politics and introduced them to the pleasures of Los Angeles. Tara, Dirk, and I are especially thankful to the following DREAMers for their support and friendship: Carlos Amador, Jose Beltran, Sofia Campos, Neidi Dominguez, Erick Huerta, Adrian Gonzalez, Jorge Gutierrez, Graciela Marquez, Nancy Meza, Jonathan Perez, Bupendra Ram, and Mariella Saba. I am forever grateful for their hospitality. If only more people could be as generous to strangers in a new land as these DREAMers were to my students! Also, I would like to thank Pocho-One and Julio Salgado who agreed to have their wonderful art be a part of this book.

The Department of Sociology at the University of Amsterdam proved to be an ideal environment to write this kind of book. The Programme Group on the Dynamics of Citizenship and Culture in the department provided important sources of funding to finance the field research. Our administrator, Cristina Garofalo, arranged for a teaching schedule that allowed me to spend time in the field and write up the findings. Colleagues, including Christian Broer, Jan Willem Duyvendak, Jan Rath, Evelien Tonkens, Nico Wilterdink, Olav Velthuis, Imrat Verhoeven, among many others, have provided important feedback on various papers, proposals, and presentations. I am especially grateful to Sébastien Chauvin, Olga Sezneva, Floris Vermeulen, and Jarrett Zigon, who were particularly generous with their time and insights. I would also like to thank my good friend Justus Uitermark of the Erasmus University of Rotterdam. Without our many conversations, I would have produced a very different book. Lastly, I would like to thank my students at the University of Amsterdam. Our discussions during the immigration and urban sociology seminars helped me work out a number of important theoretical knots.

Several student researchers provided crucial assistance. Sophie Roussel spent months collecting and organizing newspaper accounts and statements on the immigrant rights movement. She was an enthusiastic, bright, and effective assistant throughout this process. Tara Fiorito and Dirk Eisema performed additional interviews with youth activists and embedded themselves with Dream Team Los Angeles for five months. They embraced their roles as participant observers, gained the respect of the DREAMers, and showed great rigor in their research. They sent timely copies of their reports and provided constant Skype updates from the field. Their interpretations and analyses helped me think through the empirical material and develop several theoretical assertions. I would also like to thank the editorial team at Stanford University Press. Kate Wahl, Frances Malcolm, and Tim Roberts contributed to the slow process of transforming the early manuscript into a publishable book. Producing this work has certainly been a team effort.

My family has been an enormous source of support. Over the years my mother, Ana Maria Nicholls, nudged me to do what needed to be done. Her pragmatic advice helped to keep me on track in the face of many tempting tangents. My father, Julio Nicholls, stoked my interest in politics, books, and storytelling. For the last ten years he has been asking when I was going to write a book. I hope this work satisfies his expectations. My sister, Sharon Nicholls, has long been a major source of inspiration. For years she has worked with working-class immigrants in Los Angeles, first as an activist and then as an elementary-school teacher. Her deep commitment to social justice encouraged me to continue studying immigrant rights activism. I was also fortunate to have had an extended family with a rich sociological and political imagination. My aunt, Cecilia Menjívar, has dedicated her professional life to the study of immigrants in the United States. She has provided excellent feedback on countless papers and chapters. I could not have asked for a better mentor and colleague. My uncles, Oscar and Rolando Menjívar, provided me with an exceptional education in politics. At an early age my uncle, Rolando Menjívar, took me to demonstrations in Los Angeles to protest US military intervention in El Salvador's civil war. My other uncle, Oscar Menjívar, patiently tutored me in the twists and turns of Latin American politics. This socialization implanted an unwavering passion for politics. I would also like to express my deepest gratitude to my French family. My in-laws, Jacques and Anne Vandendries, have been enormously supportive of my academic work. They made their apartment in La Rochelle, France, available for long writing stints and helped my wife, Marie, with our children during extended periods in the field.

Last but certainly not least, I must acknowledge my immediate family. My children, Emile and Louise, were the primary source of relief during long hours of writing, researching, and teaching. They also motivated me to write this book. They should look at this book as the story of real people who have revealed terrible injustices and pushed hard to create a more just and equal world. The DREAMers should inspire them to grow into adults who do not accept the wrongs of our society as natural or normal. By documenting the stories of the DREAMers and other immigrant activists, I hope to provide Louise and Emile with a good example of how to be political in a complicated and deeply problematic world.

This book is dedicated to my wife, Marie, for everything she has done. She has been my closest and dearest confidant. Without her, nothing would have been possible.

Introduction

The Voice and Power of Undocumented Youths, an Unlikely Story

On May 17, 2010, four undocumented students occupied the Arizona office of Senator John McCain. This action was followed by a flurry of high-profile public actions around the country. Undocumented youths poured into the streets, occupied the offices of other leading politicians, filled up blogs and editorial pages with eloquent arguments, lobbied senators and White House officials, and worked their networks to gain the backing of some of the most powerful unions and rights associations in the country. Their immediate goal was to pressure the Senate to support the Development, Relief and Education for Alien Minors Act (DREAM Act), which would have provided undocumented youths the legal right to stay in the United States. The youths, or DREAMers as they came to be known, were making a powerful demand for residency status, but they were also "coming out" and demanding that they be recognized as human beings who belonged in the country. They were "good" immigrants who deserved permanent residency status, but they were also human beings who had the right to a public and political life. No longer would they accept their fate silently. They were asserting their "right to have rights": the right to have a public existence in a country that had banished them to the shadows.[1]

These political assertions contrasted sharply with the situation of undocumented youths ten years earlier, when, as a political group, undocumented youths did not exist. There were no arguments, messages, or rhetoric to represent undocumented youths and their cause in the public sphere. There were no organizations to sustain their campaigns and interventions in public life. And there were few if any networks that allowed individual youths to connect to one another and create a sense of themselves as political beings. Though these youths did not exist as a coherent *political* group, they certainly existed as a distinctive category of immigrants. By 2000, more than one million children and youths found themselves in a similar situation because of their shared immigration status. That is, they had migrated to the United States without authorization when they were children and they grew up without legal residency. They faced similar childhood experiences, common constraints upon entry into adulthood, and shared feelings of deep disappointment when realizing the difficulty of achieving their dreams and aspirations.[2] In spite of their different class, ethnic, sexual, gender, and regional backgrounds, the immigration system imposed upon these individuals a similar experience and fate. This made them into a group that was distinct from other immigrants and nationals alike.

Individuals within this group not only shared common constraints and feelings of frustration, but also pursued similar strategies to find a place in the only country they knew as their home. As children, they had a constitutionally protected right to attend elementary and high schools.[3] School administrators were forbidden to ask for proof of legal residency or to discriminate on the basis of a student's residency status. School was a place of refuge where children did not have to think about their immigration status on a daily basis. As their "illegality" faded into the background, they had an opportunity to play, study, explore, consume, socialize, and cultivate aspirations "just like anybody else." Through these kinds of everyday activities, they had become a part of America, just as America was part of them. So, while they were Mexicans, Filipino, El Salvadorans, Chinese, and Colombian by origin, they also developed a strong sense of belonging to the United States. They became American.

As the children moved into adulthood, the constraints of their "illegality" became more apparent and burdensome. Many went straight to work after high school. The lack of either a work permit or a social security number consigned most of them to precarious and low-paying work. The young adults who went to college struggled to find the means to do so. In many states, undocumented college students did not have access to in-state tuition and were denied the right to apply for financial aid. Many chose to go to less expensive community colleges rather than four-year universities. They struggled to find scholarships and worked a string of part-time jobs in the shadow economy. Their limited finances meant that many college students had to forego regular housing and meals. Figuring out how to eat and where to sleep was a constant concern. One youth who attended university away from home recounts, "I mean, it was survival. There were many times when I was like: 'What am I doing here?' I mean, I was going to school full-time, I was working full-time; I was doing everything you can think of. I had to, it was the only way. I was cleaning a lot of houses. I still remember some of my professors . . . I was like: 'It's fine! I don't mind cleaning your house. I really need the money.'"[4] Fulfilling basic physical needs was as much a part of college life as studying and passing exams. Many were able to overcome these barriers and finish their degrees, but still many others weren't. Those who dropped out of college joined the millions of other undocumented immigrants busing tables in restaurants, working in sweatshops, cleaning houses and hotels, performing day-labor jobs, mowing lawns. For those who finished college, most could not find a job in the areas they were trained because they did not have a work permit. After struggling and often failing to find employment in their professional fields, many were channeled back into the bottom end of the labor market.

In addition to facing these massive obstacles to the "American dream," the young adults have also had to contend with the countless forms of exclusion encountered in their daily lives. They have faced great difficulty driving, obtaining identification cards, opening bank accounts, going out and ordering drinks, traveling by plane, applying for "regular" jobs, or interacting with the police. These big and small forms of exclusion have served as constant reminders of their "illegality."[5] In the eyes of their American-born friends and peers, they were "normal" people and bore no outward signs of "illegality."[6] As such, they have been expected to engage in the things that "normal" young adults do. Their citizen friends asked why they couldn't drive, go to the college of their choice, obtain normal identification, or pursue their chosen careers. Responding to recurrent questions of why they couldn't do these "normal" things contributed to resurgent feelings of embarrassment, awkwardness, silence, and shame. One DREAMer recounted a personal experience:

> I remember one time, going out for dinner and I wanted to get something to drink and I showed my [Mexican] Consulate ID and I remember the server was like, "Well sorry, we cannot take this." And I was like, okay, no problem. You just want to ignore it. And I remember one of the girls with us was like, "Why don't you have an ID?" I didn't even know her because she was a friend of my friend. And I was like, "Oh . . . well . . . " You're trying to think of something quick, "Oh well, I'm not from here." And she was like, "What do you mean? Are you an illegal?" It was so degrading! You're out at night, trying to go out with your friends and have some fun. And then for someone who doesn't even know you to label you like that; it was horrible. This kind of thing never stops.[7]

Each of these kinds of experiences reminds the youths of the stigma they bear. No matter how American they may feel, look, or talk, they cannot in the last instance shed their "illegality." Faced with massive barriers and constant reminders of their absolute difference, many resign themselves to the impossibility of having a "normal" American life and seek to make the most of their lives on the margins of this inhospitable country.

The explosion of open, public, and assertive demonstrations across the country in spring 2010 marked their entry on the national political stage as the DREAMers. These youth activists collectively asserted that they were undocumented, unafraid, and unapologetic. They publicly rejected a life in the shadows and demanded the right to be recognized as rights-deserving human beings. They had developed a sophisticated set of arguments to represent themselves and their cause. They argued that they were raised in America, they only knew this country, and they were important contributors to its economic, civic, and moral life. They were not a "foreign" threat because they were Americans. They had played by all the rules and they now had a right to live out the American dream, just like anybody else. Denying them the right to live and thrive in the country would be a moral outrage and a profound injustice.

This was not an ephemeral cry. They did not just pierce the public sphere with one disruptive act—a demonstration, civil disobedience—and then quickly fade into silence after their fifteen minutes of political fame were up. Undocumented youths around the country, with the assistance of immigrant rights associations, formed college campus support groups, advocacy organizations in their communities, online networks through blogs, Facebook, Twitter and so on, and national organizations. This organizational infrastructure provided a safe and supportive environment for individuals to come out and talk about their status with others like themselves. Individual youths began to learn that they were not alone. They learned that there were hundreds and thousands of people in a very similar situation and that they were all facing common hopes, obstacles, fears, and dreams.

DREAMers in these organizations also extended their reach outward into their communities. They went to the media, high schools, churches, and community meetings to share their experiences and stories with others. The constant struggle to push their message out in these public arenas attracted more supporters and connected them to youths living their lives silently in the shadows. At one outreach meeting at a Los Angeles-area church, one DREAMer reported the following encounter to his organization:

> I noticed the girl on my right, Maria, wipe a tear from her eye. I looked across from me and saw a different girl, Cathy, whose eyes were getting red. . . . I asked Cathy if she knew someone who was undocumented. She nodded. I asked "Are you undocumented?" and she said "yes" tearfully. "Have you ever revealed yourself?" and she said "no." "So, this is your coming out," I added, and we applauded for her. She said she came here when she was nine, didn't bother going to college because she didn't know how. . . . It was at that point the girl to my right, Maria, started

crying. . . . She said, "Let me tell you my story. I was my class Valedictorian. I had perfect grades. I was all set to get a full scholarship to any school of my choice. It was then that they said there was a problem with my social security number. I went home and my mother said she made it up. I didn't have one. I tried to go to college, but had to work, it was too much." What's interesting, Maria and Cathy didn't know this about each other. . . . So in the end, what started out as a presentation to a group unsure of their own mission for a community project became a coming out of the shadows. . . . *I'm going to say it again, without even trying, we find the undocumented, we find allies, we get stronger. Imagine what we can do if we set our minds to it.*[8]

The constant effort to extend their organizational reach out into their communities has provided new opportunities to establish connections to isolated and unconnected youths. The complex and intertwined DREAMer organizations that developed in the latter part of the 2000s allowed individual youths to discover their group by connecting individuals to one another and providing them with enormous amounts of support.

DREAMer organizations and networks have also helped to circulate arguments and messages concerning why undocumented youths deserve the right to live in the country. Through their interactions with other undocumented youths, they learned the discourses, arguments, and messages that framed their claims to equal rights. By talking about their feelings, dreams, rights, and injustices, the youths absorbed the themes of their incipient movement. This kind of political socialization helped shape how they thought and felt about their own "illegality." They learned that there was nothing to be ashamed of. They also learned that sticking together as a group allowed them to make powerful claims for equal rights. There was power in numbers and in a morally compelling argument. Their message and commitment made it possible to occupy the offices of senators and of Homeland Security and to undertake acts of civil disobedience. Their formation into a self-conscious and an internally bounded group made it possible to gain support from broad swaths of the public and mitigate the risks of detention and deportation. Even in the most hostile states like Arizona, protesting DREAMers had become "undeportable." By coming out and saying "undocumented, unafraid, and unapologetic," they had demonstrated that a life outside the shadows was possible for themselves and all undocumented immigrants. This dramatic expression of equality was possible only after the youths had become a political group with its own representations, arguments, organizations, solidarities, and beliefs in what was good and just.

This book charts the remarkable transformation of dispersed undocumented youths into the powerful political group of the DREAMers. It intends to explain how, in the span of ten years, this group came to assume a leading role in the country's immigration debates. This is not only the story of the DREAMers but of the entire immigrant rights movement because the DREAMers did not emerge in a vacuum. They emerged from a longer-standing movement. The leading rights associations in the movement took a role in crafting the representations of the youths, setting up DREAM organizations and connecting youth activists, and training the youths to carry their messages into the public sphere. The DREAMers were conceived by these national immigrant rights associations as a way to push the general struggle for immigrant rights forward in a context where few political opportunities existed. While large and professional rights associations sought to exercise control over the DREAMers, the youth eventually asserted autonomy and control over their own struggle and their place within the immigrant rights movement. They assumed a place as first among equals within the movement, collaborating, deciding, and mobilizing fellow DREAMers alongside other groups and actors in the immigrant rights movement. Together, they would not only push for the passage of the DREAM Act but also for the rights of all undocumented immigrants living in the United States.

Producing a Voice in a Hostile Context

The formation of the DREAMers and their strong presence on the national political stage presents us with an interesting puzzle because it departs from our standard sociological expectations. Much of the recent scholarship on immigration politics from the United States and

Europe suggests that hostile environments would encourage undocumented immigrants to turn away from the public sphere of receiving countries. The scholarship suggests that growing nationalism and xenophobia offer few if any opportunities for stigmatized immigrants to make strong public claims to rights.[9] Most natives have difficulty recognizing undocumented immigrants as human beings with basic inalienable rights because they have been portrayed as threats and polluters of the national community.[10] Rather than being "persons" with inalienable rights protected by law, they are considered "aliens" whose lives are governed by arbitrary government decrees. Giorgio Agamben suggests, "In the system of the nation-state, *the so-called sacred and inalienable rights of man show themselves to lack every protection at the moment in which they can no longer take the form of rights belonging to citizens of a state.*"[11] The "illegality" of undocumented immigrants provides further justification that their basic rights can be arbitrarily rescinded by the will of the majority.[12] Under these conditions, achieving legitimacy for claims to basic rights would be difficult if not *impossible.*[13] Those undocumented immigrants who mobilized in these contexts not only would be perceived as "noise" from a foreign and illegitimate mob, but also would risk detection, detention, and deportation for themselves and their families.[14] Undocumented immigrants have, therefore, been cast into the shadows of the private arena, tending to their basic physical survival and avoiding the public and political worlds of receiving countries.

If the shadows were indeed the fate of undocumented immigrants, how could the DREAMers have created a strong and legitimate voice in the public sphere? This group of undocumented immigrants learned how to construct compelling rights claims, identify public arenas, such as campuses and the Internet, to express their claims, plan and undertake high-risk protests, and lobby public officials to support bills recognizing their rights and the rights of other undocumented immigrants in the country.

What is even more puzzling is that the DREAMers do not appear to be alone. Undocumented immigrants in countries as diverse as Spain, France, the United Kingdom, Germany, and the Netherlands have brought their cases directly into the public sphere, argued that the current system is unjust and has wronged them, and developed power-ful and broadly supported rights claims.[15] Rather than turn away from the public sphere as an arena to be avoided, these activists have trans-formed the public spheres in the United States and other countries into strategic places for making rights claims. To draw on the language of the lesbian and gay rights movement, "coming out" has become more advantageous than "staying in the closet."

We know why undocumented immigrants *should* turn away from hostile political worlds, but we cannot explain how certain undocu-mented groups like the DREAMers struggle to create a public, power-ful, and legitimate voice in hostile countries. That is, we can account for their "exit" into the shadows, but we cannot explain how such "pariahs" of law and nation create a public "voice."[16] Some recent schol-arship on the immigrant rights movement in the United States moves us in the right direction for understanding these issues, but research still falls short of providing an account of how a legitimate and public voice for undocumented immigrants is produced.[17] For example, these studies describe and analyze how activists, advocates, and supporters mobilized in massive demonstrations in 2006 to fight repressive immi-gration bills, but they do not address the core issue of how undocu-mented immigrants overcome barriers, construct a powerful and legiti-mate voice, and assert this voice in the public sphere. We learn from these studies that the making of a voice is possible, but we still lack the theoretical tools to understand how this is actually done.

In telling the unlikely story of how disparate undocumented youths became a politically identifiable group called the DREAMers, the book analyzes how a legitimate "public" voice was produced for this group. Creating such a voice was not a matter of choice, but rather was the product of a long, complicated process. Undocumented youths in 2001 did not suddenly choose to craft a voice that would trans-mit their claims for rights into the public sphere. These young adults started their battles facing a major hurdle—they were branded as "ille-gal aliens" and were therefore not recognized as legitimate claims mak-ers or holders of inalienable rights. Crafting a voice required them to undertake an arduous process of finding small cracks in the legal and moral systems of the country, making arguments for why their group deserved basic rights, gaining the support of many different allies, and asserting a certain degree of unity and discipline within their ranks.

Generally speaking, all undocumented immigrants have faced an environment made up of general hostility *and* several "niche openings." On the one hand, undocumented immigrants in the United States, especially from Latin America, have faced great hostility in the past twenty years. They have been represented as competitors for jobs and freeloaders on an overburdened public sector.[18] Their "illegality" makes them a threat to national sovereignty and the rule of law. Seen by most natives as less than fully human, anti-immigrant activists and policymakers have called for the suspension of basic rights, the rollout of harsh enforcement measures, and the enhancement of border security.[19] The "war on terror" only intensified feelings of hostility and fear, with anti-immigrant advocates and policymakers making direct links between immigrants, borders, and terrorists.[20] Hostility and enhanced enforcement during the 1990s and early 2000s therefore closed down political opportunities for big immigration reforms and elevated the risks of public protest for undocumented immigrants. On the other hand, legal, economic, and moral ambiguities have arisen over the extent to which *all* undocumented immigrants should be considered fully "illegal."[21]

Such ambiguities combine to create "niche openings" for groups of immigrants, including students, youths, children, family members, and workers in certain sectors, who may be considered deserving of some form of legal residency status. Just as the government has developed ways to further rollback the rights of undocumented immigrants, legal openings have emerged for cases protected by the Constitution, the courts, and international treaties (in the cases of families, children, asylum seekers, and so on).[22] Moreover, a number of industries have pressured the government to ensure continued access to a steady supply of immigrant labor, such as in the areas of agriculture, hospitality, and construction.[23] The rollout of more enforcement and border security measures has prompted these industries to make increased demands for exceptions for certain categories of immigrant workers. Lastly, some groups of immigrants may elicit sympathy from important segments of the native population because they may possess attributes that resonate strongly with national values and humanitarian norms.[24] Some groups of immigrants may be well assimilated, have good and useful jobs, possess families with small children, or exhibit some other attributes that resonate with the values and moralities of nationals. The public may be swayed to support exceptions for these morally ambivalent cases while still demanding that the government ensure border closure for most others.

Undocumented immigrants face a unique political environment characterized by closure for most but niche openings for some groups in possession of strategic legal, economic, and cultural attributes. In this environment, the possibilities for major reforms, amnesties, and legalizations are extremely limited, encouraging immigrant rights advocates to push for narrow groups and issues that stand much greater chances of success (that is, piecemeal measures). In 2001, national immigrant rights associations and their allies in Congress believed that a niche opening existed for undocumented youths, precipitating the creation of the decade long DREAM campaign.

Niche openings have been a necessary condition for some undocumented immigrants to gain a foothold, but they are by no means sufficient for creating a legitimate and convincing public voice. A group of undocumented immigrants, like the undocumented youths of this book, presented with a narrow opening continue to face powerful adversaries. Anti-immigrant advocates respond to the rights claims of immigrants with the slogan: "What part of illegal don't you understand?"[25] In spite of the special circumstances or situations of a group, antagonists believe that their essential "illegality" makes them totally ineligible of any rights in the country. Facing these powerful headwinds, a group of undocumented immigrants struggling to assert a voice must craft representations that counter the stigmatizing arguments of their adversaries and build a sympathetic public portrait of their group. They construct a representation of the group focused narrowly on the attributes that match the existing niche opening.[26] Their messages, talking points, and emotional stories stress the most strategic qualities of the group, silencing those other aspects that may distort their central message. These representations help transform a diverse array of individuals—with many different qualities, backgrounds, and cultures—into a coherent and deserving "group" that fits an available niche.[27] In addition to demonstrating their fit in a narrow opening, they must also demonstrate their fit in the country. This involves crafting discourses that cleanse the group of the polluting stigmas attributed to undocumented immigrants.[28] Well-placed immigrants, like undocumented youths, must demonstrate that they are not free riders, unassimilated, culpable for their illegality, or irreducibly foreign. It also helps to be able to demonstrate both conformity to national values and the ways they stand to make an important contribution to the country. Their hard work ethic, love of family, and civic engagement build on core national values and reinvigorate the moral and economic life of the nation.[29] Demonstrating *national identification* strengthens the argument that they are not a threat to the nation but an exceptional group that deserves an exemption from exclusionary immigration rules. Natives can thus begin to recognize that these exceptional immigrants are human beings who may deserve the right to reside in the country legally. Once the strategy of national identification reveals their humanity, support may broaden and the group of undocumented immigrants can transform a narrow opening into a real and sustained political opportunity.

This discursive strategy is by no means the only strategy available to a group. But under conditions of intense hostility, it is the strategy that is likely to be the most effective. More radical arguments calling for the end of borders and the immediate extension of full citizenship to all undocumented immigrants, irrespective of their attributes, would likely be rejected as the "noise" of "crazy illegals" and not the "voice" of a deserving and reasonable group of immigrants. Rights advocates are quite conscious of this. While they are by no means bound to pursue the strategy described above, many select this strategy over the alternatives because it is better able to gain the support of a leery and antagonistic public.

Good representations are important but so too are strong and supportive networks. Crafting a voice requires ties with well-established advocacy groups and rights associations. High levels of cultural and symbolic capital are needed to produce a strong and legitimate voice.[30] Rights advocates must have an intimate knowledge of the political culture of the country and understand how to pitch messages in ways that resonate with natives at intellectual, moral, and emotional levels.[31] They must also possess enough symbolic capital (that is, legitimacy) to ensure that what they say is considered reasonable and believable by the national public. Lastly, they must possess connections with media gatekeepers who can assist in transmitting their frames, messages, and talking points to the public. While these forms of cultural and symbolic capital are necessary for producing compelling representations, they are not equally distributed across the immigrant rights movement. Newly arrived or newly politicized undocumented immigrants are unlikely to possess sufficient levels of capital needed to produce effective and believable representations. The nationally specific nature of cultural and symbolic capital means that even the most sophisticated newcomers will have difficulty representing their demands and concerns in the most appropriate ways. The relative poverty of recent immigrant activists, both in terms of cultural and symbolic capital, requires them to depend on well-established advocacy organizations in possession of these scarce resources, such as professional immigrant rights associations, labor unions, religious organizations, and so on.[32] These "support" organizations provide crucial resources to immigrants including legal knowledge, knowledge of national political cultures and institutions, legitimacy, and communication expertise. They can use these strategic resources to translate the rights claims of the immigrant group into powerful arguments that resonate with the norms and values of the national public. The "voice" of the undocumented immigrant is therefore not necessarily crafted by undocumented immigrants themselves but well-established support associations, *at least in the early stages of a campaign.*

The DREAMer as a political group was not necessarily created by undocumented youths themselves. Rather, professional rights associations identified a niche for well-integrated undocumented students in 2001 and launched a campaign to pass the DREAM Act. Investing considerable cultural and symbolic capital, leading immigrant rights associations created the public figure of the "DREAMer." They argued that these youths were exceptionally good immigrants and particularly deserving of legalization. These associations were responsible for introducing the issue of undocumented college students into Congress, deciding what strategy was right for the youths, crafting and controlling their representation in the public sphere, and representing them directly to political officials and the media. While this representation was crafted in the earlier years of the mobilization (2001–8), it served as a framework that influenced how activists in later years produced messages and arguments about themselves and their cause.

Good representations need to be transmitted into the public sphere in a disciplined manner. If activists do not impose discipline on their public message, the message will neither stick nor be well received by the general public. In countless cases, the claims of protesters pierce the public sphere and then quickly fade from the public's political imagination, as was the case with the Occupy Wall Street mobilizations in 2011. In other instances, aggrieved protesters may be rejected by the public as noise from an unruly mob.[33] Creating and sustaining legitimacy for a group of stigmatized outsiders requires the leadership to impose discipline on both the message and the messengers. In the case of the DREAMers campaign, the leadership centralized message production, structured messages through the use of talking points, and silenced utterances and symbols that detracted from the core argument. Just as important, they disciplined undocumented youth activists who were responsible for carrying the message into the public sphere. Disciplining youth activists was a challenging task considering the thousands of different activists and organizations involved in various DREAM campaigns. By the second half of the 2000s, immigrant rights associations had developed a complex and integrated infrastructure to produce a common message and to train activists in localities around the country. The leaders sought to diffuse talking points downward into the grassroots. Training sessions helped socialize youth activists into the DREAMer discourse, shaped their views of their place and rights in the country, and contributed to forming individual undocumented youths into a common political subject with common worldviews, aspirations, and emotional dispositions.[34] This disciplinary infrastructure therefore kept activists on message, but it also transformed youths into actual DREAMers who saw, felt, and experienced their political worlds in very similar ways.

The steps described above—namely, identifying niche openings, crafting compelling representations, forming strategic alliances, disciplining messages and messengers—have provided a narrow path for a group of undocumented immigrants to produce a legitimate voice. Recognition of a group's legitimacy does not lead to the automatic extension of legal rights. It only makes it *possible* for this group's legalization to become an issue of legitimate public debate. However, the process that gives legitimacy to a political group also generates many contradictions. The long and arduous struggle to create a political group with a legitimate voice has rendered important cleavages between the different allies involved. These cleavages have resulted in forceful disagreements and conflicts over who deserves rights, how rights should be represented, and who should be representing immigrants and their struggles in the public sphere. While these disagreements risk fragmenting the immigrant rights movement, they also introduce new ideas about what rights are and what are the best strategies to achieve them. The disagreements resulting from internal contradictions can certainly be destructive, but they can also be moments of great creativity, where different activists and advocates discover new ways to push their struggles for equality and justice forward.

Stressing the attributes that make some groups of undocumented immigrants deserving of legalization contributes to sharpening differences with other undocumented groups. By representing individuals with select attributes as exceptional, advocates assert that the possession of these scarce attributes makes their case more deserving and pressing than others. DREAMers have stressed high levels of assimilation, education, and innocence as the attributes that make the case of undocumented youths compelling and exceptional. Other immigrants who lack these attributes, including adults, unassimilated, poor and dependent, "guilty," and so on, may find it more difficult to make arguments in support of themselves and their cause. The political success of a group can reinforce legal as well as rhetorical obstacles. Political success means establishing new categories (for example, DREAM-eligibility) with restrictive eligibility criteria (age, time in the country, education requirements, and so on). The rhetoric of the "deserving immigrant" is enacted into real legal categories, resulting in the unequal distribution of rights and privileges on the basis of one's possession of strategic attributes. Niche openings therefore provide undocumented immigrants with one of the only realistic pathways in a closed and hostile environment, but responding to these openings aggravates important discursive and legal cleavages between legalizable and unlegalizable immigrants. This gives rise to critiques directed at a strategy that seeks out exceptions for privileged groups of immigrants. Critics may then push for a more radical and universal position that rights should be granted to everybody irrespective of their exceptional attributes. This cleavage is and remains an important source of tension, disagreement, and reflection within the contemporary immigrant rights movement.

When human and immigrant rights associations assume central roles in representing undocumented immigrants to media and politicians, rank-and-file undocumented activists may give rise to another set of cleavages. Leading associations assume a central role in designing the strategy, setting up targets and priorities, creating the messaging campaign, and training the activists to deliver the message in a disciplined fashion. Leaders believe that by controlling representations, the movement is better able to produce and deliver messages and arguments in public, which in turn increases the chance of achieving the goal of legalization. However, dominance of these associations—run mostly by university-educated, middle-class citizens—over the representational process introduces an important cleavage with rank-and-file undocumented activists. Many in the rank and file may begin to question whether leading immigrant rights associations can actually represent the "true" interests of undocumented immigrants. In 2010, as leading rights associations sought to control the discourse and strategy of the campaign, many DREAMers and youth activists felt deprived of the possibilities to speak for themselves in the public sphere. Unable to express their own voices in *their* campaign led some DREAMers to rethink the meaning of their struggle for equality. If it was about gaining the legal right to stay in the country, it was now also about gaining recognition for themselves as political equals who could speak for themselves.[35] Being able to speak in the public sphere was viewed as a precondition of equality, so the act of representing became not simply a means to an end, as the association believed, but rather an end in its own right. Those blocking their abilities to speak, namely, the leading associations, were therefore viewed as blocking undocumented youths from achieving equality in the polis. DREAMers continued to criticize the government for denying them the right to stay in the country, but they now also criticized the immigrant rights associations for denying them the right to represent themselves.

The efforts of DREAM activists and their allies created a political group with a compelling and legitimate voice by 2010 and 2011. But this group was by no means unified. The process of producing the group and its voice necessarily introduced disagreements and conflicts. These disagreements have been a double-edged sword: they are destructive because they give rise to factionalism that can undermine the collective power of the movement, but they are also creative because they help generate new ideas and discourses about equality, rights, and citizenship. Debates and disagreements permit activists to discover the limits of preexisting strategies and create new ones that they believe are more appropriate, inclusive, and equal. Such disagreements disrupt the reproduction of older and sometimes exclusionary understandings of rights, for example, stressing national belonging, and point out new directions outside the well-worn strategies and notions of the past.[36] The new discourses and views that emerged since 2010 have sat beside those produced in earlier stages of the movement, resulting in a cacophony of arguments, frames, utterances, strategies, and visions in the same social movement.

The process of creating a political group with a legitimate voice does not simply result in discourses that affirm a single idea of citizenship. Rather, it produces multiple discourses, ideas, and schemas of citizenship, some of which complement one another and some of which conflict. The very difficult challenge for a mature rights movements, made up of many different factions and arguments, is to stitch together some of these discordant discourses into a compelling mobilization frame that convinces *both* the fractious activists making up the movement and the more conservative publics making up the nation.[37]

I use the term "DREAMer" to describe politically active undocumented young adults who self-identify as "DREAMers" and who have worked in campaigns to advance the rights of undocumented youth in the country. The DREAMers are remarkable for many reasons. This group has become a driving force of immigration debates and politics in spite of its political nonexistence before 2001. While the DREAMers have not yet succeeded in passing the federal DREAM Act, they enter 2013 with great momentum and have played a leading role in pushing for large-scale immigration reform. This book reveals that while there are certain networks, histories, claims, and feelings that produce a common political group, there are many differences that distinguish the individuals making up this political group. I have drawn on newspapers, the online interventions of DREAMers, interviews, and participant observation to highlight these commonalities and differences (see Appendix for full discussion of methods). The study focuses on the DREAMers in Southern California and uses them as a window for understanding the national movement. This approach makes it harder to make big claims about the "national" character of the movement, but it provides us with the depth needed to understand its microscopic dynamics. By uncovering such dynamics, we are in a better place to understand how these youths achieved a degree of unity and power in the face of all the differences making up their group.

The case of the DREAMers is unique, but I believe their struggle provides important lessons for other undocumented immigrants and marginalized peoples struggling for rights in the United States and beyond. The most important lesson is that while struggles for rights are difficult for highly stigmatized groups, they are not impossible. The process is hard, piecemeal, nonlinear, and full of contradictions and internal conflicts. We learn that even when governments take aggressive measures to exclude certain groups, cracks often open up in defensive walls and provide outsiders with small niche openings. When outsiders can demonstrate their fit in a niche, they can begin to enhance their legitimacy and expand their bases of support. As these struggles gain traction, they may open up possibilities for some groups but also introduce new closures for others. The contradictory nature of these struggles introduces questions and disagreements into these movements, which compel constant reflections over rights and the most appropriate strategies for achieving them. The book is, therefore, specifically about the DREAMers, but their remarkable case informs our general understandings of how outcast groups struggle for rights, equality, and respect in hostile countries.

[Narrator's ominous voice] They keep coming, two million illegal immigrants in California. The federal government won't stop them at the border yet requires us to spend billions to take care of them. Governor Pete Wilson sent the National Guard to help the border patrol. But that's not all: [Governor Wilson appears on screen] "For Californians who work hard, pay taxes, and obey the laws, I'm suing the federal government to control the borders. And I'm working to deny state services to illegal immigrants. Enough is enough!"

Governor Pete Wilson, campaign advertisement, 1994[1]

I have no doubt that individual minority persons can assimilate to the culture necessary to run an advanced society . . . but if through mass migration, the culture of the homeland is transplanted from Latin America to California, then my guess is we will see the same degree of success with governmental and social institutions that we have seen in Latin America.

Letter from John Tanton, U.S. Inc., to Roy Beck, Numbers USA, 1996[2]

In this new era, the single most immediate and most serious challenge to America's traditional identity comes from the immense and continuing immigration from Latin America, especially from Mexico. . . . [T]hey [Americans] have overlooked the unique characteristics and problems posed by contemporary Hispanic immigration. The extent and nature of this immigration differ fundamentally from those of previous immigration, and the assimilation successes of the past are unlikely to be duplicated with the contemporary flood of immigrants from Latin America. This reality poses a fundamental question: Will the United States remain a country with a single national language and a core Anglo-Protestant culture? By ignoring this question, Americans acquiesce to their eventual transformation into two peoples with two cultures (Anglo and Hispanic) and two languages (English and Spanish).

Samuel Huntington, Professor of Government, Harvard University,
Fellow of the American Academy of Arts and Sciences[3]

1

Finding Political Openings in a Hostile Country

The immigrant rights movement emerged in the late 1980s and 1990s during a time of great hostility toward immigrants. By that time, anti-immigration advocates had become more sophisticated, national, and legitimate. They included well-respected politicians such as Pete Wilson, scholars such as Samuel Huntington, and sophisticated grassroots activists with national-level reach such as John Tanton and Roy Beck. Many like them argued that immigrants posed an economic problem to the country, but even more importantly, they argued that their inherent culture posed an existential threat to national institutions and identity. Anti-immigration advocates in the 1990s had not only been successful in pushing the idea of the immigrant as a central threat to the country, but they also succeeded in persuading President Clinton and the Republican-controlled Congress to pass laws that rolled back rights, sharply expanded border enforcement, and required local and state officials to deny basic services to immigrants. Most politicians embraced the anti-immigrant ferment and accepted sealing borders and deporting settled undocumented immigrants as common-sense policy responses to this so-called threat. The "war on terror" only augmented hostility and reinforced the "border first" and enforcement instincts of political officials.

Facing greater penalties, restrictions, and surveillance, all undocumented immigrants encountered considerable risks to come out in public, protest, and make rights claims. How was it possible, in that environment, for undocumented youths to emerge and establish themselves as a prominent group in national immigration debates?

In a rather paradoxical way, the more the government pushed to seal the borders, the more ambiguities and cracks surfaced in the country's immigration system. Repressive measures ran up against liberal legal norms, economic needs of employers, the resource constraints of law enforcement agencies, and humanitarian and moral concerns of the public. A political landscape characterized by general hostility and many cracks provided narrow openings for undocumented groups like refugees, farmworkers, children, and young adults to make claims for basic rights and legalization. While the inhospitable environment reduced the possibilities for big and sweeping immigration reforms, small niche openings provided footholds to push for the legalization of some groups of immigrants. This resulted in an immigrant rights movement characterized by narrower mobilizations and campaigns (from El Salvadoran refugees in the 1990s to the DREAM campaign in the 2000s) aimed at pushing smaller measures that would benefit particular groups of immigrants.

The years 2006–7 marked an important shift in this political environment. After a decade of enacting one restrictive measure after another, the population of undocumented immigrants had grown dramatically and the cracks and contradictions in the country's immigration system had become unavoidable. In response to these problems and the political concerns of top Republican strategists, the Bush administration initiated an effort to pass reforms to fix what many believed to be a broken system. For many immigrant rights advocates, this new opportunity required them to rethink the past strategy of small mobilizations pushing piecemeal reforms. Even though these first efforts to pass comprehensive reform failed, immigrant rights advocates believed that they could pass comprehensive immigration bill in a friendlier Congress if the movement centralized its efforts, both organizationally and strategically, and focused exclusively on securing the 279 congressional votes needed to pass a bill (that is, 219 House votes and 60 Senate votes).[4] The DREAM Act would be part of comprehensive reform and the DREAMers would serve as an important group in driving this collective effort forward. Thus, in response to the new openings of 2006, the leading immigrant rights associations began a long effort to centralize and exert control over the many different parts of the movement, hoping that would allow them to focus their energies on pushing through a sweeping law that would benefit most undocumented immigrants once and for all.

The Hostile 1990s

Immigrants and immigrant rights advocates in the 1990s faced an extremely hostile discursive and political environment.[5] Anti-immigrant forces had begun to produce compelling messages for why federal and state governments should strip immigrants of all rights (social, political, and civil) and forcefully remove them from the country. Immigrants were presented as a core threat to national stability, both economically and culturally. They were viewed as transforming large parts of urban and suburban landscapes into ethnic spaces, making Americans into foreigners in their own country. Immigrants were accused of competing for jobs and being welfare cheats. They drove down the wages of the American working class while bankrupting the welfare state. Anti-immigrant forces argued that even if some immigrants might have sympathetic stories, it would be impossible to grant them basic rights because that would open the "floodgates" for more immigrants. In order to sustain the integrity of the nation in these global times, tight border restrictions should be put into place and no rights should be given to "illegals." This overall argument was framed as a matter of life or death for the country.

Where earlier anti-immigrant mobilizations had largely been local and fragmented,[6] in the late 1980s and early 1990s, anti-immigrant activists began to deliver their message on the national stage through the increased prominence of large and professional anti-immigration associations (for example, Federation for American Immigration Reform, Americans for Immigration Control, Numbers USA, U.S. Inc., among others).[7] These national organizations served as important vehicles for presenting a strong and compelling anti-immigration message to the media and Congress. Meanwhile, a new generation of public intellectuals began to articulate a coherent discourse that painted immigrants, particularly Latino immigrants, as a *cultural* threat, not simply an economic one, to the nation.[8] They claimed that Latinos failed to become a part of the national fabric, and because of their inability to assimilate, these immigrants threatened the cultural coherence of the country. In 1996 Stanford historian David Kennedy wrote in an *Atlantic Monthly* essay, "They [Latinos] can challenge the existing cultural, political, legal, commercial, and educational systems to change fundamentally not only the language but also the very institutions in which they do business. . . . In the process, Americans can be pitched into a soul-searching redefinition of fundamental ideas such as the meaning of citizenship and national identity."[9] Latino immigrants were, in short, *irreducibly* different from "normal" Americans. This assertion was coupled with the argument that some Latinos sought to reconquer the American Southwest (*la Reconquista*), with prominent commentators like Patrick Buchanan arguing that Mexicans were a fifth column in the country. According to Leo Chavez, the immigrant threat discourse therefore rested on three major themes: Latinos as competitors for scarce resources; Latinos as irreducibly other; and Latinos as a political force seeking the territorial dissolution of the nation.

Framed in these ways, immigration was an existential problem that required some kind of action by local, state, and national government officials. Anti-immigrant advocates presented a zero-tolerance line, arguing that recognizing even the most basic right of the most innocent immigrant introduced major risks to the national community. When governments recognized the rights of seemingly sympathetic and innocent undocumented immigrants for limited services, immigrants would use this as a toehold to make additional rights claims. This would allow them to accumulate a range of additional rights and privileges in a slow and incremental way. For instance, once primary education was provided to seemingly innocent undocumented children as the result of the Supreme Court ruling *Plyler v. Doe* in 1982, the children graduated from high school and expected the right to attend higher education and work in the country.[10] Granting these rights and privileges would eventually result in the de facto legalization of the population at best, a broad amnesty at worst. Additionally, anti-immigration advocates argued that recognizing basic rights served as a magnet for further rounds of immigration. Recognizing the rights of children born in the United States, who were called "anchor babies," opened the door to legalizing the status of parents, grandparents, aunts, uncles, and cousins through family reunification laws. Each immigrant, no matter how innocent or deserving, was conceived as a virus that threatened to spread and eventually drain life from the national host. The aim of anti-immigration advocates was therefore not only to enhance border protections and aggressively strip immigrants of all basic rights but also to apply severe restrictions equally to all undocumented groups. By building a strong and impenetrable wall through border security, enforcement, and the rollback of basic rights, undocumented immigrants would not be able to implant themselves in localities and spread to communities across America. This idea and its associated policy proposals came to be known as "attrition through enforcement" or "self-deportation."

These arguments achieved great resonance in the public sphere and helped structure the media's framing of the immigration issue.[11] National magazines including *US News and World Report, Time, Newsweek, Business Week*, and others employed the "Latino threat" discourse to frame reporting and editorials on the subject of immigration.[12] As the discourse was diffused through the media, it helped shape public perceptions on immigration. Massey and Pren note, "The relentless propagandizing that accompanied the shift had a pervasive effect on public opinion, turning it decidedly more conservative on issues of immigration even as it was turning more conservative with respect to social issues more generally."[13] The effects of media on public perceptions were most powerful in areas undergoing rapid demographic changes: "Sudden demographic changes generate uncertainty and attention. Coverage of immigration in the media can inform people about demographic changes and can politicize those changes in people's minds. Acting in tandem, local demographics and nationally salient issues can produce anti-immigrant attitudes and outcomes."[14]

In the 1990s these arguments were bolstered by the support of key politicians with national reach. Governor Pete Wilson of California played a particularly important role in 1994. Entering an election year with low levels of voter satisfaction, the one-time moderate Republican took a strong anti-immigration position in his bid for reelection and expressed strong support for Proposition 187 (known as the Save Our State [SOS] initiative). This measure aimed to deny undocumented immigrants the right to key social services and undocumented children the right to attend primary and secondary schools.[15] Wilson became one of the first national-level politicians to use publicly the term "self-deportation," and he held up Proposition 187 as a model policy to achieve these ends.[16] His overwhelming reelection was attributed to his support of the measure, giving state and local politicians around the country a blueprint to win campaigns. Proposition 187 won with 59 percent of the vote, only to be deemed unconstitutional by several federal courts.

Seeking to preempt a patchwork of local and state-level variants of Proposition 187, the Clinton administration introduced measures to enhance border security. In 1994, the government introduced Operation Gatekeeper, which reinforced the southern border by expanding the number of border agents by 1,000 per year until 2001, reinforcing the border fence, and bolstering other surveillance methods.[17] In 1996, the Clinton administration supported the Illegal Immigration Reform and Immigrant Responsibility Act (IIRIRA), which allocated more resources to border-enforcement and deterrence measures.[18] In addition to allocating more money to border protection, IIRIRA expanded monitoring of immigrant entry and exit data, expedited deportations by lowering the threshold of deportable offenses, restricted judicial discretion during deportation proceedings, and extended periods of admissibility for deported immigrants, among other things. According to Durand and Massey, between 1996 and 1998 the budget of the Immigration and Naturalization Service grew by eight times and the budget of the Border Patrol by six.[19] In this very short period, the latter agency was transformed from one of the most insignificant federal law enforcement agencies in the country into the most funded and best armed.

The heavy emphasis on border enforcement had important effects, but decreasing the number of undocumented immigrants was not one of them.[20] Between 1988 and 2002, border crossings shifted from traditional points around San Diego, California, to nontraditional areas in the eastern desert. Arizona increasingly became an entryway for unauthorized border crossings. The increased risks of crossing the border raised the monetary costs of migration, which in turn favored the expansion of the human-smuggling industry. The death rate of unauthorized border crossings also tripled as immigrants were compelled to pass through dangerous desert terrain. The growing costs and risks of crossing resulted in a lower return rate for migrants, decreasing from approximately 50 percent in 1986 to 25 percent in 2007.[21] As immigration rates continued to hold steady and return rates plummeted, more immigrants permanently settled in the country, which contributed to the rapid growth of the undocumented population. The population of undocumented immigrants, in other words, grew as a direct response to border enforcement, growing from an estimated 7 million in 1997 to 10 million in 2002 and then to 11.9 million in 2008.

Border enforcement encouraged not only permanent settlement but also families to take hold inside the country. As border enforcement raised the costs and risks of circular migration, migrants were encouraged to raise their families in the United States.[22] By 2008 nearly half of undocumented immigrant households were couples with children.[23] While 73 percent of the children of undocumented immigrants were citizens by birth, approximately 1.5 million children were undocumented. This came to account for approximately 16 percent of the total undocumented population.[24] The unanticipated consequence of restrictive immigration has therefore been to accelerate family settlement, which has given rise to households with very mixed legal statuses ranging from citizens, permanent residents, temporary residents, to unauthorized migrants and a large population of undocumented children. These undocumented children would eventually fill the ranks of the DREAM mobilizations of the 2000s.

While the population of undocumented immigrants grew and became much more complex, it faced increasingly hostile environments as rights and privileges were rolled back and better enforcement measures were developed to detect and extract immigrants.[25] In addition to expanding external border security, IIRIRA created a memorandum of understanding called the 287(g) agreements between federal immigration and local police agencies. These agreements empowered local authorities to enforce federal immigration laws. They also provided local police officials important levels of financial support and training to take on these additional responsibilities. While this program was voluntary, it provided strong incentives for local police agencies to assume a direct role in detecting and removing undocumented immigrants residing in their jurisdictions.[26] Congress, with the support of President Clinton, also passed the Personal Responsibility and Work Opportunity Reconciliation Act of 1996 (PROWARA). This law introduced key restrictions on welfare support for permanent and undocumented immigrants.[27] This measure made permanent immigrants ineligible for a range of benefits, including food stamps, Supplementary Security Income, welfare, and nonemergency Medicaid for the first five years of their residency in the United States. Undocumented immigrants were made ineligible for publicly funded state and local services. States were permitted to provide undocumented immigrants with in-state services, including in-state tuition for higher education, only if they passed a law that explicitly stated the law's support of this population.[28] These measures therefore enhanced the enforcement capacities of the federal government by integrating state and local government officials into its efforts. Local and state officials were now required to use the immigration status of residents as a criterion of detecting whether people belonged in their communities and whether they merited basic rights and privileges.[29]

Many states and municipalities not only fulfilled their new responsibilities to fight unauthorized migration, but also the new laws increased their leeway to enact their own anti-immigration laws and ordinances. Beginning in the late 1990s and early 2000s, municipalities across the country passed ordinances that specifically targeted the legal status of residents. Some of these ordinances fined landlords and businesses that entered contracts with undocumented immigrants. Other municipalities devised housing regulations to minimize immigrant residency and banned public assembly associated with day-laborer hiring sites.[30] These local measures went on to inspire exclusionary state laws beginning with the passage of Arizona's S.B. 1070 in 2010.[31] These state enforcement policies were legally premised on the grounds that they *complemented* federal authority, rather than supplemented it, and were essentially extensions of federal partnership programs like 287(g) and its follow-up measure, "Secure Communities." These federal measures provided Arizona and other states and localities with the legal opening needed to create their own enforcement policies. Localities were incorporated into federal enforcement measures, and they also began to devise their own restrictive measures to deter the settlement of immigrants within their jurisdictions. As the population and complexity of undocumented communities grew in response to border security, members of these communities faced increased restrictions, risks, repression, and surveillance in towns and cities across the country.[32] Not all undocumented immigrants, however, have been equally exposed to this hostility.[33] Adults and recent migrants were most exposed because they sought work without legal documentation, faced police stops and checkpoints during their daily commutes, bore visible signs of "foreignness" (for example, language, clothing), and were asked for legal identification in daily transactions. Adults were compelled to negotiate and think about their "illegality" as part of everyday living. Undocumented children have been partially shielded because of their cultural assimilation, and their lives have centered on the relatively protected institution of the school. The Supreme Court's *Plyler v. Doe* ruling of 1982 recognized the right of all children, irrespective of legal status, to attend public schools. This ruling barred school officials from inquiring into the legal status of children and from using such status to deny children the right to an education. As a consequence, undocumented children had a space of relative refuge where they did not have to concern themselves with the implications of their legal status on a daily basis. The issue of their own legality would become a more central issue in their lives as they moved into adulthood and faced increased demands for legal documentation.[34]

Niche Openings in Hostile Lands

The hostile context of the 1990s and early 2000s put most immigrant rights advocates on the defensive. The near-universal hostility of national politicians in the late 1990s, Democrats and Republicans alike, toward immigration reduced the political possibilities of a national measure for comprehensive immigration reform or an amnesty for undocumented immigrants. Moreover, growing restrictions and stigma directed at undocumented immigrants reduced the willingness of most immigrants to mobilize publicly and make claims for residency status or other basic rights. In this context, rights advocates identified niche openings and pushed for smaller measures that stood a greater likelihood of success. While these measures would not benefit most undocumented immigrants, they would at least provide some groups with additional protections and rights. These smaller wins were seen by many to be stepping stones that would permit the extension of additional rights and protections further down the road.

There were certain immigrant groups that were well placed to respond to niche openings. In 1990, advocates took advantage of the legal and moral ambiguities regarding the case of El Salvadoran immigrants.[35] While government officials recognized that El Salvadorans would qualify for refugee status under the United Nations Convention Relating to the Status of Refugees of 1951, admitting so would make the United States recognize the war and make it complicit in supporting a human rights-violating regime.[36] This ambiguity provided immigrant rights advocates an opening to make demands. One participant in this campaign remembered it in the following way: "The US never wanted to admit that they were funding and training the military in El Salvador. They were involved but they didn't want to admit that there was a war. So they said: 'Okay, we understand that people cannot be sent back, but we also cannot recognize this war. So we are going to give them Temporary Protective Status.'"[37] Responding to this opening, a concerted effort was made by immigrant rights activists in the late 1980s and early 1990s to represent these immigrants as "deserving refugees."[38] They did this by recruiting immigrants with the appropriate legal and cultural attributes, developing frames and stories that stressed these unique attributes, and training immigrants to tell their stories of political persecution and flight to different publics across the country.

Efforts to respond to niche openings continued throughout the decade. Farmworkers enjoyed the support of large growers associations, some Republican politicians, unions, and large segments of the public.[39] This particular group of immigrants was not only presented as contributing an important economic function to the country, but it also had developed a compelling story that dated back to the struggles of the United Farm Workers in the 1970s. In another instance, El Salvadorans and Guatemalans saw their temporary status threatened after the passage IIRIRA in 1996. During this time, Congress was also preparing to pass a measure that would legalize asylum-seekers of left-wing regimes in Nicaragua and Cuba (Nicaraguan Adjustment Central American Responsibility Act). Immigrant advocates again saw a niche opening resulting from the legal and moral discrepancy of this measure. They argued that El Salvadorans and Guatemalans should be granted the same rights as these other groups and be made permanent residents. This group of immigrants was also settled, well integrated, and making important contributions to the country. It was only fair that they should be given the same rights as Cubans and Nicaraguans.

The campaign to legalize the status of undocumented youths was an extension of such piecemeal and incremental approaches of the 1990s. Prominent immigrant rights associations, such as the National Immigration Law Center [NILC], Center for Community Change [CCC], among others, launched a campaign to pass the Development, Relief and Education for Alien Minors Act in 2001. The DREAM Act promised to place undocumented university students and youths performing community service on a path to citizenship. This initiative was a response, in part, to the fact that IIRIRA had placed enormous pressure on the country's enforcement agencies.[40] As the enforcement net encompassed more immigrants, immigration officials struggled to find better ways to allocate their resources more effectively in order to meet these growing demands. In the late 1990s senior officials argued for the need to prioritize resources by focusing on egregious cases and using prosecutorial discretion to grant deferred action (that is, temporary relief from deportation) on humanitarian grounds. This position was strongly advocated by outgoing INS Commissioner Doris Meissner in an influential memorandum written in 2000.[41] The Meissner memorandum did not become official policy, but it provided an opening for immigrant rights advocates to argue for deferred action on moral and humanitarian grounds. Additionally, indiscriminate and enhanced enforcement raised moral ambiguities among certain segments of the public, with many questioning whether all undocumented immigrants deserved to be treated with equal severity by enforcement agencies. Ramping up enforcement measures had therefore spurred cracks in the country's immigration system and the nation's resolve to enforce repressive laws equally across the undocumented population. Here were openings for those who could demonstrate a fit on moral and humanitarian grounds.

The early advocates of the DREAM Act sought to respond to this particular niche because the measure was designed to legalize a certain group of undocumented immigrants deemed to have compelling back-grounds and stories: that is, the DREAMers' unique situation as highly assimilated and well-adjusted members of their communities opened up an opportunity for their legalization on humanitarian and moral grounds. Joshua Bernstein, director of Federal Policy of the National Immigration Law Center (NILC), helped draft the original piece of leg-islation. Eligibility criteria included college students, youths engaged in community service, liberal age requirements, and short periods of US residency. These broad criteria made it easier for the bill to benefit a seg-ment of the immigrant population that extended far beyond the narrow population of youths enrolled in higher education. The original DREAM Act was designed to use an existing niche benefit the maximum number of undocumented immigrants living in the country.

The measure quickly found support among key House and Senate Democrats in 2001, with Richard Durbin becoming a major champion of the bill in the Senate and Luis Gutierrez in the House. Bernstein and his colleagues organized the campaign to build support for the bill. Central to this campaign was the recruitment of a handful of exemplary undocu-mented students with the most compelling stories to give a face to the core message of the campaign: the DREAM Act was designed to allow these good and productive youths a fair chance to achieve the "Ameri-can dream." These youths had done everything right, but because of their immigration status, they were denied the possibility of achieving their dreams and condemned to a life on the margins. During these early days, the youths told their stories to the media and personally lobbied members of Congress. Although the original bill failed, strong support by influential supporters in the immigrant rights community and Congress kept it alive through the decade. Senator Durbin would provide consistent support for the measure in Congress and NILC and the Center for Community Change provided consistent support in the immigrant rights community.

In the different cases of refugees, farmworkers, and youths, immi-gration rights advocates did not necessarily achieve their ultimate goals (permanent residency status and paths to citizenship), but they were able to use available niches to launch campaigns, negotiate with govern-ment officials, and in certain instances, extend residency (temporary and permanent) status to some undocumented immigrants. For immigrant rights advocates, this was the best one could hope under extremely hostile political conditions. In this context, immigrant rights activists were compelled to focus on the battles of groups and issues that stood the strongest chance of success, rather than invest scarce resources in the improbable goal of legalizing all undocumented immigrants.[42]

Negotiating Immigration Reform in the Age of Terror

The election of George W. Bush in 2000 introduced a very contradictory period for immigration politics. While the Bush administration embraced greater integration with Mexico and more liberal immigration policies, it also unleashed a massive buildup of border security and enforcement measures. Many in the immigrant rights community hoped for a turn away from the anti-immigration policies of the 1990s. The first several months of the Bush administration resulted in a round of high-level talks between administration officials, Congress, and the president of Mexico. The administration's receptive position was reflected in White House statements issued during this time. White House spokesperson Ari Fleischer announced, "There are people who are already in this country, contributing to the American economy even though they may not be legal, and they are paying taxes."[43] The administration's moves raised the hopes of many immigrant rights advocates. The director of the National Day Labor Organizing Network (NDLON) remembered the period in the following way: "When Bush talked about immigration it was better than Clinton. There was this synergy between Fox [president of Mexico] and Bush. Bush said, 'We're going to help our neighbor.' That was one of his first priorities—he seemed to mean it. Then Fox comes and delivers a very important speech to the Congress and there was this cheering moment. We were getting close."[44]

The attacks of September 11, 2001, shifted the administration's attention to the "war on terror" and immigration was quickly reframed as a security issue.[45] The events of the early 2000s provided anti-immigrant advocates with an important opportunity to define the problem of terror as lax border security. Dan Stein, the president of Federation for American Immigration Reform (FAIR), argued that the terrorist attacks were the direct result of what he called "open-borders advocates."

"The nation's defense against terrorism has been seriously eroded by the efforts of open-border advocates, and *the innocent victims of today's terrorist attacks have paid the price.*"[46] The link between terrorism, immigration, and border security was echoed in public statements by prominent government officials and leading Republican activists. Four years after the attack, Secretary of State Condoleezza Rice cited intelligence reports of terrorists using the Mexican border to gain access to the country. "Indeed we have from time to time had reports about Al Qaeda trying to use our southern border." She went on to argue for the need to bolster border security as a central element of the country's "war on terror": "I note worries that terrorists would use the Mexico border as a back door to the United States, and there is the need for closer cooperation and the use of better technology to stop illegal crossings."[47] A leading Republican activist, Grover Norquist of Americans for Tax Reform, reiterated the position: "Immigration reform and border security are not competitors; they are the same thing."[48] Terrorism and border security had become central discursive frames through which immigration policy would be interpreted and evaluated by conservatives and moderates of the time.

Advocates of the DREAM Act continued their efforts in the early 2000s, but intense anti-immigration hostility and the "border-first" position presented them with powerful headwinds. While many of Senator Durbin's moderate colleagues favored the DREAM Act, adversaries believed that the eligibility criteria of the DREAM Act would benefit many more undocumented immigrants than just undocumented students. Moreover, without any strong restrictions on family reunification, the DREAM Act would contribute to the mass legalization of family members in the country and provide families outside the country with access to legal residency status. The DREAM Act was criticized as a Trojan Horse because it would open the border to a "flood" of immigration at a time when the country was securing its borders against terrorists. Its adversaries dubbed the measure the Nightmare Act. Senator Durbin responded by expanding bipartisan support and introducing more restrictive eligibility criteria. The revised measure dropped the provision for community service, introduced age caps, denied eligibility to youths with poor moral character (that is, those with criminal records), extended the probationary period for full permanent residency status, and placed restrictions on family reunification. These changes to restrict the number of "DREAM eligible" youths aimed at broadening Republican support in the Senate and House. In spite of these changes, the DREAM Act failed to pass as stand-alone bills or as attachments to omnibus bills in 2003, 2004, and 2005.

This political and discursive climate closed down narrow openings for measures like the DREAM Act but encouraged the enactment of increasingly repressive measures. Between 2001 and 2005 three new restrictive immigration laws were passed by Congress,[49] and six different operations were initiated by Homeland Security.[50] These initiatives combined with IIRIRA to accelerate deportation rates, increasing from a rate of less than 200,000 immigrants per year in 2001, to 300,000 in 2005, and finally to 400,000 by 2009.[51] The discursive coupling of immigration and terrorism played an instrumental role in driving restrictive immigration policies and directing them disproportionately at Mexican immigrants. "None of the terrorist attacks involved Mexicans, and none of the terrorists entered through Mexico. Indeed, all came to the United States on legal visas. . . . Mexicans nonetheless bore the brunt of the deportation campaign launched in the name of the war on terrorism."[52]

The "border-first" and enforcement-only push in the first half of the 2000s exposed several important cracks in the immigration system. The growing demands placed on border security and enforcement stretched thin the resources of federal law enforcement agencies. This raised concerns among immigration officials that expanding the scope of enforcement was undercutting their abilities to guard the country from high-priority risks. Officials sought ways to use their discretionary powers to prioritize certain cases and violations over others and welcomed efforts to ease border pressures by expanding legal avenues of migration.[53] Moreover, senior Republican strategists had wanted to build their "permanent majority" by attracting Latino voters. The government's singular focus on border security and enforcement would push Latino voters away from the Republican fold. Lastly, ramped up enforcement was cutting into the supply of labor for several industries heavily reliant on immigrant labor. These industries had begun to express their concerns to Republican leaders in Congress and the White House.

Responding to these pressures, President Bush made immigration reform a central part of his second-term agenda. In 2005, the White House worked with Senate allies John McCain and Edward Kennedy to introduce the Secure America and Orderly Immigration Act (commonly known as the "McCain-Kennedy Bill," S. 1033). At the center of the bill was a tightly regulated guest workers program that would provide temporary visas with limited rights to workers in specific industries. The administration prioritized the guest workers program over the DREAM Act because of pressures from the hospitality, agriculture, and food-processing industries. The Republican chairman of the Senate Committee on Health, Education, and Labor expressed these economic concerns: "There are not enough visas for temporary workers. We need a plan to offer more visas for temporary seasonal workers."[54] In spite of the narrow scope of the bill and the additional resources made available for border security and enforcement, the bill faced stiff resistance by conservative Republicans who preferred a plan that focused only on border security. The general sentiment of these Republicans was conveyed by Tom Delay, the powerful Whip of the House Republican caucus: "I don't think I'm betraying a confidence. The White House hasn't done a very good job in being clear to the American people where he [the President] is coming from. *You've got to convince the American people that we're going to secure our borders, that we will actually enforce the laws passed, and only after that can you get to a guest worker program.*"[55] Delay and other conservative Republicans rejected efforts to introduce a guest worker program without having first sealed the border and enforced existing restrictions.

The White House responded by reframing immigration reform as a measure to enhance border security. "Border security is one of the President's highest priorities. The President recognizes that we need to be placing as much emphasis on communicating our ongoing efforts to strengthen border security as we are on immigration reform, and he told members [of the House] he wants to continue working with them on this."[56] The guest worker program would provide the government with better means to monitor and regulate immigrant labor in specific industries. "I'm for a bill that strengthens our border by providing people with a tamper-proof identity card to let them work in America for jobs

Americans won't do, on a temporary basis, and then go back to their country."[57] This program would also reduce pressures on the border, enabling enforcement agencies to focus their resources on truly threatening immigrants. Secretary of Homeland Security Michael Chertoff expressed the White House position:

> And the fact of the matter is people are rightly upset and distressed about the prospect that we do not have control of our border the way we should. An increasing enforcement along the nation's borders will not alone repair the nation's immigration system. I urge the adoption of a temporary-worker program. . . . It [reform] is a three-legged stool. It requires tough enforcement at the border, tough interior enforcement, and a temporary-worker program to deal with the very real draw.[58]

The guest worker program would therefore strengthen borders by enhancing the capacities of the government to regulate immigrant flows and allowing enforcement agencies to better direct their resources at more threatening migrants.

As the Senate struggled and failed to overcome Republican resistance in this chamber, the House passed a bill that only addressed enforcement issues. The House bill was given the apt title, Border Protection, Anti-terrorism and Illegal Immigration Control Act ("Sensenbrenner Bill," H.R. 4437). The bill aimed to expand the border fence, make it a felony to be undocumented, increase substantially the fines for hiring undocumented workers, require employers to use electronic verification to check the legal status of workers, require federal agencies to take into custody undocumented immigrants held by local agencies (ending "catch and release"), and criminalize assistance to undocumented immigrants.[59] James Sensenbrenner described the bill, saying, "It will help *restore the integrity of our nation's borders* and *re-establish respect for our laws* by holding violators accountable, including human traffickers, employers who hire illegal aliens and alien gang members who *terrorize* communities."[60] The bill was strongly supported by the Republican caucus, with 92 percent of House Republicans voting in favor of it. One member of the House expressed his support for the bill: "Our constituents are berserk with fury over the unprotected borders. The borders have been entirely unprotected for far too long. But *until we get the borders under control, we'll never win the war on terror,* and it's pointless to discuss the guest worker program."[61]

The failure of the Bush White House and its Senate allies to win over conservative Republicans in the Senate and House led it to pursue another strategy aimed at expanding Democratic support in the Senate. The McCain-Kennedy Bill was reintroduced by Senator Arlen Specter (R) as the Comprehensive Immigration Reform Act of 2006 (S. 2611). The proposed bill combined the border security and guest worker measures of the previous plan with a strategy to legalize the status of millions (but not all) undocumented immigrants in the country. The DREAM Act would now be incorporated into this larger reform bill. The Senate bill was substantially more liberal than the Sensenbrenner bill that had passed in the House in late 2005. The aim was to design a bipartisan Senate bill that would gain overwhelming Democratic support and some moderate Republican support. A compromise between the House and Senate bills would then be negotiated in conference. In spite of criticisms from both sides of the aisle, the Senate succeeded in passing the bill on May 25, 2006.

The next step for immigration reform to become law was to find a compromise between the Senate and House bills. The Bush administration now needed to convince conservative House Republicans by highlighting the restrictive nature of the Senate bill. First, President Bush reminded Republicans that enforcement was central to the Comprehensive Immigration Reform bill: he claimed, "We'll add 6,000 agents by 2008 to build high-tech fences and new patrol roads, and to end 'catch and release' once and for all on the southern border of the United States."[62] Second, the president argued that the path to legal residency was not an "amnesty" program. For conservative Republicans, "amnesty" undermined the rule of law by rewarding people for "illegal" conduct, and it served as a magnet for millions of more migrants. "We must face the reality that millions of illegal immigrants are already here. *They should not be given an automatic path to citizenship. That is amnesty. I oppose amnesty.*"[63] The bill was not an amnesty program because it would not provide "an automatic path to citizenship." It introduced strict criteria to qualify for legal status including language acquisition, long-term settlement (more than five years), the payment of a fine for having broken the law (more than $2,000), payment of back taxes, steady employment, and no criminal record. Third,

President Bush stressed that the guest worker program enhanced the government's capacities to govern immigration because it allowed officials to monitor labor migrants, steer the movement and economic activities of migrants in the country, reduce possibilities of permanent settlement, and free up enforcement resources by reducing pressures on the border. "We must reduce pressure on our border by creating a temporary worker plan. Willing workers ought to be matched with willing employers to do jobs Americans are not doing on a temporary —temporary — basis."[64] Comprehensive Immigration Reform would therefore eliminate "illegal" immigration and enhance security by legalizing the status of deserving immigrants, redirecting new immigrants into a restrictive temporary program, and enhancing the enforcement powers of the government against undeserving, criminal, and truly "illegal" immigrants.

The effort to find a compromise for the House and Senate bills failed. House Republicans proved to be unwavering regarding their "border-first" and enforcement position. Speaker of the House Dennis Hastert expressed the Republican position: "Before we can look at other immigration issues, we must first secure the borders."[65] Though the Comprehensive Immigration Reform Act failed, Congress passed yet another law to reinforce the border fence in October 2006.[66]

In spring 2007, Senate Republicans and Democrats supporting comprehensive reform began their efforts again. In the hope of reaching a compromise with conservative Republicans, a stricter version of the Comprehensive Immigration Reform Act was introduced by its supporters. Senator Edward Kennedy announced, "I'm shifting gears in hopes of winning Republican support and speeding the passage of immigration legislation this spring."[67] Senate Republicans talked of a "grand bargain" that hinged on a policy trigger. Legalizing eligible undocumented migrants (that is, the pathway to citizenship) would only begin once new border security and enforcement measures were firmly in place. "Negotiators have reached what they called a grand bargain. It includes a series of triggers that require new border security measures to be up and running before the start of any programs to give legal status to people in the country illegally."[68] The "grand bargain" also introduced restrictions on the temporary-worker program, greater resources for enforcement, and severe restrictions on family reunification. Under this version of the bill, only spouses and children of new citizens could apply for a visa under the family-reunification provision. The influx of new temporary immigrants would therefore be offset by restrictions on permanent family reunification.

Concerns with this version of the bill were expressed by immigrant rights advocates and many Democratic Senators (including presidential candidates Hillary Clinton and Barack Obama). Barack Obama criticized the bill, arguing, "Without modifications, the proposed bill could devalue the importance of family reunification, replace the current group of undocumented immigrants with a new undocumented population consisting of guest workers who will overstay their visas, and potentially drive down wages of American workers."[69] Anti-immigration activists also mobilized against the bill. Numbers USA, an anti-immigration advocacy group, took up a leading role in this effort. "The bill had support from the opinion elite in this country. But we built a grassroots army, consumed with passion for a cause, and used the power of the Internet to go around the elites and defeat a disastrous amnesty bill."[70] Failing to garner support by Democrats and Republicans in the Senate, the bill never made it to the Senate floor for a full vote. Senator Edward Kennedy lamented the defeat with the following statement, "We know what they [conservative Republicans] don't like. What are they for? What are they going to do with the 12 million who are undocumented here? Send them back to countries around the world? Develop a type of Gestapo here to seek out these people that are in the shadows? What's their alternative?"[71]

After several years of struggling and failing to reach a compromise on comprehensive reform, some members of Congress pivoted back to the strategy that focused on smaller and piecemeal measures that stood greater chances of success. Even with the support of a Republican president, Republican Senate leaders, and party elites, hard-line conservatives continued to reject any measure that provided undocumented immigrants with some form of legal status (temporary or permanent) in the country. The only measures conservatives would support were those that enhanced border security and the enforcement capacities of federal and local police agencies. Facing this overwhelming resistance, the best way forward was to identify those parts of the larger comprehensive package that stood a greater chance of success. "The agriculture and student measures have a decent chance of passing this Congress because they have strong champions, broad bipartisan support, and they have been around for a long time."[72] Senator Richard Durbin, the longtime champion of the DREAM Act, mobilized on its behalf immediately after the failure of the Comprehensive Immigration Reform bill in 2007. With regard to agricultural workers, employers' lobbies argued the need to reform the existing visa programs. "We urge changes like speeding up the H-2A application process, easing housing requirements for guest workers, reducing the required wage for these workers and increasing the types of work they are allowed to do."[73] The Bush administration addressed these concerns through executive decree rather than the legislative process: "The Department of Labor is now in the process of identifying ways the program can be improved to provide farmers with an orderly and timely flow of legal workers while protecting the rights of both U.S. workers."[74] Thus, in the face of unwavering conservative hostility, a string of reforms failed between 2005 and 2007. This prompted reform advocates to resume the old strategy of pushing for narrower measures that stood less resistance from conservative political forces and a better chance of success.

The Evolving Strategies of the Immigrant Rights Movement

The hostile context of the 1990s encouraged immigrant rights associations to mobilize in response to whatever niche openings were available to them. A context of general hostility and few niche openings did not favor a unified and centralized social movement. Advocacy in the 1990s to the early 2000s was characterized by relatively small coalitions of different interest groups seeking to push narrow measures for particular groups of immigrants (for example, refugees, agricultural workers, youths, and so on). Coalitions and alliances were formed and broken as different issues and opportunities came to the fore.

Beginning in 2004, efforts were made to create greater unity and coherency across the countless immigrant rights organizations and associations in the country. The Center for Community Change helped create a national network to coordinate immigrant rights campaigns. The new immigrant rights network, called Fair Immigration Reform Movement

(FIRM), was a Center for Community Change project housed in its Washington, DC, headquarters. Other prominent advocacy associations, like NILC, National Council of La Raza, and the Mexican American Legal Defense and Educational Fund, were connected to FIRM but were not formal members. The principal members were regional and local immigrant rights organizations like the Center for Humane Immigrant Rights of Los Angeles, Illinois Coalition for Immigrant and Refugee Rights, and the New York Immigration Coalition.

The rapidly changing political context of 2005–7 intensified efforts to create a more unified and centralized movement to advocate for immigrant rights. In his second term, President Bush moved to gain bipartisan support for the Comprehensive Immigration Reform Act. Simultaneously, powerful anti-immigration advocates in the House had successfully pushed for a string of restrictive laws and policies. In particular, James Sensenbrenner was using the House Judiciary Committee to produce a series of bills that would not only rescind rights and enhance enforcement but also criminalize undocumented status. This particular juncture presented national and local rights associations with strong incentives to coordinate their efforts. The massive demonstrations in opposition to the Sensenbrenner bill in March 2006 provided one of the first opportunities to coordinate efforts on a national scale. FIRM played a role connecting local and national organizations, transmitting information between these organizations, and providing local and regional activists with a common messaging frame. Nevertheless, local immigrant rights organizations took the initiative to plan protest events and mobilize massive turnouts in cities throughout the country.[75]

While efforts were made to protest the most restrictive immigration measures, the leading national organizations (Center for Community Change, National Immigration Law Center, National Council of La Raza, and so on) were also coordinating lobbying efforts concerning the Comprehensive Immigration Reform Act. These organizations, in consultation with their congressional allies, agreed that the DREAM Act should be passed as part of the comprehensive package. The students were one of the most well-liked and least stigmatized groups within the broader immigrant population and their stories resonated well with the moral and humanitarian sentiments of the media, politicians, and the general public. They were, in this context, held up as the "poster-children" of the general immigrant rights movement and employed as a way to gain broad popular support for Comprehensive Immigration Reform. Just as importantly, the youths had revealed themselves to be extremely effective and energetic grassroots organizers. Their continued participation was viewed by the leadership as important for the passage of the immigration reform bill.

Soon after the failure of Comprehensive Immigration Reform in 2007, Senator Richard Durbin immediately reintroduced the DREAM Act as a stand-alone bill. Durbin believed that a more limited bill stood a greater chance of success. Durbin's move triggered an important debate among leading immigrant rights groups and their political allies. Prominent rights associations argued that the Senate leadership should reintroduce the Comprehensive Immigration Reform Act with the DREAM Act as a part of the larger bill. They feared that introducing a stand-alone bill for students (or farmworkers for that matter) would split the movement and remove the best-supported and most energetic groups from the comprehensive campaign. An incremental strategy of passing narrower bills for undocumented students or farmworkers would peel off these strategic groups and undermine the unity needed to pass the broader Comprehensive Immigration Reform Act.

The leading immigrant rights associations, politicians, and funders came to a consensus on a strategy to focus their efforts on winning the 279 Congressional votes and 1 presidential signature needed to pass the Comprehensive Immigration Reform Act. The focus was now on Congress passing a single all-encompassing bill. Efforts were also made to centralize key decision-making functions and the infrastructure of the movement. Major foundations like the Atlantic Philanthropies encouraged the national associations to create a new coalition in January 2008. They provided that new coalition, called Reform Immigration for America (RIFA), with $3.5 million to direct a national campaign to push for the passage comprehensive reform.[76] While the coalition would include many national and local rights associations across the country, the principal organizations making up the leadership circle were Center for Community Change, National Council of La Raza, and the National Immigration Forum, with the Center for Community Change assuming the directing role. Other major immigrant rights associations like NILC, MALDEF, and National Day Labor Organizing Network (NDLON) were also important stakeholders of RIFA but played less central roles. In this context, the DREAM campaign was viewed as an integral part of the general struggle to achieve comprehensive reform.

In 2007 NILC had asserted its influence over the DREAM campaign and sponsored the creation of the United We Dream Coalition to support the passage of the DREAM Act as part of a comprehensive bill. The coalition was then supplanted by an organization with the same name. The staff of United We Dream was made up primarily of undocumented youth, but NILC served as its fiscal sponsor and its office was located in NILC's Washington, DC, headquarters. Also, Joshua Bernstein continued to play an influential role in shaping the political and communication strategy of the group. Another RIFA member that developed a strong youth wing was the Los Angeles-based Center for Humane Immigrant Rights of Los Angeles (CHIRLA). This association had developed a youth wing in the late 1990s called Wise-Up, and in 2007, it received a grant to create a statewide network of undocumented support groups on college campuses (the A.B. 540 groups).[77] CHIRLA worked closely with NILC's United We Dream and was a strong advocate of RIFA's comprehensive strategy. This provided RIFA with direct access to the largest network of undocumented youth activists in the country.

Though the new centralized structure and strategy was able to impose some order over the many different actors and tendencies within the immigrant rights movement, these actors continued to face varied constraints and openings that pulled them in different directions. Maintaining internal unity in the face of the various interests and priorities was a central challenge to RIFA's leadership. Three major factors presented RIFA with important challenges. First, some RIFA associates including NDLON and MALDEF started to shift their attention to draw attention to local, state, and federal enforcement measures. While RIFA insisted that all coalition partners should focus their energies on passing the Comprehensive Immigration Reform Act in Congress, these other associations began to initiate campaigns directed at federal enforcement measures (287[g] and Secure Communities) and repressive state-level laws (Arizona's Support Our Law Enforcement and Safe Neighborhoods Act [S.B. 1070]). Second, these cracks in the movement's unity widened when key undocumented groups, the DREAMers in particular, became pessimistic about the prospects of passing Comprehensive Immigration Reform in 2010. If there was little possibility of passing a comprehensive bill, many undocumented youths began to argue that RIFA should redirect its support for smaller measures like the DREAM Act, which stood a better chance of passing. Lastly, associations like MALDEF and NDLON argued that comprehensive reform could only be achieved at the cost of accepting major restrictions on who could qualify for legalization and future migration flows. Winning enough support for a supermajority in the Senate and a majority in the House would be difficult if not impossible without accepting major concession on punitive enforcement measures. This raised questions about the costs of passing comprehensive reform in terms of accepting restrictions and new enforcement measures and how these costs would affect different groups of undocumented immigrants in the country. Thus, in spite of RIFA's major efforts to centralize the immigrant rights movement, a number of factors continued to pull the movement in different directions. These tensions would explode in spring 2010 soon after RIFA's first major effort to push the Obama administration and Congress to pass Comprehensive Immigration Reform.

The anti-immigration hostility of the 1990s resulted in the introduction of new government policies to enforce borders and roll back the rights to immigrants, both documented and undocumented. It also resulted in localizing immigration policy by making local officials increasingly responsible for policing undocumented populations in their jurisdictions. For immigrant rights advocates, growing hostility and strong enforcement tendencies shut down hopes for the introduction of a bill in Congress to legalize the status of undocumented residents. Instead, enforcement trends gave rise to legal, political, and normative ambiguities for immigrant groups that could not be easily classified as fully "illegal." Certain refugees (Cubans and Nicaraguans at first, then El Salvadorans and Guatemalans), workers (those in agriculture and increasingly hospitality industries), and youths (those enrolled in higher education) possessed strategic attributes that made them more deserving of some kind of legal status than others. Immigrant rights advocates during the 1990s to the early 2000s therefore organized smaller campaigns to legalize the status of those who stood the best chances of success rather than invest their scarce resources in the unrealistic goal of legalizing the status of all undocumented immigrants in the United States. The strategic response by the rights community was therefore appropriate and well suited for a context characterized by hostility, enforcement, and slight niche openings.

The growing possibility of comprehensive immigration reform in 2005–7 resulted in a move away from this incremental and piecemeal strategy to a comprehensive one based on centralized unity. The failure to pass comprehensive reform was for some, including funders and leading rights organizations, the result of the movement's inability to unify and exert its influence in a more effective way. Fragmentation, it was believed, limited the movement's abilities to use its collective resources in a more concerted manner to influence public debate and pressure key politicians. Centralizing the strategy and the movement's infrastructure was therefore seen as the only way to overcome the political-ideological hurdles facing them.

The election of a Democratic Congress in November 2006, a Democratic supermajority in the Senate in 2008, and a Democratic president in the same year raised expectations that comprehensive reform could pass in 2009 or 2010. This new window of opportunity reinforced the view that unity, discipline, and centralization were needed to win the 279 votes needed to pass comprehensive reform. While RIFA's mandate was to centralize and discipline the different components of the movement, there were important forces that continued to fragment the movement. Certain groups continued to face niche openings (youths, farmworkers) and other groups started to direct their attention to new battles over local and federal enforcement measures. As factions within the movement were pulled in different directions, the leadership of RIFA worked to maintain control and unity. Those efforts in the face of these centrifugal forces only magnified tensions between the movement's central leadership and the multiple groups, factions, and activists making up the movement. These tensions exploded in spring 2010 when DREAMers lost faith in RIFA's capacities to represent their interests. This was a cathartic moment that marked an important shift in the evolution of the immigrant rights movement and the birth of the "DREAMer" as fully autonomous political group.

2

The Birth of the DREAMer

Before 2001, "DREAMers" did not exist as a political group. There were hundreds and thousands undocumented youths facing a unique set of problems resulting from their position of being "in-between" countries.[1] As children, they went to school in the United States, played in the streets, watched television, rooted for their home teams, navigated fashions, and developed aspirations to move on to bigger and better things. They absorbed the feelings, dispositions, tastes, and values of America through the everyday interactions that made up their childhood.[2] They were certainly immigrants, but most felt and knew themselves to be of this country. This feeling of being home in the United States, of being "normal" Americans, was disrupted as the children transitioned into early adulthood and tried to pursue activities like applying for a driver's license, opening a bank account, looking for a job, and submitting college applications.[3] Each of these activities required demonstrating proof of residency, a process that precipitated difficult and recurrent discoveries that they did not formally belong in this country. One youth described this type of experience:

I came to the US when I was six, but I didn't know about my status until I was seventeen. My senior year at high school I tried applying for the FAFSA [Free Application for Federal Student Aid], and that's when my parents finally had to tell me about the lack of the social [social security number]. I didn't really have an idea. I had no idea what was going on. I had no idea why it was happening to me. There was this overwhelming feeling of being so alone and so, like just "aarrrgh." All of your hopes and dreams are being taken away for no particular reason, and you can't know who to blame. There is nobody to blame and there is nobody you can appeal to. It's just this whole sense of being lost, inside and out. You are so lost. I was so lost. I was really just going through the motions. I was seventeen years old, and I ended up in that space, and I don't know. It just happened.[4]

In addition to being cast out of the national community, the "hopes and dreams" that many grew up with were suddenly "taken away." This sudden experience produces a trauma and consciousness that is shared by many undocumented youth and that is different from immigrants who migrated to the United States as adults.[5]

These common experiences have made undocumented youths a sociologically distinct group of immigrants, but they did not exist as a political group before the 2000s. There were no labels to mark the group's political existence ("DREAMers"), there were no common arguments and stories to express a singular political voice, and there was no infrastructure to foster political connections and consciousness between dispersed youth. There had been several campaigns to win in-state tuition for undocumented youths in the 1990s, but these campaigns were mostly led by state legislators, administrators, and rights associations. Undocumented youths only played residual roles within them.[6] Their nonexistence as a political group at the start of the decade stands in sharp contrast with their major political presence after 2010 when DREAMers emerged as a central player in immigration debates and became a driving force of the immigrant rights movement.

This remarkable development over such a short period of time stems from early efforts to pass the national DREAM Act. During the early 2000s the National Immigration Law Center (NILC) and Center for Community Change played instrumental roles in raising the issue in Congress, developing a strategy to push for the DREAM Act, crafting a representation of undocumented youths and their cause, and representing them directly to political officials. Given the lack of experience of undocumented youths in national-level activism, immigrant rights associations possessed the resources needed to transform the grievances of undocumented youths into a legitimate political voice in the public sphere.

Operating in a rather hostile and xenophobic environment, the leading associations of the early DREAM campaigns needed to craft representations of undocumented youths that would convince liberal and conservative audiences alike. They stressed the youths' deep cultural and social ties to the United States and their ongoing contributions to the country. By representing them as virtuous Americans, immigrant youths would be transformed from threats to the national community into sources of economic, civic, and moral rejuvenation. Although this strategy was successful in building public and political support, activists and advocates confronted a new dilemma because of it. By stressing the attributes, such as cultural assimilation and being college students, that made undocumented students into "good" and deserving immigrants, those who failed to possess these same attributes were by default less deserving. Crafting a compelling message was extremely important, but developing a method to "stay on message" was just as important. The leading associations also developed an infrastructure to train and discipline undocumented youth activists to stay on message in the public arena. These training sessions helped inculcate youth activists into the DREAMer discourse and shape their views and feelings concerning their undocumented status and their position in the country.

The process described here helped transform thousands of different undocumented students into the political group of the DREAMer.[7] It was a group that bore a common label, infrastructure, and goals, but it was also a group with common subjective and emotional dispositions. As individual youths became DREAMers, their common subjectivities, identity, and emotions fueled commitment to their cause.

Undocumented Youths as the Exceptional Immigrant

The large immigrant rights demonstrations in 1994 were a messaging debacle. In the demonstrations against California's punitive Proposition 187, marchers carried flags from Mexico, Central America, and other immigrant-sending countries. To the immigrant rights activists the display of flags was empowering and reinforced their ties to one another. But to their opponents, the flags were seen as defiantly foreign.[8] Anti-immigrant forces used images from these demonstrations to bolster their arguments that immigrants represented an existential threat to the country. Having learned the lessons from these demonstrations, immigrant rights advocates looked to craft a message in the 2000s that stressed assimilation over distinction and conformity over difference. American flags were now widely disseminated at public demonstrations and flags from other countries were pushed out of sight. The move to embrace American symbols and silence displays of foreignness and otherness has been a central plank of the movement's representational strategy.

This strategy has strongly influenced how national immigrant rights associations represented undocumented youths and their cause. Lead organizations believed that if they were to gain support from conservative and liberal publics alike, they needed to establish a direct connection between undocumented youths and core American values. The authors of the original piece of federal legislation developed the DREAM acronym (Development, Relief, and Education for Alien Minors Act) to create a direct connection between the cause and core national values associated with the American dream. Rather than being a foreign threat to the country, these immigrants were presented as the exact opposite: extensions of the country's core historical values and a force of national reinvigoration.

The immigrant rights associations leading the DREAM campaign crafted a discourse of undocumented youths that rested on three main themes. These themes have intersected to form the "master frame" through which undocumented youths and their cause would be represented in the public sphere for years to come.[9]

First, it has been important to embrace American symbols and mark the group's distance from foreign symbols. One DREAM activist remarks on the importance of American symbols in representing themselves and the cause, observing, "We have brought in the Statue of Liberty into the recent campaign. Why? Because this is important to remind people what we stand for as a country."[10] They not only stressed national symbols like flags and the Statue of Liberty but also national values. Another DREAMer adds, "The key values that we stressed were fairness, hard work, and self-determination. Those are our key values that we always try to come back to. Like, 'The DREAM Act is a policy that supports fairness and rewards hard work.' These are key American values. We were talking about the values that this policy supports."[11] The emphasis on national symbols and values has been aimed at winning over the support of a broad and sometimes hostile public. "Yeah, that whole spiel about being 'good Americans' is strategic messaging.[12] The aim of it all is to gain support from people in conservative places."[13] The flip side of stressing national conformity is to stress distance with "foreign" symbols:

> *That is something we all agree on. You can never have a Mexican flag waving at your rally.* One time we said, "Hey, wouldn't it be cool to have a rally showing our different flags, you know, flags from Mexico, Korea, Honduras, etc." But then we said, "No, we have to be careful because we're in Orange County [a very conservative area of southern California] and people are going to take it the wrong way." *We thought it would be nice to celebrate the fact that we are from all over the world but we didn't want to risk it.*[14]

Stressing the qualities that make these youths wholly "American" requires the use of overt national symbols (for example, flags, statues of liberty, graduation gowns, and so on) and rhetoric. Demonstrating national belonging has also encouraged the display of tastes, dispositions, tacit knowledge, and accents that would be considered distinctly American by natives. They have been shown to engage in the same activities, eat the same foods, cheer the same sports teams, and embrace the same aspirations as any other American in their peer group. They are cheerleaders, they love the Lakers, they speak perfect English, and they dream of becoming middle class, just like any "normal" person. By stressing their American cultural attributes, they demonstrate that they have internalized American values and that these values are inscribed in bodily dispositions. To use Norbert Elias's term, they have deployed their "national habitus" in strategically purposeful ways.[15] For many early supporters of the DREAM Act, their qualities as "de facto" Americans made the youths exceptional and deserving an exemption from the country's exclusionary immigration laws. "These children are de facto Americans but their hopes are being dashed on a daily basis."[16] Demonstrating national identification has been a means for this "other" to reveal its "normalness" and common humanity with the native. It allows them to present themselves not as breaking with or "threatening" the norms of the country but ensuring continuity.

Second, in addition to stressing the attributes that make undocumented students "normal" Americans, DREAM advocates have also drawn attention to their most exceptional qualities. They are indeed "normal" American kids, but they are also the "best and the brightest" of their generation. The former director of the California Dream Network explained:

> This message comes from the facts because that is their experience. Many of these students are going to school and succeeding in spite of terrible barriers. The only strategic part is that we have focused on the crème de la crème, the top students, the 4.3, the valedictorian. We have always been intentional of choosing the best story, the most easily understood story, the most emotionally convincing story. So, we have always been intentional but that story also runs true: young person comes, realizes they are undocumented, faces terrible constraints but does good anyway because those are the things their parents taught them.[17]

The image of the straight-A immigrant student rebuts the stereotype of immigrant youths as deviant and delinquent. Moreover, because these students are the "best and the brightest," they stand to make an important contribution to the country. Senate Majority Leader Harry Reid has drawn on this line to justify his support of the DREAM Act. "The students who earn legal status through the DREAM Act will make our country more competitive economically, spurring job creation, contributing to our tax base, and strengthening communities."[18]

Third, the stigma of illegality has long been used by anti-immigrant groups to undermine the legitimacy of immigrant rights claims. DREAM advocates and supporters have sought to cleanse youths of this stigma by absolving them from the "guilt" of having broken the law. The youths cannot be considered fully "illegal." They did not "choose" to cross the border and therefore cannot be held accountable for breaking the law. A DREAMer in the 2007 campaign argued, "I didn't ask to come here, I was brought here. With kids like me, you're truncating their future."[19] The phrase, "no fault of their own" became a standard talking point used by DREAM Act advocates in various campaigns. This talking point has resonated widely with the media and national politicians. "The bill could pass the Senate because it is intended to benefit young people who grow up in the United States and are illegal immigrants as a result of decisions by their parents."[20] This theme has shown to be extremely resilient and continues to be used by leading officials and politicians supporting the DREAM Act. The secretary of homeland security reiterated this point in her support of the DREAM Act in 2010. "The students who would gain legal status under the bill have no fault for being here in the United States because they were brought here when they were children by their parents."[21] Senate Majority Leader Harry Reid employed a similar argument to voice his support of the bill: "If there is a bipartisan bill that makes sense for our country economically, from a national security perspective and one that reflects American values, it is the DREAM Act. This bill will give children brought illegally to this country at no fault of their own the chance to earn legal status."[22] Another DREAM Act supporter, the president of Arizona State University, argued that passing the act would be a way for these youths to vindicate their "innocence": "There are thousands and thousands of students who were successful in public school, who did everything right and didn't do anything wrong on their own. *The bill is their pathway to innocence.*"[23]

These themes highlight the attributes that make this group exceptional and deserving of legalization. By countering stereotypes, the themes cleanse the youths of the three main stigmas attributed to undocumented immigrants. The undocumented youths are normal Americans (and not irreducibly foreign), the best and brightest (and not free-riding welfare cheats or terrorizing gang members), and bear no fault for their immigration status (and not truly "illegal"). One longtime activist notes, "Everything is pretty clear-cut. We know what we need to say and we need a solid image. We're basically debunking all the stereotypes, promoting ourselves as people with good character—to counter all the bad stereotypes of immigrants. You don't want to give the media any reason to be against us."[24] While these themes structure the representations of undocumented youths, advocates transmit variants of these themes through an emotionally compelling "storyline."[25] The storyline maintains that undocumented youths were brought to the country as children (no fault of their own), learned to become good and hardworking Americans, have overcome major barriers in the pursuit of the American dream, and were now not allowed to realize the dream because of their immigration status. By connecting the personal difficulties of individuals to a very public storyline, activists have been able to articulate their argument in an emotionally compelling way.

This representation has been crafted for the primary purpose of producing an exceptionally good front stage persona of undocumented youth in an inhospitable political environment.[26] The more the campaign sought to convince conservatives in hostile areas of the country, the greater the need for clear, simple, and sympathetic representation of these youths and their cause. A former organizer of United We Dream notes:

> Yeah, we need to stick to the DREAM Act talking points that have been in place for ten years. You know, no fault of their own, best equipped, positive for the economy, and of course the pro-America thing. You have to say these things because we are trying to reach people in Iowa, Missouri, Utah, and North Carolina. If you want to reach these people, you have to stick close to these talking points because they work really well with people in these places.[27]

Producing a good front-stage persona of the DREAMer also requires silencing utterances, acts, and symbols that would raise doubts about their legal innocence, contributions to the country, or loyalty to America. The backstage complications and identities of *real* immigrant youths, their complicated national loyalties, sexualities, conduct, and so on, could not be allowed to seep onto the public stage because they would complicate the core message and imperil the cause.

After establishing youths as an exceptional and deserving group of immigrants, advocates argue that it would be an injustice to deny them the right to stay, live, and thrive in the country. They have done everything right and played by the rules. In spite of their efforts to overcome enormous hurdles and be good and contributing members of society, they are denied the legal right to stay in the country. The DREAM Act is about fairness and justice because it provides people who have fulfilled their part of the bargain an equal chance to realize the American dream. Denying these exceptional youths, these de facto Americans, the right to stay in the country would not only be a profound injustice but it would also be moral lapse of the country. President Obama drew on this argument to express his support of the DREAM Act: "It is heartbreaking. That can't be who we are. To have kids, our kids, classmates of our children, who are suddenly under this shadow of fear, through no fault of their own."[28] What makes the case of these youths morally shocking for President Obama is that these are "our kids" who are forced to live in the "shadows of fear" due to factors that are "no fault of their own."[29]

DREAM advocates have not only won over strong supporters among traditional allies, but they have also won over the support of some traditional adversaries. As a candidate in the 2008 Republican presidential primaries, former Governor Mike Huckabee spoke sympathetically of the youths and their cause, "In all due respect, we're a better country than to punish children for what their parents did."[30] Even more telling, the director of the anti-immigrant association Numbers USA was willing to cede ground when it came to undocumented students, saying, "I could support legal status for some young immigrant students. However, I would do so only if Congress eliminates the current immigration system based on family ties and imposed mandatory electronic verification of immigration status for all workers."[31] During the 2012 Republican presidential primaries, Governor Rick Perry justified Texas's policy of granting in-state tuition to undocumented youths on moral grounds: "If you say that we should not educate children who have come into our state for no other reason than they have been brought there by no fault of their own, I don't think you have a heart."[32] The effort to create a compelling representation of the youths as exceptional immigrants has in fact swayed some leading conservative figures to recognize the attributes that make them deserving of an exemption from restrictive immigration laws.

Differentiating Between "Good" and "Bad" Immigrants

The representation of undocumented youths and their cause has presented advocates and DREAMers with an important dilemma.

Stressing the attributes (normal Americans, best and the brightest, no fault of their own) that made undocumented youths into exceptional immigrants who deserve legalization helped make their cause a legitimate political issue. However, those not possessing such attributes (for example, unassimilated, recent arrivals, adults, poor and low skilled, "criminals") could be seen as less exceptional and therefore less deserving of legalization. Moreover, demonstrating belonging in America has been coupled with efforts to distance themselves from the stigmas associated with the general immigrant population. The process of de-stigmatizing undocumented youths has therefore contributed to differentiating between "deserving" and "undeserving" immigrants.

The representation of undocumented youths has rested on the effort to stress the group's assimilation into the American value system and its break from the cultural and moral worlds of sending countries. During the 2007 campaign, one DREAM activist noted, "All I'm hearing now is that I'm Colombian, but I've never really been there. I have no memories of the country where I was born and I do not speak articulate Spanish. They are taking me from my home in America and sending me to a dangerous country that I don't even know."[33] Arguments like these have stressed that youths are wholly assimilated and that the countries of their parents are as foreign and other to them as they are to any "normal" American. The director of United We Dream maintained, "Maybe our parents feel like immigrants, but we feel like Americans because we have been raised here on American values."[34] Differentiating youths from the countries of parents helps reinforce a message of national conformity, but it also reinforces dominant representations of these places and their peoples as other, foreign, and incongruent with the American value system.

DREAM Act advocates have also sought to cleanse undocumented youths of the stigma of "illegality." They have argued that youths cannot be held accountable for their legal status because they did not choose to migrate to the country. However, in making such an argument, the assumption is that those who made the "choice" (parents) are culpable for crossing the border and staying in the country "illegally." Claiming innocence for youths has inadvertently come at the cost of attributing guilt to parents. This has allowed youths to be cleansed of the stigma of illegality, but it has also reinforced the stigma for parents. The double-edged nature of this rhetoric has continuously been reflected in public expressions of support by liberal political officials:

- "It's [current immigration law] penalizing children for *mistakes* that were made by their parents."[35]
- "It's unfair to make these young people pay for the *sins* of their parents."[36]
- "The bill could pass the Senate because it is intended to benefit young people who grow up in the United States and are *illegal immigrants as a result of decisions by their parents.*"[37]

On Senator Richard Durbin's web site, a link prompted undocumented youths to submit their stories as part of the broader campaign to pass the DREAM Act. The link stated, "The DREAM Act would allow a select group of immigrant students with great potential to contribute more fully to America. *These young people were brought to the U.S. as children and should not be punished for their parents' mistakes.* If you are an undocumented student that the DREAM Act would help, I hope you will share your story with me."[38] This request for stories also provides youths with a model to structure their own personal narratives. This double-edged rhetoric has also resonated with media supporters. Lawrence Downes, a frequent editorial contributor to the *New York Times*, provided the following sympathetic portrait of an undocumented youth: "Ms. Veliz is here illegally, *but not by choice.* She arrived from Mexico with her parents in 1993 on a tourist visa. She was eight. She had never lived in the United States before but has lived nowhere else since. By all detectable measures, she is an American, a Texan."[39] Thus, the assertion of innocence for undocumented children and youths has been coupled with the attribution of guilt for parents.

The discursive differences drawn between deserving and less deserving immigrants plays into the categories used by policymakers to decide where to draw the line between legalizable and unlegalizable immigrants. They employ these categories to inform where to draw the real line between immigrants who deserve legalization and those who deserve deportation. In an early statement of support for the DREAM Act, Senator Richard Durbin argued that it would help the government to better distinguish between good immigrants and criminals: "We have to distinguish between those who would do us harm and those who came to our country to pursue the American dream and are contributing members of our society."[40] Six years later, Janet Napolitano used a similar argument: "Passing the DREAM Act would help immigration authorities focus their resources on deporting dangerous criminals."[41] Support for devising a path to citizenship for "good" immigrants (youths) has therefore been justified on the grounds that it enhances government capacities to direct its resources against truly threatening immigrants.

Most of the leading DREAMers have been conscious of the dilemma posed by this discourse and have found no easy way to resolve it. The former director of the California Dream Network remarked, "It perpetuates the good immigrants and the bad immigrants, and that the good immigrants are the ones who look like me and talk like me. And the bad immigrants are ones who don't know the language and choose not to learn it."[42] Most DREAMers place responsibility for this dilemma on the national rights associations and politicians, which developed the messaging strategy of the early campaigns. One prominent DREAM activist notes, "Painting us as the good immigrant has not necessarily been a positive thing. We were painted that way by people who were working hard to pass the DREAM Act but not necessarily the DREAMers themselves."[43] Another DREAMer goes on to note, "We noticed that at the federal level, politicians, activists, and national organizations highlighted those students at the top, the cream of the crop but they forget that there are more students at the bottom than at the top."[44] The former director of the California Dream Network nuances these assertions by stressing that the strategy emerged at an early phase when immigrant rights leaders were uncertain of what they were doing and cautious about the hostility facing all undocumented immigrants in the country. "Much of this was a reflection of the early strategies. It was all very new to talk about these things. In this context it was important to cover all your bases, to show this top student, let them know that we're not what they think."[45]

Since 2010, there have been concerted efforts to rectify the problems associated with the past discursive strategy. "Now, when we come
up with messages, we try to highlight everything, the many different
realities of undocumented students. We try not to highlight only one
section of the reality and generalize from that."[46] Describing the complex and messy lives of youths generates a more realistic representation,
but it is a representation that is less compelling than one highlighting
the few attributes ("one section of the reality") that make these youths
exceptional. The image of the good immigrant that was constructed in
the earlier period is reinforced by the media's strong preference for the
more traditional representation of the DREAMer. "It's an old strategy
and it just stuck because the media likes it and wants it. This is a good
thing because we get our message out there and people like what we present. But, it's not good because it doesn't leave room for anything else. If
we try to veer from the message and present something else, the media
will say, 'Oh, can we just talk to a real DREAMer?'"[47] By "real," the
journalist implies the sympathetic public figure (de facto American, best
and brightest, innocent) crafted in the earlier mobilization cycle. When
DREAMers deviate from the script and assert a more accurate portrait
of their lives and struggles, the media loses interest and pushes them
back into the public and front-stage persona. The master frame used to
represent immigrants in the early cycle of mobilization has constrained
the messages and representations of a newer generation of activists and
advocates. This newer generation finds itself bound in a particular discursive path that contributes to the reproduction of the themes and their
associated dilemmas.

Controlling the Message and Messenger

The ability of rights associations and DREAMers to forge an effective political voice has depended on generating a compelling message, but
equally, it has depended on controlling the ways in which thousands of
diverse activists and advocates talk about the cause in the public sphere.
Sticking to the talking points has been just as important as the talking
points themselves. Poorly disciplined activists produce a cacophony of
different utterances, acts, and performances in the public sphere. The

general public would more likely see this as the "noise" of a threatening foreign mob than a compelling and legitimate "voice" from a deserving group of immigrants.[48] The importance of message control encouraged the leading associations to build an infrastructure to discipline how thousands of activists across the country have talked and represented the struggle.

Prominent national associations like National Immigration Law Center and the Center for Community Change helped form a network of DREAM-friendly associations called the "United We Dream Coalition" in 2007. This coalition was made up of youth activists and immigrant rights leaders seeking to pass the DREAM Act as part of Comprehensive Immigration Reform. Participants in this coalition and its follow-up organization, United We Dream, connected through weekly conference calls to discuss the political and messaging strategies of the campaign. After failing to pass Comprehensive Immigration Reform in 2007, rights associations and youth activists developed a permanent organization to support the youth component of the struggle. United We Dream has played an important role in controlling the DREAM message. It served as a site where national rights associations worked with youths to produce core messages. Professional communications experts working for national associations helped create compelling frames and stories that resonated with politicians, the public, and the media. They knew how to tap core values, convey values through convincing frames, identify strategic targets, and modulate arguments for different audiences. Through their good relations with influential journalists and producers covering immigration issues, they also enjoyed access to local and national print, radio, and television media. They used this access to put stories "out there" and frame the ways in which these stories were told in the media. These communications experts possessed a unique set of resources that allowed them to exert a degree of control in shaping the message and representations of the DREAM campaign. United We Dream not only was a center for producing messages, but also it became a central training center for activists around the country. It attracted talented youth activists to its Washington, DC, office for workshops and internships. These DREAM activists were trained in the nuts and bolts of producing effective messages and running campaigns. Once youths were provided with extensive training, they were expected to go back to their home organizations and diffuse these skills to local activists. Lastly, United We Dream also reached outside of their office in Washington, DC, In addition to holding regular retreats and conventions for DREAMers nationwide, the organization sent staff and interns from the central office to perform training sessions across the country.[49] This national reach made it an important node for producing and diffusing the DREAM message across activist networks.

State and local DREAMer organizations also arose during this time, connecting up to and complementing the work of United We Dream. The Center for Humane Immigrant Rights of Los Angeles (CHIRLA) spearheaded one of the most prominent and well-developed of these organizations. CHIRLA was a member of the national Reform Immigration for America (RIFA) and an ally of the leading immigrant rights associations. In 2007, CHIRLA initiated an effort to integrate A.B. 540 groups (college-based support groups for undocumented students in California) into a single statewide network. The California Dream Network played a similar role as United We Dream, but the organization was more formal, centralized, and vertically integrated. The organization was made up of three regions—Northern, Central, and Southern California—with each region connecting most of the A.B. 540 groups in their respective areas. Each region selected a steering committee of three representatives, and they coordinated activities and discussions with the network director, a paid employee of CHIRLA.

To ensure the autonomy of the campus organizations and the Network from CHIRLA, a measure was introduced into the network's by-laws to guarantee autonomy in decisions concerning strategies, campaigns, and actions. The network director's role was not to impose the "CHIRLA-line" in a top-down fashion but to use information provided by CHIRLA to help inform the network's actions, messages, and campaigns. The director functioned as a mediator and broker between the needs of the network and CHIRLA:

> We are Network organizers but we are also CHIRLA staff. CHIRLA as a larger organization has needs. This is a 50/50 responsibility. So, let's say the Network develops a strategy and message that differs from CHIRLA, then I

have to be the bridge between both. I'll say to CHIRLA, "Well, the students say this." And then I'll go to the Network and say, "Hey, CHIRLA staff thinks this." You try to maintain a neutral ground but at a certain point you have to take a position on these matters and try to find a solution.[50]

Another one of the founding members of the network stressed the ambivalent nature of this relation. CHIRLA intended to create an autonomous political space for undocumented youths, but it would also benefit from its control over one of the largest networks of DREAMers in the country. "Even though their [CHIRLA] intention was the right one, to create a space for all these groups to talk to each other, they were also smart. Providing that space for the youth to talk to one another would provide them with some control over it. So whenever a bigger campaign was initiated, they would be the ones able to move a statewide youth network to do the work and get the message out there."[51] As political officials sought out DREAMers for events and campaigns, CHIRLA became the "go-to" organization within the immigrant rights community. "People [politicians] come down to find the student groups because they knew that the student groups were a good media sell and they were good organizers. They were just vying for that grassroots base."[52] CHIRLA was able to enhance its power in the field of immigration politics by becoming the gatekeeper to one of the country's largest grassroots networks of DREAMers.

The California Dream Network and CHIRLA worked with national associations to produce messages, and these messages were diffused through the network's statewide infrastructure. Message diffusion was performed through bimonthly meetings (telephone and in-person) between the network director and regional steering committees. Workshops, regional summits, and retreats have become very important methods to diffuse the messages and messaging frames to individual DREAMers across the state. These events assembled individuals from different communities and backgrounds and provided them intensive training in messaging. Training in "storytelling" has been a particularly important part of these events.[53] Immigrant rights advocates have long understood that the most effective method to deliver a message to the general public was through a morally compelling story.[54] This understanding of the unique power of the story strongly informed the messaging strategy of the DREAM campaign. "We tell them that storytelling is the most important way of getting our message across, in organizing, lobbying, in media outreach, in everything."[55]

A good story depends on a person's abilities to blend their own compelling life histories with the generic narrative employed by the campaign. The generic narrative stresses several main points: the hardships facing them as children, their abilities to overcome difficult barriers and continue to strive for the American dream, and the burdens posed on them by an unjust, immoral, and broken immigration system. Placing one's personal life within this general narrative structure enables the DREAMers to convey their message in a morally and emotionally compelling way to the general public. For new recruits, telling a compelling story has not been natural. The personal peculiarities of one's real life have tempted most new recruits to veer "off-message" or to personalize the story too much. This has required intensive and ongoing training in storytelling. "We've gone through several trainings. Your story has to show how this legislation will benefit you personally, how it will benefit others in your community, and how it will benefit the country. Now, when people ask me how to write their story, I say to include something about themselves but also tie it to everybody. Don't personalize it too much."[56] Another DREAMer confirmed the importance of training sessions for telling a good story: "This is a training that we provide. We tell them how to tell their story in a compelling way. How to connect it to the national level, how to connect it not only to their own personal problems but also to society as a whole."[57] After new recruits develop stories with the right balance of the personal and general, they perform their stories repeatedly to their fellow DREAMers. These sessions allow DREAMers to comment on each other's stories and share techniques in crafting and performing stories. One veteran DREAMer recounts the importance of training sessions in constructing his story:

> For me, the members at that time really empowered me too—because I didn't even know how to tell my story. There was no beginning or middle or end for me. And so, through them I was able to structure my story, and be able to tell it. Within a few months, I was empowered to share my story,

not only here, but also publicly. For me, that became very real. Once I began sharing my story, it became something else. I was ready to be involved, to risk more than I thought I could risk.[58]

Through a process of telling and retelling their stories to one another, newly recruited DREAMers have internalized the general narrative into their own thinking and feelings about their lives as undocumented youths in the country. This enabled them to become highly effective and committed deliverers of the DREAM message in the public sphere.

Following these training sessions, DREAMers have been expected to return to their local colleges to diffuse the messages and messaging skills to members of their local campus support groups. Having acquired the message and skills, they are expected to impart these skills on to new recruits coming up through local campus organizations. More experienced members of the network have also visited campus groups and provided additional training and support. For example, one DREAMer recounts:

Interviewer: And learning storytelling has occurred through workshops on campus?

DREAMer: Yeah. We had an organizer come to one of our meetings to talk about how storytelling is done, and then after he explained what the story was, we then went ahead with one-on-one trainings.[59]

Well-trained activists with the network visited localized campus groups and trained new recruits to employ the generic discourse of the DREAM campaign in compelling ways.

Making the DREAMer Through Networks

The formal infrastructure created by United We Dream and state and local-level organizations like the California Dream Network has also helped expand the social networks of DREAMers. These organizations created real spaces, such as support groups, retreats, meetings, conventions, and so forth, where undocumented youths could connect to others like themselves, discover commonalities, and apply the DREAM discourse to interpret their common realities. By connecting individuals to a broad and supportive community, these networking spaces create nurturing environments that enable individual youths to "come out" about their status in public and begin to think of themselves as DREAMers.

Networking spaces have provided opportunities for emotionally intensive exchanges between youth activists. These have been important moments in which youths share the trauma of discovering their status, the shame and stigma associated with it, and the countless barriers they face. At its regular retreats and workshops, California Dream Network has consistently organized "ice breakers" and other emotionally intensive activities. These exercises have been described by participants as "therapy sessions" because they provide participants a safe space to share their stories and feelings with others. One member of the California Dream Network described an activity:

> We have a training called "Step Up to the Line." This training helps students see their differences but also their similarities. Sometimes we say, "Step up to the line if you have a family member who is currently in the process of deportation." So we do those trainings to highlight the fact that everyone is in the same boat and that all of us are being affected by the broken immigration system. That allows them to open up and see the human aspect and connect emotionally to other people.[60]

Lead organizers therefore built connections between individual youths by revealing commonalities through emotionally intensive exercises and activities.

For most participants, these sessions were the first times they spoke openly about their undocumented status in public. While many youths have been quite apprehensive about this, they learned that they could trust other participants to validate their feelings, fears, and hopes. One DREAMer recounts her first experience in a student meeting:

> I was so scared but I did it—I don't know why I would ever do it. Just being in those spaces and meeting people, and *feeling like it was okay to be me* and it was okay to be involved, it wasn't as hard as I thought it would be. I felt good. I saw that my status didn't need to limit me in the ways that I thought

it would. And it didn't need to stop me. It didn't mean that everybody would hate me or would want to stop me from doing things. *It was the opposite: I was doing things because of my status. I was giving a speech in front of people and they were all, happy for me, supporting me. I think feeling that really helped me a lot.*[61]

The group provided this youth with a safe and supportive space to come to terms with her newly discovered status. This was an important and cathartic moment. The support provided by this group of undocumented youth made it possible for her to be herself ("feeling like it was okay to be me") and to view her status as a source of empowerment and not just a stigma and constraint ("I was doing things because of my status").

These intensive interactions have infused participating DREAMers with high levels of "emotional energy,"[62] which has helped reinforce commitment to one another and to the general movement. One DREAMer describes how attending California Dream Network retreats made him feel "pumped up" and more dedicated to the cause: "We encourage new members to go to the retreats so they come back pumped. This happens very often and that is how I got more involved in the movement. I was a member of my campus group. Then I went to a retreat; I got very pumped up and got much more involved in the community."[63] When asked why the retreat pumped him up, the respondent stressed the importance of developing connections to other people like himself: "You see that you are not just working by yourself on your college campus. There are people in Santa Barbara or Berkeley who are going through the same struggles. You realize that you are not alone and that if you bring more people on board, you can make bigger changes. We learn that we are not alone and this pumps us up to keep up with the struggle."

Emotionally intensive interactions harness strong bonds between DREAMers, but these emotional interactions also facilitate their abilities to internalize the discourse and develop a political and social identity as a DREAMer:

> It's like when I had a gay friend tell me "it's like coming out of the closet"— to say you're undocumented is a really big thing. But as they become more involved in the movement, they eventually embrace it—not all of them, but the majority of them embrace their identity. They realize that "undocumented" is just an imposed identity by the Government, and that is not who

they are—that they are human beings and they shouldn't be afraid of saying that they are undocumented. They are students and human beings. I think this process takes months, years. But they eventually get to that point where they don't feel afraid of saying, "I am an immigrant from this country. This is my culture and this is who I am."[64]

Some undocumented students had been active in politics before entering college, but few had developed a distinctive political identity on the basis of their undocumented status. Emotionally intensive workshop, retreats, parties, and "coming-out" events have fostered collective recognition of themselves as undocumented students with politically distinctive goals, needs, and cultures.

Geographical proximity has allowed DREAMers in the same city to sustain their contacts through regular meetings and socializing events. In the Los Angeles area, CHIRLA has become a regular meeting point for DREAMers across Southern California. Network members from metropolitan Los Angeles gather there regularly to work, socialize, and address issues about various campaigns. The organization has a formal meeting space for the DREAMers and work cubicles for activists spending the day at the office. Geographical proximity has also enabled the DREAMers to connect to one another through social events like parties, fundraisers, and informal leisure activities. While these activities have often been fun and social, they have also played an important role in strengthening bonds between activists and commitments to one another and the struggle. One DREAMer remarks on the importance of these socializing events

DREAMer: At the end of every event we decide, "Okay, let's organize a social party at someone's house," and that helps us to keep developing the relationships. So, I think our lives revolve around having fun too, not only organizing but also spending time with friends. That is another critical component.

Interviewer: Do these kinds of relations help your organizing work?

DREAMer: Yeah, definitely. I have been able to develop very personal relationships where they trust me, where I trust them, and where if I ever need something from them, they show up.

> And they do the same thing with their own members. And when we say, "We're having a fund-raising party at someone's house and we need people to show up," I just call them and they say, "Oh don't worry: we'll be there."[65]

Interactions in intimate spaces of daily life (CHIRLA office, campus clubs, parties, events, and so on) have functioned as moments where activists share their fears with one another, celebrate accomplishments, reinforce their belief that their cause is just and right, and express doubts about their situations and concerns over the movement's direction. These face-to-face interactions foster feelings of trust in other DREAMers and emotional commitment to their general cause.

The Internet has also been an important medium for producing and sustaining social networks. Facebook, Twitter, web sites, online petitions, and blogs have connected individuals. The Internet has provided a straightforward means to transmit basic information concerning campaigns, scholarships, and options for undocumented youths. Web sites, blogs, and social media have become important sources to diffuse the messages and talking points of the movement across the country. Highly frequented web sites employ standard frames, talking points, and sound bites. The web site of United We Dream, for instance, employs a tight narrative to describe the situation of undocumented youth. It also provides activists with scripts and talking points to address the media, legislators, and members of the public.[66] In addition to transmitting messages and information, social media tools have been instrumental in coordinating meetings between the leading DREAMers. One member of the network's steering committee discussed the centrality of this function:

> I have brought up many tools to help the Steering Members organize the Network more efficiently. The use of technology is our most important tool—we use Facebook, Gmail, Yahoo, and Google groups and also Wiggio. Wiggio is very important: imagine Facebook, Twitter, Gmail, Skype combined. It helps small groups to facilitate and collaborate. It's a really powerful and useful tool. We've been using Wiggio and Gmail as one of our primary tools to organize, and it has proven extremely useful and effective.[67]

In addition to coordinating meetings, social media services like Twitter,

Facebook, and blogs provide DREAMers opportunities to discuss the arguments, messages, and symbols generated by the leading activists of the movement. When messages or arguments are posted to Facebook, for instance, DREAMers have the opportunity to assess, critique, or support them. Participating in these constant online deliberations concerning messages and strategies, DREAMers remain engulfed in the movement in their everyday worlds. Their online social experience becomes consumed by DREAM talk and exchanges. The boundary between the private world of youths and the public world of the DREAMer breaks down as the activist is constantly enmeshed in dialogue and exchanges over what it means to be a DREAMer.

Online and offline networks are strategic mechanisms for socializing new activists into the discourses of the DREAM mobilization. They learn the discourse, assess the meaning and value of particular messages, and come to understand their own particular circumstances through the narrative structure and themes of the movement. They learn not only to speak the language of the movement but also to feel the language.[68] An organizer from the California Dream Network remarked:

> I knew my status was a really big obstacle, but I never felt comfortable saying that I was undocumented. But then after becoming involved in IDEAS [his campus support group] and the California Dream Network, I think *it changed the way I think and the way I see life.* Eventually, in less than a year, I saw the whole picture and I became extremely involved. *Building those relationships with other students, listening and hearing what they had to say about their own personal experience—it took time.*[69]

The process of becoming a DREAMer has therefore been as much an intellectual process as it is has been an emotional and social one. Networking spaces functioned to support youths negotiate and undergo their complicated struggles of coming to political terms with their immigration status.[70]

Spreading the DREAM Across Public Arenas

The organizations and social networks have helped connect scattered campus-based groups to one another and bring dispersed youths into the public sphere. As new recruits have been taken from their private worlds and brought into the public sphere, this organizational and social infrastructure has provided them with the discourse and training to present their arguments for rights in a disciplined and consistent fashion:

> Before we [his campus support group] joined the network, we thought about messaging but not strategically. We just focused at the campus level; we were basically living in a bubble. When we became part of the California Dream Network, it just opened doors and helped us see the larger picture. *So now when we talk about messaging, we see the California Dream Network, we get updates from the network, we decide what we should be doing, what we should be saying.*[71]

These experiences have trained DREAMers to become disciplined messengers in different public arenas, for example, schools, campuses, public meetings, media, and so forth. Armed with a tight message and excellent training in message delivery, DREAMers entered their public worlds and worked to shape ideas and gain support within them. DREAMers have been quite effective in penetrating and framing their message to the English- and Spanish-speaking media. They have also been extremely effective in penetrating the smaller and more obscure arenas that constitute public life.

DREAMers have targeted college campuses. They have used their messaging skills to recruit supporters among campus administrators and faculty; to enter public debate through tabling, participating in campus-based forums, and writing letters to campus-based newspapers; and to recruit new undocumented students. When informal campus groups have gained sufficient levels of support, many have gone on to establish charters and become formal student organizations. The formalization of support groups has permitted access to institutional resources and support from colleges and universities, including money, office space, technology, organizational assistance, and public space. Access to these resources enhanced their abilities to strengthen their public presence on these college campuses. This has by no means been an easy process and often involves protracted conflict with a range of hostile campus-based adversaries, such as conservative clubs, students, administrators, and faculty.

Campus-based DREAMers in California have also advanced their struggle off campus. They have spent much of their time visiting community meetings, public events, churches, and schools to tell their story. Direct communication to local audiences increases support and draws in recruits and allies to the struggle. By telling their compelling stories at different community events, DREAMers can also shape local narratives and the ways the public thinks about DREAMers and their cause. High schools have also been an important part of outreach efforts. DREAM activists use their personal relations with old teachers, counselors, and administrators to gain access to high schools. They visit their former schools, talk to teachers and counselors, tell their stories to the students, and provide important information concerning the possibilities of attending community college and university. UCLA's campus-based group IDEAS, which had been an important affiliate of the California Dream Network, has developed one of the most sophisticated outreach strategies in the country:

> First it started with the same schools that we went to. Even until today, when new students come, we encourage them to go back to their schools and give workshops in their schools—even giving information if they don't feel comfortable giving a workshop. We will go with them. And I think that is the encouragement that a lot of our members feel. It's not just that they should go do it, but "we'll go with you to do those workshops." We also have a Counselor's Conference, and so outside of helping students with recognizing that they can continue going to school, we also acknowledge that a lot of the times there needs to be a systematic change with how things are run in the school district. So we also target counselors. This past year we had over one hundred counselors from LAUSD [Los Angeles Unified School District] and the OC [Orange County] school district come to UCLA. We gave them a workshop on what it means to be undocumented students and what it is that they can tell their students. We don't tell them to tell the students that everything is going to be perfect, but to tell them that it's possible.[72]

Each contact with high school students, counselors, teachers, and administrators has provided another opportunity for DREAMers to re-tell their stories to familiar and new audiences. This has influenced the ways in which school personnel and students think, perceive, and talk about these youths. It has also provided undocumented high school students important support to know that there are many other people in their situation, there is no shame in being undocumented, and there are still ways to achieve their dreams in spite of their legal status. Spreading the DREAM message through these highly localized public arenas has therefore influenced the identities and aspirations of undocumented high school youth; provided counselors, teachers, and administrators the language and information to support these youth; and served to recruit students, teachers, and counselors into the general struggle.

The infrastructure used to produce and diffuse the messages therefore enabled leaders and activists to achieve a high degree of messaging control. The experience and cultural resources of the leading immigrant rights associations enabled them to retain control over how messages were produced and expressed publicly. They used their central position within the infrastructure to produce messages and diffuse those messages to state and local organizations across the country. This downward diffusion process enabled the leaders to retain a certain degree of control over how DREAMers thought and talked about their struggles nationwide. It also allowed leaders to penetrate and influence the discourses in highly localized and scattered public arenas around the country (campuses, schools, churches, community organizations, local media markets, and so on). The process of downward diffusion largely rested on the constant training of undocumented youth in the art of effective messaging, with many DREAMers being directly or indirectly trained to become well-disciplined messengers. By training students to play these roles, they have gained the capacities to frame the ways in which people on their campuses, communities, cities, states, and country have thought about the DREAM Act and the injustices facing undocumented youth.

The training of DREAMers also imparted cultural and symbolic resources away from the leaders and to the newly activated DREAMers. The DREAMers have learned how to construct effective messages, transmit these messages to the media and other important publics, and use language and symbols in highly effective ways. In a very short period of time, these inexperienced youths acquired the cultural and symbolic capital to make them highly skilled and professionalized activists in their own right. Soon, they would become less dependent on the immigrant rights associations to construct and spread their messages, becoming leaders of their own movement in both name and deed.

The DREAM Act arose as a central issue during the presidential election in 2012. Both Barack Obama and Mitt Romney expressed their admiration for this group of immigrants and provided different ideas to resolve problems concerning their status. While the Republican candidate advocated the hard-line of no exemptions for any undocumented immigrants during the primaries, he shifted to a more mainstream position of supporting some kind of exemption for this group during the general elections. Considering that this political group of immigrants simply did not exist twelve years before, their emergence as a central figure in national immigration debates is a remarkable feat.

The process of constructing this group involved creating an effective message and social and organizational infrastructure. This not only gave the group a public presence, but also it provided opportunities for undocumented youths to connect to one another and become acquainted with the discourses framing the group in the public sphere. By being brought in through these networks, they became familiar with the language of the DREAM campaign, using the language and stories to construct their own political subjectivities and identities. Through such a process, individual undocumented youths became a political group of DREAMers, with common ways of performing, feeling, and expressing themselves in the public sphere. Such a process empowered the group to become an important force in national immigration politics, but it also planted countless splits in the group. These splits would quickly grow into gaping cleavages between the different individuals, organizations, and factions making up the DREAMers. Cleavages posed important risks to their struggle and to the broader immigrant rights movement while at the same time introducing new opportunities for the evolution of both.

3

Taking a Stand

By 2010 the DREAMer had emerged as a political group. DREAMers had established a public identity, possessed distinctive interests and solidarities, and articulated their interests with a powerful and compelling voice. As the group grew more concrete and powerful, some DREAMers became displeased with their continued subordination to larger immigrant rights associations. They were no longer the "kids" of the immigrant rights movement. They should be able to take a seat at the table and assume an equal role in making decisions about the strategic direction of the immigrant rights movement. Dismissed as petulant and impatient by some leading associations, dissident DREAMers broke from their traditional supporters and developed their own strategies and methods to advance their cause. By fall 2010, the dissidents had shifted the strategic focus of the whole immigrant rights movement from the Comprehensive Immigration Reform Act to the DREAM Act as a stand-alone bill and asserted themselves as an autonomous force in the movement. Through these struggles, DREAMers began to win recognition as first among equals within the immigrant rights movement.

The views of this self-conscious group of DREAMers were expressed in an explosive op-ed piece (a veritable DREAMers manifesto) in *Dissent* magazine, published in fall 2010:[1]

We are undocumented youth activists and we refuse to be silent any longer. The DREAM Act movement has inspired and re-energized undocumented and immigrant youth around the country. In a time when the entire immigrant community is under attack, and increasingly demoralized, stripped of our rights, the DREAM movement has injected life, resistance and creativity into the broader immigrant rights struggle.

Until we organized this movement, we had been caught in a paralyzing stranglehold of inactivity across the country. We were told that the Comprehensive Immigration Reform Act, or CIRA, was still possible. Yet we continued to endure ICE raids and we witnessed the toxic Arizona S.B. 1070. Meanwhile, CIRA had lost bipartisan support and there was no longer meaningful Congressional or executive support for real reform.

Youth DREAM Act activists stopped waiting. We organized ourselves and created our own strategy, used new tactics and we rejected the passivity of the nonprofit industrial complex. At a moment when hope seemed scarce, we forged new networks of solidarity. We declared ourselves UNDOCUMENTED AND UNAFRAID!

Differences over strategy precipitated the break, but the break was also a reflection of deeper cleavages concerning position, power, and recognition in the immigrant rights movement.

Negotiating these cleavages and conflicts marked an important step in the evolution of the DREAMer as a political group. Throughout the 2000s, many DREAMers stayed in the shadows and were represented by the immigrant rights associations and political supporters. Their early struggle was about gaining legal-juridical rights to stay in the country, but as this struggle advanced, it also became about gaining recognition for themselves as legitimate subjects capable of making claims on their own behalf.[2] For these DREAMers the struggle for equality was as much about winning residency status as it was about winning recognition as political equals. It was during this time when the slogans "I Exist!" and "Undocumented and Unafraid" became prominent in their messaging. They were now engaged in a two part struggle: a struggle directed at the government to win legal-juridical rights, and a struggle directed at the leadership of the immigrant rights movement to win the right to speak for themselves in the public sphere.

Disagreements over Strategy

DREAM Act advocates were presented an important strategic choice in 2006 and 2007: Should they push the DREAM Act as a stand-alone bill, or as part of the Comprehensive Immigration Reform Act? NILC was the most prominent association supporting the DREAM campaign. It had pushed for the DREAM Act as a stand-alone bill in the early 2000s before there was ever talk of comprehensive reform. By 2006–7 the general consensus among the leading associations had changed. Most believed the time was right to push for the most they could possibly get from Congress (Comprehensive Immigration Reform) and only fall back to smaller measures like the DREAM Act if their initial demands were not met. They also believed that pushing for the DREAM Act as a separate bill would weaken their efforts because political leaders could use it as an easy way to placate immigrant rights and Latino activists while leaving the status of millions of other undocumented immigrants unchanged. Passing the DREAM Act as a stand-alone bill would also remove the most dynamic and well-liked part of the immigrant rights movement from the struggle, making it all the more difficult to extend residency rights to other undocumented immigrants. When the leading associations formed the RIFA coalition in 2008, their strategic line was that the different organizations, factions, and advocates making up the immigrant rights movement needed to stick together to pass Comprehensive Immigration Reform and legalize the status of most undocumented immigrants in the country. As the fiscal sponsor of United We Dream, NILC was asked to tone down its past support for a stand-alone bill and follow the general strategic line of the coalition. "People knew that it was the go to organization for DREAM. When the word came down from RIFA that these organizations should stop talking about DREAM, NILC was the first organization they went to."[3]

There were also debates over these strategic issues within the California Dream Network. CHIRLA encouraged the California Dream Network members to vote in support of the RIFA strategy during one of its early retreats. CHIRLA's leaders believed that this was the best way forward for the undocumented immigrants and for the organization's standing within the national immigrant rights movement.[4] "It was framed in this way: 'We cannot be selfish and think only about our-selves. We have to think about our parents and everybody else. So, do we continue to push for the DREAM Act as our legislative goal or do we go for legislative reform for everybody?' That was the framing. That was the moment in which Comprehensive Immigration Reform became the principal legislative goal of the Network."[5]

In 2008, rights associations temporarily shifted their attention from the national legislation to the presidential elections of 2008. Once Barack Obama was elected, many believed that he would support Com-prehensive Immigration Reform after his signature health care bill had passed. In late 2009, RIFA initiated a new campaign to pass Comprehen-sive Immigration Reform before the congressional elections of fall 2010. It was believed that vulnerable congressional Democrats would want to rally the Latino base in the face of a difficult election. Moreover, a Republican victory in November would make it impossible to pass Com-prehensive Immigration Reform. Many in the immigrant rights commu-nity looked to President Obama's State of the Union speech in 2010 for a sign of his support for comprehensive reform. However, instead of using the speech to make a bold announcement, President Obama dedicated only thirty-eight words to immigration reform at the very end of his speech. Disappointed members of RIFA approached the White House to discuss its lukewarm support of reform. The White House responded by encouraging RIFA to pressure House and Senate Democrats to take the lead.

RIFA organized a massive immigrant rights demonstration in Washington, DC, in March 2010. Coalition members invested millions of dollars and mobilized more than one hundred thousand people to the event. In spite of this impressive show of force, the event was overshad-owed by the passage of the Affordable Care Act and a Tea Party protest of one thousand people. Media coverage of the immigrant rights dem-onstration was minimal. The weak support from the White House and the failure of the costly demonstration led many to question the viability of RIFA and its strategy to achieve comprehensive reform. "They [RIFA] didn't get the headlines and they spent a lot of money on the demon-stration. That is when they lost the support of a lot of community orga-nizations around the country. These community organizations struggle mightily. They are understaffed and overworked. Here the big national organizations are spending tons of money for this march that doesn't even make the news. That was the beginning of the end for RIFA."[6]

Soon after the Washington demonstration, several critical immigrant rights associations shifted their attention from Comprehensive Immigration Reform and began mobilizing against federal and state-level enforcement measures. In particular they targeted the federal government's 287(g) program and the passage of Arizona's punitive anti-immigration bill, S.B. 1070. The National Day Laborer Organizing Network (NDLON), Mexican American Legal Defense and Education Fund (MALDEF), and local Arizona associations assumed a leading role against this state-level measure. RIFA resisted their efforts because their focus on state-level antienforcement battles deviated from RIFA's central message and siphoned resources away from the campaign for Comprehensive Immigration Reform. The Director of NDLON recounts a mediation session between NDLON and RIFA:

> The director of Center for Community Change says that the enforcement messaging is essentially taking away from their messaging, that it's not the messaging that we need to communicate to America, that it's going to hurt us in the long-term. So, obviously, we said, "We're very sorry for that, but the thing is we're not going to use the fight in Arizona and the suffering of people to help this failed effort. We're not going to do that. S.B. 1070 [the Arizona measure] is wrong on its own merits. It's not wrong because it's going to stop you from promoting CIR [Comprehensive Immigration Reform]. If you can use it, go ahead and use it. . . . We're going to fight it because we need to bring justice to the people of Arizona—no question about it. There is nothing to discuss here." I strongly believe that. So that's it. We couldn't come to terms with them.[7]

NDLON and its allies went on to organize a large march in Arizona that was said to divide the focus of the immigrant rights movement. "So while they spent millions of dollars to bring 100,000 people to Washington, DC, we put 150,000 people in the streets with about thirty-five thousand dollars. And then we invited the funders to come to Arizona: 'You got to come here and see.' So they saw. . . . It was one of the most beautiful marches ever of the immigrant rights movement."[8] Following the Arizona march, NDLON helped launch a large-scale boycott of Arizona and initiated an effort to build up the organizational capacities of local activists in the state.

Associations like MALDEF and NDLON became more vocal with their criticisms of RIFA's strategy and began to outline an alternative strategy. They needed to fight against repressive enforcement measures and push for smaller measures that stood much better chances of passing (like the DREAM Act). The target should not only be Congress; they also needed to target local and state-level institutions. Local and state officials in conservative jurisdictions had become bolder in passing repressive immigration-related measures.[9] By focusing on smaller wins at local, state, and federal levels, the immigrant rights movement would take slow and incremental steps toward advancing the rights of immigrants. Lastly, they feared that winning bipartisan support for the Comprehensive Immigration Reform Act would require RIFA to accept major restrictions and enforcement measures as part of the compromise. A close associate of NDLON and MALDEF noted:

> You know, they [NDLON] and others predicted that the CIR strategy [Comprehensive Immigration Reform] was not going to work and it was going to lead to what we have today. And that we should have from the beginning taken on these issues piecemeal. . . . Right-wing conservatives have always done everything piecemeal, by attrition. They take on issues one-by-one, place by place. They have taken on issues at local levels, from taking away housing to audits to working with local-level law enforcement. They have been more effective at their strategy, and NDLON began to argue that we should have pushed that strategy from the beginning.[10]

As RIFA mobilized all the movement's resources to push for Comprehensive Immigration Reform at the federal level, anti-immigrant groups had developed a sophisticated strategy to pass local and state-level measures that rolled back the rights of immigrants across the country.

> We're in a worse situation now than when we embarked on CIR. What happened is that all the resources and focus on CIR took us away from all the stuff that was happening on the side with local law enforcement, local

initiatives, audits, etc. We didn't get CIR, but we fell so far behind in our response to these other initiatives that now we are way behind in even forming a strategy.[11]

A stand-alone DREAM Act coincided well with the strategic preferences of these critics and their vision of incremental immigration reform. In January 2010, MALDEF was the first of the large national associations to come out in support of a stand-alone DREAM Act. It believed that all the proposals in circulation for comprehensive reform were overly punitive and ceded too much ground on enforcement.[12] The only reasonable way forward was through piecemeal and incremental struggles. The DREAM Act should be given priority because of the strong momentum in its favor.

Building Support for Dissident DREAMers

DREAMers were also frustrated with RIFA's position. Many believed that RIFA was sticking to a strategy that was very costly and not bearing any fruits. DREAMers began to strike out on their own. The first such action was initiated by four undocumented students in Florida. The students embarked on a four-month walk from Miami, Florida, to Washington, DC (the "Trail of Dreams"). On May 1, they participated in a civil disobedience action in Washington, DC, which ended with the arrest of one hundred supporters, including several members of Congress. The students attracted massive media attention, which helped place the DREAM Act once again into the public debate. Having witnessed the success of the "Trail of Dreams" campaign, dissident DREAMers in Los Angeles, Chicago, Michigan, and New York felt the time was right to escalate the struggle. This group adopted the name, "The Dream Is Coming." They embraced aggressive, public, and confrontational tactics to push for the DREAM Act as a stand-alone bill. In their view, there were clear signs that the DREAM Act stood a much greater chance of passing in this Congress than Comprehensive Immigration Reform. Many of these DREAMers were also tired of waiting for the passage of comprehensive reform. They feared that if they waited too long the window of opportunity for the DREAM Act would close. One dissident DREAMer remembered the process of assessing political opportunities:

Everybody was like: "Alright, cool, that [Comprehensive Immigration Reform] is like the ultimate end goal—that's what we all want. But, you know what? It's not going to happen. We need something a little smaller but big enough to bring about change." And for us that was the DREAM Act. That is the first step to immigration reform. And for us it was a much easier campaign. We're all grassroots, we're all students and we're part-time activists, part-time brothers and sisters—a lot of part-time jobs. So our time is very limited. For us, it was like: this is what we know how to do and we believe in ourselves and we know what we have the resources to do it. So we were being realistic.[13]

These DREAMers believed that pushing the DREAM Act now would legalize the status of hundreds of thousands while providing grounds to push for more extensive reforms later.

The DREAMers also felt confident with their own abilities to direct and manage a campaign without the guidance of the traditional immigrant rights associations. They were careful to set up the legal and political groundwork leading up to the civil disobedience actions. Extensive planning went into place in order to reduce the risk of long detentions and deportations for DREAMers arrested during the actions. Among the activists willing to participate in these actions, they identified those with the strongest immigration files. They anticipated what would happen after arrests and how the legal support team could intervene to ensure a rapid release. Additionally, they created national and regional response teams to support the arrestees. These teams provided legal, political, and emotional support for DREAMers engaged in civil disobedience, but they also led the messaging campaigns and mobilized massive petition drives to ensure the rapid release of arrestees.

In addition to developing this sophisticated support network, they also developed an alternative network of allied supporters:

We created our strategic ally committee. These were people that we had long relations with and knew would support us. They got an email from me saying that big actions were coming soon. So they all came to the meeting. I remember [the director of the UCLA Labor Center] was there with his hands on his head. He asked, "Is there any way we can talk you out of this?" We answered no. He then immediately asked, "What do you need from us?" The director of MALDEF was also at the meeting. We asked him to be the one making the calls to Washington [DC] once the actions started. We thought NDLON would be the right fiscal sponsor because they have an independent position from RIFA. I remember [the director of NDLON] sat in the back, just taking notes and saying yes to everything. And from them [UCLA Labor Center], we just asked them to provide us with a space at the Labor Center to do our work.[14]

Preexisting ties encouraged these associations to provide important levels of support to the dissident DREAMers. The DREAMer who called the meeting had strong personal and political relations with these individuals that dated back to her childhood. Her parents were longtime activists in the Los Angeles immigrant rights community, and she had been an active member of Southern California Institute of Popular Education and CHIRLA's Wise-Up and California Dream Network.[15] Her networks were extremely helpful in developing this alternative base of support within the immigrant rights movement.

MALDEF came out in strong support of these efforts. "They [MALDEF] believed that the whole nature of the debate needed to change and the best way to change it would be to highlight the DREAMers."[16] In addition to helping change the debate, NDLON saw the passage of the DREAM Act as a stepping stone for more difficult immigrant groups like day laborers. "They [NDLON] realize that in promoting day laborers out there . . . you know, the public is not biting. But if they support the students and they get the DREAM Act passed, then it helps them in the long-term, because they open the door for other reforms."[17] Considering the unlikely chances of passing Comprehensive Immigration Reform in spring 2010, the dissident DREAMers and the critical associations agreed that a stand-alone DREAM Act was the best way forward:

I think NDLON and MALDEF were one of the few that really came out and said, "No, a comprehensive approach is not possible and we need to take a piecemeal approach and incremental wins. One of the wins or the first win should be the DREAM Act as a step forward for immigration reform." And that was also our language. That's when we started saying we need to have a stand-alone bill and we need to push the DREAM Act separate from CIR because if that doesn't happen, it will never happen. We will never be able to push CIR as it is, or as it's being given. There was no political will for that. There was a lot of lip service, but there was no political will. So we understood that and we decided to move forward.[18]

The convergence of strategies and the belief that these youths were the future of the immigrant rights movement prompted these associations to lend strong support to these DREAMers. This support was crucial for mounting a campaign for the DREAM Act as a stand-alone bill.

Providing support to dissident DREAMers needed to be handled delicately because of potential conflicts with individuals and associations in the immigrant rights community. The director of NDLON remembers:

> This more radical group came to us to ask us for their support as they were breaking off from the rest. This became the most potent and dynamic element of the movement. But I didn't want this to split the DREAMer movement or start a big fight with CHIRLA or the other big groups. We wanted to support them without contributing to more conflicts in the movement. We quietly made the infrastructure of NDLON available to the youths. We said, "If you need office space, we have an office in Washington, DC, here it is. If you need a place to stay around the country, here is a list of our organizing staff, you can stay in their houses." We have made everything we have available to them: here are our lawyers, here are our contacts, use them. And, they did.[19]

Groups like NDLON, MALDEF, and the UCLA Labor Center provided important support to the dissident DREAMers, but they were also careful to provide support without aggravating cleavages and conflicts in the movement. They held different strategic visions than others, but they also recognized that they were all still fighting for the same long-term goal.

These allies also provided political support to the dissident DREAMers. MALDEF had extensive connections to local and national officials and the UCLA Labor Center had strong ties to labor unions. The director of the Labor Center used his ties to urge Richard Trumka, the president of the AFL-CIO, to support a federal DREAM Act:

> We have been very instrumental in educating labor unions about this issue. . . . Last spring, Richard Trumka had a press conference with the

Teachers Union to aggressively support the DREAM Act. They didn't have to say "stand-alone," but clearly, when you have a major press conference of that nature, it was a huge signal that labor was coming out to say that we have to move the DREAM Act forward. That was an extremely important event. It was the first such press conference of this sort. There were many in the CIR movement who attacked that press conference and tried to block it from happening.[20]

Trumka's strong support for the DREAM Act played an important role in shifting the balance of forces in favor of the dissident DREAMers. It signaled to congressional leaders that the national labor movement was now supporting the DREAM Act as a stand-alone bill. "You know, getting the AFL-CIO and the presence of the two major education unions in the country behind these students, you cannot ask for more powerful allies in Congress. And that gave them so much power and leverage in Congress when that press conference happened, because it opened people up. 'What is the president of the AFL-CIO doing with these students and supporting the DREAM Act?'"[21]

These associations supported the dissident DREAMers, but they were also conscious about respecting their autonomy. One DREAMer remembers, "If we needed help with money or doing anything, they would come in like in a big brother role to help us out. They never tried to change our direction or our minds or stalled us on anything. It was like: 'We believe in you and we're going to help and support you. That's it.'"[22] One supporter stressed the importance of respecting the autonomy of the DREAMers when providing support, "So our goal has been trying to find the resources for them. They already know what they want and they already have the strategy and analysis, so *we're not going to impose our thinking on them.*"[23] Nevertheless, some associations in the broader rights movement worried that the DREAMers were ill equipped to negotiate the DREAM Act by themselves. Passing the DREAM Act would require some concessions on enforcement. Associations working on these issues expressed concern about the abilities of the DREAMers to negotiate these matters in an effective manner. They argued that DREAMers should relinquish their place at the table when it came to these delicate and complicated negotiations. The director of NDLON countered that

the more experienced associations should play a supportive role in negotiations and not a dominant one:

> The Republicans were saying that "we'll go for the DREAM Act but you
> have to go for these other things," and border enforcement was one of those
> things. People in our movement were saying, "Who are these students to
> negotiate enforcement." And that point was right, but our position was to
> connect border enforcement organizations to the DREAMers rather to tell
> the DREAMers to stop it. I wanted to have orgs that specialize in enforce-
> ment issues present at the negotiations but I am not going to tell these kids
> what to do.[24]

The associations that came out in support of the dissident DREAMers
respected their autonomy, refused to co-opt them, and resisted efforts to
sideline the youths during important negotiations. Dissident DREAM-
ers were therefore able to gain support without having to cede autonomy
and control. This kind of support not only provided the DREAMers
with the support needed to launch their own independent campaign, but
also helped create a tight alliance between dissidents DREAMers and
the more critical associations of the immigrant rights movement. This
vigorous alliance precipitated the decline of the comprehensive reform
strategy and RIFA's central position within the immigrant rights movement.

The Rupture

Dissident DREAMers launched a series of high-profile and aggressive actions from late spring 2010 onward. Their first major action on
May 17, 2010, was the occupation of Senator John McCain's office in
Arizona by four undocumented students and one citizen ally. On May
20, Dream Team Los Angeles (DTLA), a group created in 2009 by university graduates and dissident DREAMers, organized the occupation
of the Federal Building in Los Angeles, which resulted in the arrest of
nine DREAMers and allies. Several weeks after this action, DREAMers
initiated a hunger strike and "die-in." On July 20, DREAMers occupied congressional offices in Washington, DC, which led to the arrest of
twenty-one undocumented students. Two weeks before this action, Los

Angeles activists organized a Freedom DREAM Ride across the country, building support bases in strategic states before their arrival for a mass action in the capitol. In addition to these actions, other DREAM groups launched their own actions in localities across the country. One DREAMer recounts this chain of events:

> So we shut down Wilshire Boulevard on May 20th in front of the Federal Building on the West Side. And then all these actions started happening across the nation, of people . . . Florida, Texas, then we started the hunger strikes. Here in LA, we did a hunger strike in front of [Senator] Feinstein's office. At the same time that the hunger strike was happening, we were traveling from California to DC in two vans doing the Freedom Ride. This was in July. But we were really traveling to DC to do the actions in the Senate Building. But along the way we did meet with organizations, we made all the contacts, we were preparing people to respond—but we couldn't tell them for what. Then we get to DC—that was July—and twenty-two undocumented students take over the Senate Building, literally. We had several Senate Office sit-ins and then one big one at the atrium lobby area of the Senate Building. Twelve students formed a circle and sat in the middle. And I was in there; I was a police liaison. I got interrogated by FBI folks and everything when it happened. It was really crazy! And that's when I was like: okay, it's really happening.[25]

The civil disobedience actions demonstrated the power of the students to come out in public, criticize government policy, and successfully fight the deportations of their comrades. "These students took over the Senate Office Chambers in DC, and not one of them got charged for a crime. So, it really empowered them and helped them develop this belief that they have political power."[26] (See Figure 1.)

Facing these dissident DREAMers and their defiant calls for a stand-alone bill, RIFA attempted to assert unity in its ranks. One DREAMer recounts RIFA's response, "Yeah, they were pissed. They called up . . . [NDLON] and . . . [MALDEF]—but they never told them they knew! To this day, I will never forget that from these folks. It was more like: 'This is their movement. You've got to listen and respect them.'" When asked about other supporters from the immigrant rights movement, the respondent went on to note, "Later, after it happened,

FIGURE 1 *A Call to Arms by the "Dream Is Coming."*

yes. But the first supporters before it had even happened were in LA. NILC did but not openly, because they were in a funky situation. They kind of still do their own thing and are kind of critical of RIFA sometimes, but they are part of RIFA too, so they kind of step in and out. She [the director of NILC] eventually did though, and I have a good relationship with her."[27]

RIFA also targeted key activists with United We Dream and pressured them to stick to RIFA's strategic line of comprehensive reform. "Those people [RIFA leaders] tried that approach with Carlos, who was the national coordinator of United We Dream. They were telling him that he was hurting the cause by making X or Y statements. He's the one who was wined and dined for all of that."[28] While leaders of United We Dream faced pressures from above, the dissident DREAMers pushed them to come out in open support of their strategy and actions. Positioned between these conflicting positions, United We Dream expressed its support for a stand-alone bill, but it did so in a cautious way:

> There was hesitation in UWD [United We Dream] because some were saying that we shouldn't be too loud on this issue. There was a shift, but they were also dependent on these larger organizations. The leadership of UWD was a little bit slow because of that. It was the organizers and activists within this network who started to push for a stand-alone bill. One of those groups was Dream Team LA and other groups were the Michigan, New York, and Chicago groups.[29]

United We Dream eventually became a strong and vocal advocate of the dissident position. In summer 2010, its director made public statements in support of a stand-alone bill and the direct-action tactics of the dissident DREAMers: "What we have seen with these actions is that it is better to be out there."[30] While this organization had become vocal in its support of a stand-alone bill, it did not provide direct support for civil disobedience actions until November 2010. "They were coming out very strong in support of the actions, but they weren't taking part in the more militant actions until the end. . . . They didn't play a role in the militant protests until November during the lame duck session of Congress. This stemmed from a partnership between UWD and the Dream Is Coming."[31]

CHIRLA sought to influence Los Angeles-based DREAMers leading up many of these dissident actions. "And we were criticized by CHIRLA, by the Network, by the RIFA campaign of pushing DREAM Act and not CIR. We've been blamed for killing CIR. We were blamed or accused of being selfish and not caring about our parents."[32] Because many of the dissident DREAMers had been trained and brought up in CHIRLA's Wise-UP and California Dream Network, debates were held between old friends and allies:

> They were saying, "What are y'all doing? You should be with us, helping us, instead of trying to be divisive and doing your own thing." These were

meetings with everybody—executive directors from RIFA, the executive director of CHIRLA. It was super charged with everybody meeting in one room, our people meeting with them—which is funny because all of the people in our group, all the leaders, they all came from CHIRLA. They taught them everything they know. So here we are a few years later down the road, and they are getting mad at them for doing something they taught them to do. So it was a weird space. We just wanted what we wanted; that was our goal.[33]

CHIRLA also sought to exert its influence directly on the student members of the California Dream Network. During one of its retreats in 2010, the California Dream Network held a debate over which strategy to pursue. CHIRLA laid out its strategic position: "CHIRLA was very clear: we ask for everything. And we ask for everything because we need it for everybody. Now when it's a strategic time to push for DREAM Act, then let's push for DREAM."[34] One participant of the retreat summarized CHIRLA's argument:

> We tell them [the students], "Look, we have two options: we can go for CIR which has the DREAM Act, but it's seen as a larger component that is going to help more people at the end. Or we have the DREAM Act, which might be easier to pass but it's only going to help a very small number of people." So the students voted and the majority of them voted for CIR.[35]

The retreat was a tipping point because several important campus groups recognized their differences with the CHIRLA's and RIFA's strategy and broke off from the network: "That was the breaking point, this retreat. They said 'we really think it's DREAM and we really feel that it was unfair the way you did the process.' We were open to the critique, but we also made a decision and took a vote."[36] The outcome of the vote prompted the most prominent and politicized campus organizations (UCLA, UC Santa Cruz, UC Berkeley, CSU Long Beach, among others) to split from the California Dream Network and align themselves with dissident groups like Dream Team Los Angeles and the Dream Is Coming.

The actions and claims of the dissident DREAMers seemed to be winning the debate. Their bold actions and compelling message resonated well in the media. The *New York Times* editorial board, a longtime supporter of Comprehensive Immigration Reform, wrote a glowing piece following the takeover of Senator McCain's office in May 2010:

> Four young immigrant students risked everything on Monday when they sat down in Senator John McCain's office in Tucson and refused to leave. They were urging passage of the DREAM Act, a bill offering a citizenship path to illegal immigrants who, like them, were brought to the United States as children, too young to have willfully broken the law. . . . Who else has shown such courage in the long struggle for immigration reform?[37]

High-ranking senators also expressed preference for a stand-alone bill over comprehensive reform. Republican Senator Richard Lugar's spokesperson announced there was still a possibility to pass the DREAM Act but not Comprehensive Immigration Reform during the congressional session. "The senator does not support any effort to advance a comprehensive immigration overhaul this year, but he believes the DREAM Act can be doable."[38]

Facing a shift in political momentum toward a stand-alone DREAM bill, RIFA began to change its position in summer 2010. "They [RIFA] lost control. They started to talk openly about pivoting and the issue becomes how to pivot correctly. They were saying, 'We have to do this thing right, we have to pivot together.'"[39] By late summer and early fall, the national associations and their allies in Congress threw their full support behind the DREAM Act. While most DREAMers welcomed this shift, many also saw it as an effort to reassert RIFA's control over the DREAMers and the immigrant rights movement:

> CHIRLA and these big organizations like Center for Community Change, America's Voice, and NCLR [National Council of La Raza] were pushing for CIR all this time, but when it came time for the DREAM Act to come for a vote [in September 2010], they were there in the front, in the press conferences and the releases. *They were using the same talking points that we had created*, like "The DREAM Act is a step forward for comprehensive bill" or "The DREAM Act is a down payment." They were first criticizing us for doing that, and if you look at their press releases, that is the language they

were using. It's since September 21st—that's when the first vote happened—so the week before is when they started coming forward.[40]

While the leadership of the immigrant rights movement threw its support behind their cause in fall 2010, many DREAMers continued to distrust their motives.

In spite of the momentum of the campaign, the DREAMers failed to overcome Republican-led filibusters in September and December 2010. These were devastating blows for all undocumented youths, DREAM activists, and their broad range of supporters. In spite of these devastating losses, many also believed that the mobilizations of 2010 gave birth to the "DREAM Movement" because the youths asserted leadership over their struggle and pushed the DREAM Act to the center of the political stage. For the first time in the immigrant rights movement, undocumented immigrants had developed their own leaders, assembled their own network of supportive allies, and developed their own messaging campaign. The national media also recognized the important role played by undocumented youth in pushing the DREAM Act forward: "If the DREAM Act passes, credit must go to those who have fought for it most strenuously: the young people whose futures it will decide."[41] The DREAMers were conscious of their capacities to shape the political debate and their improved position in the immigrant rights movement:

> I think we have become an important player in the rights movement. *We were not just making noise for the sake of making noise.* We did have a strategy and a structure. We were able to move things forward when we were told by the immigrant rights associations that wouldn't be able to do that. *With almost no resources, we were able to put the DREAM Act on the agenda.* That was because of our effort.[42]

In describing the next steps forward after the congressional defeat, the director of United We Dream struck an empowered and combative tone, saying, "We have woken up. We are going to go around the country letting everybody know who stands with us and who stood against us."[43] The DREAM Act and the undocumented youths pushing it were now at the center of all future talks of immigration reform. "I think these students have realized their political power. . . . I think they have really turned it around, the whole immigration debate. You cannot have an immigration debate in this country without talking about the DREAM Act. And they put that out there. It wasn't the CIR folks—it was them who put that out there in the public."[44] The campaign failed to pass the DREAM Act, but the complicated struggles to pass a stand-alone bill transformed the DREAMers into a leading group and voice in the broader immigrant rights movement.

Representational Cleavages

The conflicts between the youths and the national rights associations were over strategic issues, but they also reflected deeper cleavages over the power to represent. Many DREAMers were deeply frustrated that their calls for a stand-alone bill in spring 2010 were not taken seriously by RIFA. This led many to question whether these rights associations could legitimately represent undocumented immigrants in the public sphere. The struggle continued to be about winning legal-juridical rights to stay in the country, but it also went beyond that. Now it was also about winning the right to make their own claims in the public sphere. For these dissident DREAMers, equality meant *both* gaining legal rights to stay in the country *and* gaining recognition as political equals.[45] As the struggle expanded in this new direction, the immigrant rights associations, which had long assumed a dominant role in representing the DREAMers, were now criticized by the dissident DREAMers for denying them recognition as political equals.

These deeper "representational cleavages" were reflected in the op-ed article in *Dissent* magazine. The DREAMers argued that the traditional leadership of the movement was not undocumented and did not face the same pressures resulting from this status. If they could not understand where the undocumented youths were coming from, the rights associations could not legitimately represent their interests in the public sphere. "Our so-called allies need to realize that they are not undocumented and, as such, do not have the right to say what undocumented youth need or want. Our progressive allies insist in imposing their paternalistic stand to oppose the DREAM Act and tell us that this is not the 'right' choice for us to acquire 'legal' status in this country."[46] The leading figures of the immigrant rights movement were not faced with the constant fear of detention and deportation. They did not have to organize their everyday lives—how they move around, find a job, cash their checks, and so on—around their unauthorized status. The legal status of the leadership provided them with the privilege of patience: they could wait for the right time to push for the right bill. Undocumented immigrants did not have this privilege. Living in a state of permanent "illegality," the DREAMers did not have the privilege to wait patiently for a massive immigration reform that would legalize most immigrants in some uncertain and distant future. Their extremely precarious status required them to respond to whatever openings were available to them now. Undocumented youths had neither the time nor patience to wait for a better time to push for the DREAM Act:

> We are tired of our third-class status, and we are tired of the social jus-
> tice elite dictating what we can and cannot do, all the while speaking
> on our behalf and pretending they represent our interests. . . . The social
> justice elite have posed the argument that because of the current state of
> public education it is unwise for the DREAM Act to pass because it will
> force undocumented youth into the military. So should we wait until
> there are no more wars? Should we wait until our public school systems
> are perfect?[47]

The 2009 and 2010 versions of the DREAM Act also contained age caps of twenty-nine and thirty, respectively. Waiting too long would make many youths ineligible. This deep frustration with waiting was echoed by a DREAMer who participated in the occupation of John McCain's office: "I've been organizing for years, and a lot of my friends have become frustrated and lost hope. We don't have any more time to be waiting."[48] The legal status of the immigrant rights leadership gave them the privilege to be patient, placing them in a very different position than undocumented immigrants to assess the timing of the movement's strategy. The leaders misrecognized the impatience of the DREAMers as petulance from spirited youths rather than legitimate frustration with exclusion from "normal" life. If the legal status of the leadership made it impossible for them to recognize the true needs and feelings of undocumented youths, how could they legitimately prescribe strategies and represent them in their struggles?

The leadership was also accused of using DREAMers in their broader power plays. Many felt they were treated like "puppets." "This immigration movement was being led by politicians and allies and never by undocumented people. We were kind of following what they were saying. Whenever a politician needed one of us, they would say, 'Hey, bring a student, we need him at this press conference.' There were many among us who felt like puppets, like we were being used."[49] Others argued that immigrant rights associations benefited significantly from serving as the representatives of the DREAMers. In playing this role, rights associations gained greater access to the media, politicians, and funders, which in turn enhanced their power in the field of immigration politics. RIFA resisted an autonomous DREAMers movement because autonomy would deprive the larger associations from an important source of power. "Because if we accept and embrace the current undocumented student movement, it means the social justice elite loses its power—*its power to influence politicians, media and the public debate. The power is taken back by its rightful holders.*"[50]

Lastly, dissident DREAMers criticized immigrant rights associations for acting more on behalf of the interest of large national funders than the needs of actual immigrants. Funders preferred large and well-choreographed demonstrations over the direct action and civil disobedience tactics of dissident DREAMers. In a follow up to their essay in *Dissent* magazine, the DREAMers provided an analysis of funders' influence on the strategies of immigrant rights associations:

Although we have very strong critiques of the nonprofit industrial complex, many of us have strong ties to grassroots organizations here locally in CA [California] that are 501(c)(3)s and do amazing work. We would go so far as to say necessary and life-preserving work. It is precisely because we have those close relationships to those organizations and understand the way they work from the inside, that we know firsthand that the direct action work and activities we were organizing were never going to be funded by a foundation. *Nor did we want any of our actions to be dictated by an organization that was beholden to a foundation and their rules.* Locally, we knew of youth being held back by organizations that were providing them with support and resources to engage in direct actions for immigration reform. *We wanted to have complete autonomy to organize and decide what we wanted and felt was strategic.*[51]

This statement distills an increasingly influential analysis of the "non-profit industrial complex" and its constraining effects on immigrant rights activism. The funding structure restricts the possibility of what rights associations can do and say. These associations in turn constrain the actions and discourses of undocumented activists working with them. The existing order of things restricted the abilities of undocumented youths to express their true voice, requiring them to break from these constraints and strike out on their own. The statement finishes by stressing that their aim was "to have complete autonomy to organize and decide what we wanted and felt was strategic."

The dissident DREAMers employed terms to label the leaders of the immigrant rights movement such as "the nonprofit industrial complex," the "social justice elite," and even more aggressively, "poverty pimps." Labeling allowed the DREAMers to draw a sharp line between undocumented youth and the traditional leadership of the immigrant rights movement. Labeling not only identified the leaders as adversaries but also attributed qualities to them that suggested a parasitic and exploitative power relation. The leaders were framed as systemic elites who gained power at the expense of undocumented people. These representations resonated with many DREAMers during the 2010 mobilizations. The critical analysis and labels were widely disseminated through Facebook, Twitter, and the blogosphere. They helped frame other critical interventions within this discursive space. In a blog entitled "The Non-Profit Industrial Complex Eats Reform and Spits out DREAMs," another DREAMer employs a similar formulation to express her criticisms of the leadership of the immigrant rights movement:

> While private prisons fight amongst themselves for contracts with the Federal government and cut corners that usually equal abuses against those housed behind concrete and barbed wire, nonprofits fight amongst themselves for money given out by corporate tax shelters and cut corners by watering down what should be revolution for reform and the end result is abuse against those whom orgs claim to represent and help in their mission statements.[52]

In another blog posting, an employee of a nonprofit association maintains that the assertions of the DREAMers were largely accurate. "Too many DOCUMENTED, privileged, often white and often men do too much of the talking, framing and decision making in the Non-Profit Industrial Complex (which is a fair term and accusation in this current staffer of a nonprofit's opinion). Even in my nonprofit, ultimate say on what work does and does not happen on the immigrants' rights front is not in the hands of a person of color or migrant for that matter."[53]

A prominent DREAM activist and blogger criticizes the power of associations to control the undocumented student movement and force them into the narrow discursive "boxes" used to define DREAMers in the public sphere:

> Along with undocumented youth from across the country, I've worked to rip the DREAM Act from the clutches of the nonprofit industrial complex. . . . *It's taken a whole decade to build a movement that is not hinged on the nonprofit industrial complex framing our stories in ways that are damaging and containing our migrant bodies in neat boxes with pretty labels.* There was a time when national immigration reform groups would refuse to help with deportation campaigns. Now they receive foundation money to run such campaigns. It is the movement bringing the DREAM Act full-circle to meet with the nonprofit industrial complex again and becoming a mainstream idea that is co-opted by our "leaders" such as Barack Obama even while he continues to deport members of our community.[54]

The blogger asserts that associations support undocumented youths because of funding opportunities and politicians support them to win the Latino vote. In addition to these standard critiques, the blogger stresses the role of these associations in producing discourses that restrict the ways in which undocumented youths present themselves and their cause in the public sphere. She argues that the mainstream rights associations produce "neat" discursive boxes that contain "migrant bodies" with "pretty labels."

These critical arguments, analyses, frames, and labels have saturated the discursive spaces of DREAMers (for example, Facebook, blogs, web sites, and so on). They have become influential in shaping the ways in which everyday activists analyze the role immigrant rights associations play in their cause. The co-chair of one of the largest campus-based support groups draws directly from this critical discourse to frame her own analysis of immigrant rights associations: "You do realize that certain immigration rights organizations are not always looking out for your best interests as an undocumented immigrant. So they will manipulate the system, they will have behind the scenes conversations with the Presidential Office or administration, and you won't know what they're talking about, or they won't invite the undocumented youth organizations to the meeting."[55] Leaders of campus groups play an important role in diffusing these critical discourses to newly recruited DREAMers. As the leaders of campus groups use this discourse to talk about rights associations and the "nonprofit industrial complex," new recruits adopt it as a standard framework to interpret the political dynamics of the immigrant rights movement. The critical discourse becomes the normal way of talking and thinking about relations between undocumented immigrants and the mainstream immigrant rights associations.

The development and diffusion of this critique occurred with extraordinary speed. While these kinds of criticisms existed in December 2009, they continued to be marginal and expressed in private conversations between frustrated DREAMers. By fall 2010, these critiques and labels became a part of the normal DREAMer lexicon and were used by many to interpret power relations within the field of immigration politics. The viral diffusion of these critical discourses was largely a function of social networking applications, blogs, and web sites. The critique and labels described above have come to dominate the ways in which many DREAMers now think about their relations to rights associations. It has, in Antonio Gramsci's terms, become the "common sense" of dissident DREAMers.[56] In producing this critical discourse, the dissidents have carved out a space for themselves as the legitimate representatives of the DREAMer mobilization. Making public arguments against leaders, drawing a sharp line in the sand between us and them, and labeling immigrant rights leaders as having antagonistic interests with the DREAMers have been important discursive moves to undermine the legitimacy of the traditional leadership of the movement.

Conflicts over strategy therefore opened a Pandora's box as undocumented youths went on to question "who has the right to represent whom" in the immigrant rights movement. These undocumented activists began to view their struggle as extending beyond the goal of gaining legal-juridical rights to stay in the country. The struggle was increasingly about gaining recognition for themselves as legitimate political subjects capable of making rights claims on their own behalf.[57] While government policies were criticized for blocking their abilities to gain legal-juridical rights, the immigrant rights associations were criticized for blocking DREAMers from expressing their own "authentic" voice in the public sphere.

Throughout the 2000s, national immigrant rights associations worked to craft a powerful discourse and infrastructure to represent the voice of undocumented students in the public sphere. Without the effort and investment of these associations, it is unlikely that undocumented students would have come to constitute themselves as the political group of the DREAMer. However, as the dominant strategy failed to win students formal legal-juridical rights, many called for a change in strategy and a push for the DREAM Act as a stand-alone bill. The reluctance of leading associations to recognize the concerns and grievances of these students prompted many DREAMers to question not only the strategy but also the representational hierarchies within the movement. Dissident DREAMers appreciated the importance of the leading rights associations, but they resented their continued reluctance to recognize their concerns, grievances, preferences, and voice. The effort to assert their voice in the public sphere expanded the scope of the struggle from one focused narrowly on gaining legal rights to one that sought recognition for the DREAMers as a legitimate and equal political subject. The assertion of autonomy did not mean the abandonment of alliances with established associations, as made clear by their effort to reach out to NDLON, MALDEF, and the UCLA Labor Center. Rather, their assertion of autonomy was seen as a means of gaining the right to make rights claims in the public sphere.

4

Rebirth from the Grassroots Up

Several nights after the DREAM Act failed to overcome a Republican-led filibuster in the Senate on December 18, 2010, members of different DREAM activist groups in Southern California met at MALDEF's headquarters in downtown Los Angeles. The youths were distraught. During the 2010 lame-duck period, there was a Senate supermajority, the House had already passed a version of the bill, there was a supportive president, Homeland Security expressed strong support for the bill, the principal adversaries of the DREAM Act were divided, and public opinion supported the Senate version of the bill. Even under these optimal political conditions, they failed to overcome the filibuster by five votes. They were also distraught because they were moving into an unfavorable political climate. In January 2011, anti-immigrant and Tea Party-inspired Republicans would take control of the House and Democrats would lose their supermajority in the Senate. These new political conditions would favor neither the DREAM Act nor Comprehensive Immigration Reform. Their window of opportunity had closed.

The DREAMers also exhibited exuberance and a powerful sense of hope, which was surprising considering the defeat and gloomy political outlook. The youths felt they had achieved the power to speak and express themselves in the public sphere. The emotional energy in the room reflected a sense of collective awe at their own abilities to bring the DREAM Act this far. Most were undocumented, most were in their late teens or early twenties, most were the first in their families to have attended university, and most were experiencing political engagement for the first time in their lives. They had not only pushed the DREAM Act to the pinnacles of political power, but they established themselves as an important voice within the immigrant rights movement. In the speech from one of Dream Team Los Angeles's leaders, he expressed the sentiment, reflecting, "The process is what is important. They [unspecified adversaries] are afraid of the power we built from the bottom up! We're going to be attacked. Before, we didn't have the power to protect ourselves. Now we have the power to protect ourselves."[1] Similar themes were stressed by the lead attorney of NDLON, who said, "You guys were at the table this year when nobody else was! *Before others used the DREAMers, others represented your interests, now you represent yourselves.* Just keep doing what you're doing and ignore the critics."[2]

The DREAMers were filled with a sense of hope and amazement because they had asserted themselves as first among equals within the immigrant rights movement. They now represented themselves in politics and the public arena. Having asserted their autonomy from national immigrant rights associations, the new generation of DREAMers has had to draw upon its own resources and build a new infrastructure from the grass roots up. They needed cultural and symbolic resources to craft effective messages, arguments, and frames; they also needed an organizational infrastructure to connect activists to one another, train new recruits, mobilize their forces in different campaigns, and so on. Without this infrastructure, the voice of the new DREAMer would have been ephemeral; it could pierce the public debate but it would not be able to achieve the consistency and coherency needed to shape and drive the public debate over an extended period of time.

DREAMers have discovered alternative ways to build a voice and infrastructure. Small activist organizations with few funding options have drawn in resources from their immediate surroundings. They ask for assistance from friends, families, churches, schools, college administrators, immigrant organizations, and so on. These grassroots resources provide the means to sustain basic and often tenuous operations. As local DREAM organizations gain some footing by drawing on localized resources, they also branch out to ensure that weaker organizations are provided support and assistance by stronger organizations. The process of branching out between DREAM organizations facilitates the flow of resources and energy through this network. The emergent infrastructure has enabled them to assert their continued autonomy and maintain a disciplined voice. The infrastructure is the body that provides the DREAMers with a clear, determined, and disciplined voice in the public sphere.

The Resources to Speak

Pierre Bourdieu argued that the creation of a powerful public voice does not come naturally.[3] To voice political desires and demands, groups must possess high concentrations of cultural and symbolic capital. Actors need cultural insights of the national public and the political field to know what messages, tones, and performances work best to gain broad support. They also need symbolic skills and a certain degree of legitimacy to present messages that are not only compelling but also believable. The inexperience of many undocumented youths in the early years of DREAM campaigns deprived them of these essential cultural and symbolic resources, resulting in their dependence on immigrant rights associations. However, they have been able to acquire these resources over time, which has allowed them to express a powerful and autonomous voice on the national political stage.

In the earlier cycles of the DREAMer mobilization (2006–10), the leading rights associations produced a message to gain broad public support. Their strategy required the creation of an infrastructure that trained undocumented youths to deliver the message in a compelling and disciplined way. This infrastructure required intensive training of undocumented youth activists. DREAMers also had many opportunities to hone their representational skills through countless campaigns, Internet communications, campus-based discussions, community outreach activities, and media interviews. Each of these activities provided activists with opportunities to work out messages, think about what worked and what didn't, and refashion their language, symbols, and tones to enhance the power and resonance of their public arguments.

While this infrastructure was designed to produce messaging discipline, it allowed DREAMers to acquire the cultural and symbolic skills needed to become effective communicators. After two to three years of involvement with the movement, these activists came to understand the rules of the game and how to frame messages in ways to maximize their symbolic power in the public sphere. Thus, the infrastructure that was used to create disciplined activists and messengers helped transmit the skills and resources needed to produce a voice of their own.

Most active DREAMers were also raised in the United States. Undocumented youths were very familiar with the cultural underpinnings of American politics (for example, discourses, values, symbols, and moralities) because this culture was part of their national habitus.[4] Unlike recent immigrants, they did not have to learn new cultural rules and how to convincingly deploy these cultures in the public sphere. Most were able to tap cultural codes and express them easily through their speech, acts, and performances. They could make believable claims about being good Americans because they *were* American. They did not risk exposing their "foreignness" through the inappropriate use of terms and conduct in public. In addition to being "real" Americans, most of the leading DREAMers were university students and recent graduates who had spent years learning how to use language and analyze complex phenomena. Many of the leading activists were trained in political science, sociology, law, and history. They spent years studying American electoral politics, the civil rights and LGBT movements, communication and rhetoric, and feminist and cultural theory. They made direct use of this education to analyze political opportunities, develop strategies, craft messages, and forge legal tactics. Their advanced analytical skills enabled them to quickly learn the discursive and symbolic rules underlying the field of immigration politics. They understood the importance of cultural rules, skills, and tricks and became talented players in this field. Their university training also transmitted "middle-class" cultural attributes to many students raised in working-class families and neighborhoods. Many learned middle-class codes of language, dress, and taste through their university experiences, which allowed them to cleanse themselves of the stigma associated with immigrant and inner-city working-class worlds. They could draw upon this culture to present themselves not just as any Americans but as "nice, middle-class" Americans. Their national and educational background therefore provided DREAMers with a wealth of cultural capital.

After their graduation from university, well-trained undocumented youths have had difficulty finding work in their fields because they lack work permits.[5] This has been an extremely frustrating and dispiriting experience. Contributing to the DREAMer movement has provided many with an important outlet to use their talents in a satisfying way. One of the most prolific artists of the movement has remained a fully dedicated militant because of his commitment to the cause but also because opportunities in journalism, his college major, were closed to him. After his graduation, he was not able to take internships and jobs for news organizations because of his legal status. Employment opportunities for this talented young man were limited to the lower ends of the service industry. He dedicated much of his free time to the DREAMer movement because of his passion for the cause, but also because the movement served as an outlet for his many talents:

> When you graduate from college, there's a feeling of going back to square one, of asking yourself what's your place in society. My co-workers at the restaurant always ask, "Why did you go to college? You can't do anything with it." Not being able to use my degree was the worst feeling ever. So, I was waking up every morning and going to my job at the restaurant and hating every single minute of it. It was driving me crazy. . . . So, I started working with other recent graduates in Long Beach to think of ways to use our skills to get our stories out there. So we created a web site "Dreamers Adrift" to produce videos that tell our stories. . . . Drawing was my other outlet. I started to post my illustrations to Facebook and received great feedback from fellow DREAMers. Then people all over started to ask me if they could use my images. I would then go to demonstrations and people would come up to me and say, "You're the guy who draws."[6]

Most talented undocumented graduates experience a similar situation.[7] They face a sharp disconnect between their high aspirations, on the one hand, and the legal reality prohibiting them from working in their professions, on the other. The frustration felt by many DREAMers is captured well in one illustration depicting an undocumented college graduate in the agricultural fields under the constant surveillance of the Immigration and Customs Enforcement (see Figure 2 below).

The gap between the high aspirations of the youths and the legal barriers to the job market has made the DREAMer community a social space where undocumented university graduates can use their talents in satisfying ways. Dedication to the movement provides an opportunity to struggle for a just cause and it provides a space where talents can be deployed and aspirations fulfilled. Their participation in the movement also allows them to interact with broader political and cultural worlds than would otherwise be possible. They engage with the media, negotiate with political and social movement elites, and gain recognition and respect because of their work with DREAM campaigns. While legal barriers block the ability of students to employ their skills and develop professionally through the mainstream labor market, they can become respected legal experts, artists, journalists, communicators, and political strategists through their participation in the movement.

The lack of professional opportunities for highly skilled undocumented graduates has been a disaster for individual undocumented youths.[8] However, it has created a large pool of highly talented and mostly voluntary labor for the undocumented youth movement. The voluntary nature of their activities is important for incipient organizations with few to no resources to pay professional staff. Weekly Dream Team Los Angeles meetings are attended by approximately twenty to thirty-five activists, depending on the time of year and events being organized. Most of the regular attendees volunteer for various committees covering legal issues, communications, art, self-healing, among other issues. Volunteers dedicate themselves to their areas of specialization with a high degree of professionalism. The legal barriers to the professional labor market also contribute to retaining the best and brightest of these volunteers. Rather than student activists moving out of social movement politics to pursue middle-class careers, which is the case with most student-based movements, DREAMers have few choices but to stick to their movement. Blocked upward mobility for undocumented graduates has therefore provided the movement with a rich and deep reservoir of talented mostly voluntary labor to draw from.

FIGURE 2 *DREAMer in the Fields. Image by Julio Salgado.*

Sharing and pooling the resources of individual youths has been important. The DREAMers constantly connect to other talented youths and combine their skill sets in new and innovative projects. The artist from Dreamers Adrift recounts how he came to work with the communications leader of Dream Team Los Angeles: "There was this big United We Dream retreat in Memphis. I was hanging out with people from California. I met her through these people. She was like, 'Dude, we need new images!' She has been very enthusiastic about using my images and getting them out there. Yeah, so ever since that, we work closely to get new messages out into the media and to our fellow DREAMers."[9] Prior to this, the artist was collaborating with other DREAMers on producing videos and creating a web site, dreameradrift.com, about undocumented youth and their struggle for legalization. The constant networking between DREAMers has been important because it has spurred constant innovations in the production of messages, images, and other cultural works. Just as important, networking encourages the collectivization of individual resources and skills.[10] The talents of individuals are certainly their own, but the constant participation of these activists in reciprocal exchange networks makes their talents available to the broad collectivity of DREAMers.[11] Individual talents are seen as a collective resource of the movement, enabling organizers to call upon each other's assistance in different campaigns. DREAMers create a powerful and autonomous voice because these networks allow them to combine their cultural and symbolic skills in new and innovative ways.

The concentration of advanced skills, talent, and sheer drive has enabled DREAMers to assume leadership roles of their own movement and its different campaigns. One DREAMer with Dream Team Los Angeles has taken a leading role in devising the legal strategy of civil disobedience actions.[12]

> And basically anybody who's been arrested for civil disobedience is because our member . . . initiated the project of creating the "how to get arrested" resource guide. "Alright, you're going to do civil disobedience? These are the things that are going to happen." She kind of formulated strategies on doing X, Y, Z and after doing X, Y and Z, this is going to happen. She and others came up with everything and they figured out the kinks too. "Once we do this, we have X amount of time to do this. After that we have X amount of time to do that. And after that, it's going to take X amount of time for the cops to come. When the cops come, this is how you talk to them, this is what you say." It's almost like reading a book.[13]

Another DREAMer assumed a general leadership position, taking an active role in convening meetings, devising the major strategic lines of the group, and representing Dream Team Los Angeles to outside organizations and politicians. Others have become specialized in messaging and communications. The communication specialist of Dream Team Los Angeles has worked to provide trainings to DREAM activists in California and across the country. As head of the communications committee, she has also cultivated good relations with reporters and producers in the English- and Spanish-speaking media. These good relations have provided her with direct access to the media and opportunities to push key messages, sound bites, and talking points into the public sphere. "What we found is that it was really important to have good relations not only with reporters but also producers. The producers were important because they were the first ones to see the press releases, frame the story according to our messaging, and tell the reporter how to talk about it."[14] Thus, the acquisition of cultural, analytic, and symbolic skills has enabled DREAM activists to assume central leadership functions within DREAMer organizations like Dream Team Los Angeles and United We Dream. They no longer depend on immigrant rights associations to speak on their behalf because they have developed the means to represent themselves and create their own voice in the public sphere.

Building a National Infrastructure from the Grassroots Up

The DREAMer infrastructure before 2010 was largely top-down in design and execution. By contrast, the new infrastructure is grounded in local DREAM organizations firmly rooted in their local environments, namely, college campuses, community organizations, networks, and so on. Drawing resources up from the grassroots, they also connect to other groups and to state and national organizations. Rather than depending on resources to trickle down from parent associations to dependent undocumented activists, DREAMer groups acquire their own resources and circulate them to other activists in their networks. This flatter structure depends on constant reciprocal exchanges between DREAMers and a diverse range of allies.[15]

Many campus-based support groups in California have continued to operate under the auspices of the California Dream Network. The more militant of these campus groups have either broken off from the network entirely or maintained their affiliation with the network but also allied themselves with Dream Team Los Angeles or other Dream Teams in California.[16] A member from UCLA IDEAS described this relation:

And so, for a while, we maintained our participation in the California Dream Network and we maintained ourselves as an affiliate organization, but we had different strategies so you wouldn't see us as active there. That's one of the dynamics also. It's about maintaining your involvement in a coalition where you don't really agree with the strategies, right? But understanding that it is important to maintaining communication.[17]

Campus-based groups have provided this new generation of DREAMers with access to university and college resources, including office space, funding, administrative support, and a well-developed communications infrastructure. An activist with the Orange County Dream Team remembers that during the 2010 campaign, his group was able to employ the resources of its affiliated campus-based groups: "When the federal DREAM Act campaign was happening last year [2010], we were able to get resources from the campuses to do things like phone banking, print out flyers, and pressure chancellors to support the DREAM Act."[18] These college resources have been available to all chartered undocumented student associations.

Colleges and universities also function as a relatively safe space to cultivate basic organizational skills of undocumented youth. Student organizations provide newly recruited DREAMers the time (two to four years) and space to incubate basic skills. New recruits learn how to raise and allocate funds, how best to make collective decisions in an open and democratic way, how to stay responsive to members' needs, how to create solidarity and emotional energy, how to create alliances, and how to recruit new members to the cause. The communications director of Dream Team Los Angeles remembers that her messaging skills were refined through her engagement in UCLA IDEAS. By her senior year, IDEAS had developed a powerful messaging operation that would rival most immigrant rights organizations in California. Other undocumented immigrants (for example, day laborers, domestic workers, and so on) do not have a comparable space to develop their organizational and social movement skills. Difficult and fractured work environments present other undocumented immigrants with more barriers to cultivate organizing skills and capacities.[19]

Some campus administrators and campus institutions have taken a special interest in the situations of undocumented students and provided them with additional levels of support. At UCLA (IDEAS), UC Santa Cruz (SIN), and CSU Long Beach (FUEL), campus-based associations received important levels of support from administrators and faculty. The level of support for UCLA IDEAS has stood out among these. The vice chancellor of student affairs at UCLA has met on a quarterly basis with UCLA IDEAS to discuss the development of the organization and outreach to undocumented students. The Student Affairs Office has provided resources to support the living conditions of undocumented students while providing IDEAS with support for their many activities including advocacy work and outreach to high school counselors. The chancellor of UCLA has been particularly receptive to IDEAS:

> We're lucky to have a supportive chancellor. Every year either we request or the chancellor requests a meeting with IDEAS. Throughout the year we have constant communication with the administration at Murphy Hall [the administration building]. That is something that other undocumented organizations in California lack. IDEAS has been so instituted into the school that we feel comfortable and at home here. We feel more comfortable in school than anywhere else.[20]

In addition to administrative support, the UCLA Labor Center has collaborated with IDEAS since 2006 on several projects including cotaught courses on undocumented immigrants and two book projects. Support by administrators, faculty, and the Labor Center has made UCLA IDEAS one of the largest campus-based undocumented associations in the country.

Campus-based DREAMers have fed into off-campus DREAM organizations like Dream Team Los Angeles and Orange County Dream Team. While campus-based groups perform most of their work at their universities or colleges, Dream Teams in California were designed as community-based organizations for recently graduated DREAMers. After having developed their skills and talents in their different campus organizations, recent graduates have transferred those skills to off campus organizations like Dream Team Los Angeles and Orange County Dream Team. While there are strong personal and institutional ties between Dream Team Los Angeles and UCLA IDEAS, the former organization is not a UCLA-only group, with many of its core members having attended other institutions including UC Santa Cruz, East Los Angeles Community College, CSU Long Beach, CSU Northridge, among other California colleges and universities. The campus-based organizations feed into off-campus groups and networks like the Dream Teams, allowing these off-campus groups to capture and harness the skills of well-trained undocumented university graduates.

The Dream Teams have also drawn support and resources from associations and institutions in their surrounding areas. This support has helped to build organizational capacities. Organizations like NDLON, UCLA Labor Center, and MALDEF have been instrumental in providing day-to-day resources to Dream Team Los Angeles. The Labor Center has provided Dream Team Los Angeles with basic support largely because of its long ties to UCLA IDEAS (since 2006) and its commitment to the DREAMer cause. It has provided office space, communication support, legal advice, and most importantly, paid internships. The director of the Labor Center stressed the importance of the internships for developing the organizational capacities of the DREAMers:

> The difference in providing internship opportunities for the DREAMers is that for the first time you have a situation in which, instead of being in school full time and working in the underground economy with two or three jobs, these students have the time to dedicate to this. We are giving them that space to use their energy to do this and build this. This has been a huge factor.[21]

One DREAMer stressed the importance of this support for Dream Team Los Angeles: "So, four people were working doing internships there and they were heavily involved in the DREAM Act stuff. You were actually having some people focusing most their time on the DREAM Act, and that was really cool because it gave us the opportunity to just kind of have people that are always going to be there. It's almost like paid staff, which is very interesting!"[22]

NDLON has also provided Dream Team Los Angeles with fiscal sponsorship. Sponsorship allows the Dream Team to gain access to foundation grants. In addition to this, NDLON's proximity to Dream Team Los Angeles (both are headquartered at the UCLA Labor Center) provides its members with regular contact to NDLON's staff attorneys and strategists. "In addition to fiscal sponsorship, they [the NDLON director and staff attorney] have been able to sit down with us a lot and provide help with political analysis. They often go to Washington, DC, so they help keep us informed about the broader political picture."[23] Additionally, MALDEF has provided important levels of organizational support to Dream Team Los Angeles. Before moving to the UCLA Labor Center, MALDEF provided this incipient group of DREAMers with an office and equipment. MALDEF has continued to provide it with critical legal and political advice in its various campaigns. The resources provided by the Labor Center, NDLON, and MALDEF have provided Dream Team Los Angeles with a strong base to build a resilient organization. It has subsequently become a powerful hub in regional and national networks and an independent ally of the California Dream Network headquartered at CHIRLA, less than a half mile down the street. While Dream Team Los Angeles has benefited from its ties to uniquely well-endowed organizations in its vicinity, other Dream Teams have largely employed the same model of drawing on the support and assistance of community organizations and other ally supporters in their immediate vicinity. These resources have been crucial for creating basic support such as office space, phones, meeting place, and so on for fledgling organizations.

While Dream Team Los Angeles has been able to draw from local support networks and become a strong organizational hub, it has also developed a strategy to redistribute resources to allies throughout DREAM activist networks. Dream Team Los Angeles has worked especially close with Orange County Dream Team. Operating since 2004, the Orange County Dream Team was one of the first community-based DREAM organizations in the country. It was run by undocumented youths (mostly recent university graduates), drew supporters from community-based organizations, and had long been an advocate of the dissident line. DREAMers affiliated with CHIRLA and UCLA IDEAS attempted to create a similar off-campus, "community-based" organization for recent graduates in 2008 ("Los Angeles Dream Team"), but this initial effort was not successful. When Los Angeles DREAMers made another attempt in 2009, they turned to their Orange County friends for support. A DREAMer who had been a member of Orange County Dream Team and became a member of UCLA IDEAS as a graduate student, brokered relations between Los Angeles and Orange County activists.

Once Dream Team Los Angeles gained firm organizational footing and strong support, it shared resources with allies in Orange County.

> Because Dream Team Los Angeles is centered at the UCLA Labor Center, it has access to resources that obviously we don't have. They were able to provide us with very specific trainings in leadership development and messaging. We don't have the resources to provide formal trainings to our volunteers. Much of what they learn happens through practice. These kinds of formal trainings are important because they allow volunteers opportunities to develop their skills. So through DTLA, we have been allowed to have those opportunities.[24]

The Los Angeles and Orange County groups also worked closely with one another to create a state-level network of Dream Teams (California Dream Team Alliance). The alliance would complement the campus-based California Dream Network by providing an outlet for recent graduates. They organized the first retreat in February 2011 and created a string of new Dream Teams throughout the state. The partnership between Los Angeles and Orange County Dream Teams has therefore provided the organizational backbone for a new, statewide network. Both organizations have sought to distribute their organizational resources, knowledge, and expertise through this network.

The California Dream Team Alliance has been strongest in Southern California because of the presence of Dream Team Los Angeles and Orange County Dream Team. Several Dream Team chapters in Southern California (San Fernando Valley, San Gabriel Valley, and the Inland Empire) have been created by activists with close ties to the Los Angeles Dream Team. Having gained organizing experience through this group, activists developed new Dream Teams in their own communities. They sought out the support of allies in community organizations and churches, recruited members through their own personal networks, and launched smaller campaigns in these communities. Two DREAMers from Los Angeles were instrumental in creating the San Gabriel Valley Dream Team. Both were active in Dream Team Los Angeles and powerful voices of the dissident wing of the DREAMers movement. In

March 2011, they decided to create a new Dream Team branch in the San Gabriel Valley (ten miles northeast of downtown Los Angeles). One of their mothers had been a longtime organizer in the area and was affiliated with a prominent immigrant association in Los Angeles. She helped this new Dream Team by allowing the group to use her own organization's facilities in Pasadena. The other organizer used friendship networks with students at Pasadena City College to recruit undocumented students into their new group. While this Dream Team now has regular meetings and a stable membership, it still lacks the resources of the Los Angeles group. Efforts have been made by Dream Team Los Angeles to provide trainings, workshops, and site visits to this and other newer Dream Teams in Southern California.

Dream Team Los Angeles has worked to distribute resources outward, but access to their resources has depended on geographic proximity and personal connections. Dream Teams in the San Gabriel Valley and the San Fernando Valley have become relatively sustainable organizations. They have stable members, a network of supportive community allies, and robust outreach operations. Both Dream Teams benefited from good relations with Dream Team Los Angeles and frequent contacts made possible by geographic and social proximity. The lead organizer of the San Fernando Valley Dream Team was able to take the metro from the San Fernando Valley to Los Angeles (a fifteen-minute ride) to attend weekly meetings. Accessibility to the center permitted her access to valuable information and skills while reinforcing her strong personal ties to the leaders of the movement. By contrast, the Dream Team in the ex-urban area of the Inland Empire has had greater difficulty establishing itself. A founding member of this Dream Team explained that organizing in the Inland Empire was difficult because of the more hostile political environment. While this area was adjacent to Los Angeles, it bore greater resemblance (demographically and politically) to inhospitable Arizona. This hostile environment has compounded organizing problems associated with the massive geographic size of the area because it constrains the mobility of DREAM activists in this region. Undocumented immigrants in California are prohibited from obtaining a driver's license, there are many police checkpoints in the Inland Empire, and public transportation options are poor and limited. This political geography has made it difficult for DREAMers in the Inland Empire to meet on a regular basis. Such a terrain has also inhibited regular meetings with DREAMers in Los Angeles and Orange County. This has denied the opportunities to build deeper solidarities and gain access to needed training, knowledge, and resources.[25]

The local and statewide infrastructure has connected to the national organization of United We Dream. Dream Teams in Los Angeles and Orange County are important affiliates of United We Dream. United We Dream had had strong ties to RIFA-affiliated associations and struggled during the painful internal conflicts of 2010. It eventually embraced the dissident line, but it did so more slowly than other groups. The power shifts in the immigrant rights movements since 2010 have encouraged youths in United We Dream to assume greater autonomy while continuing their alliance with traditional rights associations. It continues to have a formal connection to the National Immigration Law Center. Though NILC continues to exercise its "sway" over United We Dream's advocacy work, United We Dream has sought to exert its autonomy from this and other national associations.[26] It has moved its Washington, DC, office from NILC to the United States Student Association. It also planned to end NILC's fiscal sponsorship and become its own 501 (c)(3) tax-exempted nonprofit association.[27] Moreover, it has plans to become a powerful fundraising force in its own right. "As far as the grant period, a lot of the funding that RIFA lost has gone to United We Dream. Not any of the big grants yet but United We Dream is lining itself up to get major funding from organizations like Ford and the Atlantic Philanthropies."[28] The ability of UWD to gain fiscal independence by becoming a 501(c)(3) and applying for large grants will reduce its dependence on the national rights associations.

Groups like Orange County Dream Team and Dream Team Los Angeles continue to take an active role in this national organization because it allows them to stay connected to national campaigns and conversations. "DTLA and almost any other major group in any other major city have connections to United We Dream, just to be able to be like: 'We want to be part of that conversation, even if we don't agree with your policy or your strategy or your politics, whatever.' It's more about having your voice in the campaign, being part of the process."[29] United

We Dream provides direct connections between the different DREAM groups and networks across the country, enables regular communication between DREAMers in different locales, circulates important information from well-placed activists in Washington, DC, and invests important resources in training and leadership-development workshops. The Internet and regularly scheduled conference calls have been instrumental in coordinating relations between the national organization and these local affiliates.

The local affiliates of United We Dream also draw upon grassroots resources to provide important levels of support to the national organization. Dream Team Los Angeles has not only supported different campaigns and the annual conventions but also worked with United We Dream and the UCLA Labor Center to support a summer internship program called "Dream Summer" in 2011 and 2012. They aimed to expand the internship model developed at UCLA's Labor Center. They recruited unions and social justice associations and encouraged them to provide paid summer internships to these one hundred DREAMers. Dream Team Los Angeles and the Labor Center also hosted the one-week training that preceded the internships. Thus, local affiliates draw upon their grassroots resources to support major projects of the national organization. This reflects a much flatter network structure than that which existed before 2010.

The National Immigrant Youth Alliance (NIYA) was formed by the more "radical" DREAMers of the movement in January 2011.[30] Many of these youths were affiliated with the Dream Is Coming group that initiated the break with RIFA in spring 2010. This group has stressed its complete independence from immigrant rights associations and the "non-profit industrial complex." Its scarce resources have limited its capacities to perform the same functions as UWD, but its advanced communication capacities have allowed it to establish an important presence in DREAMer networks and the public debate. "I think they have a really strong communications infrastructure. [The communication director] is excellent. He has all these producers and reporters on his cell phone. As far as pushing out the message, he is one of the best equipped people in the movement."[31] As a radical and totally independent association, it employs the most confrontational methods to pursue its goals. "The folks in NIYA just don't care. They want to be super out there and break every law they can. They have already been in jail and see this as a badge of honor and courage. But, if you do that kind of activism, then you really have to operate outside the nonprofit industrial complex. United We Dream, by contrast, is very much inside the complex."[32] The radicalism and idealism the National Immigrant Youth Alliance has resonated with many youth activists and allowed it the organization to position itself as an alternative to the more mainstream United We Dream.

This new generation of DREAMers has therefore developed a largely decentralized infrastructure. Three principal mechanisms tie this infrastructure together: local DREAMer organizations draw on resources from their local environments (college campuses and supportive progressive organizations); the more prominent of local DREAM organizations become hubs that circulate scarce resources and information to others in their networks (for example, Dream Team Los Angeles redistributing resources to allies across the state); and lastly, national organizations connect to local and regional networks. Each activist group within this flatter and more decentralized network acquires certain competencies and resources that are then circulated to others within this activist space. Campus organizations enable activists to acquire certain resources (from material resources to organizing skills) that can then be transferred to community-based groups like the Dream Teams or to support national campaigns. Community organizations like Dream Team Los Angeles circulate their own concentrated resources outward to campus groups, to other Dream Teams in the city and state, and to national organizations. In a resource-scarce network where no particular organization has achieved a monopoly over precious resources, the only way to build an autonomous and powerful group has therefore been through constant reciprocal exchanges between allied DREAMers.

Youth activists acquired the cultural and symbolic resources needed to express a voice in the public sphere over time. Highly acculturated and educated youths were able to acquire the cultural capital needed to craft effective messages in the public sphere. As these youths learned to become skilled, cultured, and disciplined activists, the movement became one of the only arenas where they could deploy their talents in satisfying ways. The movement could draw on a pool of talented, committed, and motivated activists to continue the struggle. The acquisition of these essential resources allowed them to assert their autonomy from the leading immigrant rights associations and become an independent group within the general movement.

This new generation of youth activists has also developed an infrastructure that would allow them to mobilize and voice new claims over an extended period of time. It is this infrastructure that permits the sustained presence of the DREAMer in the public sphere. Whereas mobilizations like Occupy Wall Street were able to pierce the public sphere with their bold actions and broad Internet reach, they ultimately lacked the concrete infrastructure to support their presence over months and years.[33] Without this infrastructure, the new generation of DREAMers would have shared the same fate as Occupy Wall Street: after a series of highly visible and disruptive acts of civil disobedience, they would have dissipated into a political afterthought. Their abilities to develop a grassroots infrastructure saved them from this fate and allowed them to remain a potent force in the field of immigration politics. The infrastructure has drawn resources out and up from the grassroots (local associations, colleges, churches, and so on) and circulated these resources horizontally to other DREAMers operating at local, statewide, and national scales. Their abilities to tap these grassroots resources allowed the new generation of DREAMers to stay politically relevant and also to sustain their autonomy within the broader immigrant rights movement.

5

Undocumented, Unafraid, Unapologetic

The dissident DREAMers had repeatedly stressed their frustration with how they were represented in earlier campaigns by national rights associations. They were tired of being made to cower in the "shadows" of the public sphere. They wanted to come out, stand proudly, and speak for themselves. They were also frustrated with having to silence those aspects of themselves that veered off message. The youths struggled against the closets and the shadows of the past. They were now seeking to reconstruct the DREAMer in a way that moved beyond the narrow "boxes" of the good and exceptional immigrant.[1] However, many of these DREAMers were also realists. They understood that their abilities to win legal residency for undocumented youths depended on following certain "rules of the game." This meant that they had to produce an image of youths that resonated with values of the broader American public. They certainly wanted to forge representations that were true to themselves, but they also needed to represent the DREAMer in a way that would advance their fight for legalization.

Striking a balance between these competing representational needs has become one of the central dilemmas facing this new generation of autonomous DREAMers. The DREAMers needed to be more open about their multiple selves and radical about their claims, but they also needed to make sure that their message would resonate with their targeted publics. Trying to strike a balance between these discourses and arguments has precipitated intense reflection, debate, monitoring, and policing over what should or should not be said in public. The DREAMers have assumed the principle responsibility of policing and disciplining their ranks. They actively train youths in messaging, monitor how activists deliver carefully crafted stories, and exact sanctions against those who deviate from established understandings of the positive representation of the DREAMer. As certain leaders have assumed a role in instilling order and discipline within their ranks, the critiques and grievances of deviating youths are directed at those charged with ensuring a positive representation of the DREAMer in the public sphere. This revives representational cleavages and conflicts over who has the right to represent the true voice of undocumented youths.

Representing the DREAMer

Crafting compelling discourses to represent themselves and their cause has continued to be a central task. "Even before we plan an action, we think about what our messaging is going to be. We go through a process of brainstorming: framing our messaging and deciding key sound bites. When the media asks what the action is about, we need to make sure that everybody has the same sentence, everybody has the same sound bite, and everybody sticks to the same frame."[2] Winning support from the public continues to depend on creating a sympathetic portrait of DREAMers and their cause. The "iron rule" of the hostile public sphere requires activists to cleanse themselves of the stigmas attributed to immigrants and demonstrate conformity with the values of the national public. For nationals to recognize undocumented immigrants as rights-deserving human beings (rather than threatening enemies), immigrants must demonstrate their "common" humanity by showing that they have the same values, aspirations, and tastes as any "normal" American. The core discursive themes of the good and exceptional immigrant had been effective in the past because they were premised on simple binary distinctions that resonated with the public and politicians. Undocumented youths were assimilated Americans and not foreigners; they were contributing to America and not taking from it; and they were innocent and others were guilty. Stressing these binary themes made this segment of the undocumented population sympathetic in the eyes of many Americans.

Most leading DREAMers recognize the effectiveness of the past messaging strategy. The discourse of the good immigrant made it possible for many Americans (allies and adversaries) to view undocumented youths as deserving the right to stay in the country:

DREAMer: I think the function of messaging is really to start to get people to think differently, especially those on the right and have this very antagonistic and very hostile point of view of immigrant rights and immigration. If the messaging is correct and effective, then the message will be able to trigger hearts and minds, for them to be able to start thinking differently. And that has been really key for the DREAM movement.

Interviewer: What would you characterize as an effective message to change hearts and minds?

DREAMer: This whole idea of DREAMers being part of the system, that we are "Americans"; that we have so much talent to give back to our communities. But because of this very outdated immigration system we have in place right now, we're not able to give back. I think this whole idea of belonging here, being part of here and really having to decide to give back to our communities, economically but even with our values and culturally. So those messages really have been very strong and have worked very well.[3]

Changing "hearts and minds" of a hostile public requires a message that stresses national belonging. Another DREAMer agrees but emphasizes new efforts to deploy this message in a more nuanced way, "We know that the 'good immigrant' strategy works. It works extremely well! But, we also believed we needed to be more strategic in the way we use it and not just throw it out there. 'I graduated from UCLA with a 4.0.' *So, we use it but we are also careful not to demonize our parents or other immigrants at the same time.*[4] This DREAMer knows that there are "rules of the game" that govern the production of compelling discourses in a still hostile public sphere but also believes that DREAMers have flexibility in how these discourses are produced. They need to stress the attributes that make undocumented youth good, exceptional, and deserving immigrants, but they also need to avoid reinforcing stigmas attributed to other immigrant groups (parents, recent arrivals, adults, and so on).

In spring 2010, a major innovation in framing the DREAMer was the introduction of the "undocumented and unafraid" theme. Several dissident DREAMers argued that they should cease being ashamed and openly state their undocumented status in public.

> Last year was the big push for us to come out as "undocumented and afraid." For us involved in this, this was important because we needed to put a face to a human issue and stop hiding behind the pseudonyms we used in the past when we spoke in public. We were able to do that because over the past ten years undocumented students have built political clout and have built solid political alliances. This makes it possible so that we can come out and say that we are undocumented.[5]

"Coming out" as undocumented was viewed as a way to defiantly assert one's dignity in a world where hiding in the shadows had become the norm. They were undocumented, unafraid, and unapologetic. Publicly asserting one's status has also been a way to assert one's existence as rights bearing human beings. The DREAMer and artist Julio Salgado expressed this feeling in his "I Exist!" illustration series (see Figures 3 and 4 below).[6] "We're doing this to make presence, to make people know that we are here, to say, I exist! The worst feeling that any human can have is being made to feel nonexistent. We have been told for so long, 'You are not like me, you're different, you don't have a right to exist.'"[7]

Coming out also provides emotional support for undocumented youths. When DREAMers come out about their status, they reveal to undocumented youths everywhere that they are not alone. Responding to the suicide of an undocumented youth, one DREAMer reiterated the importance of coming out in a Facebook posting: "If you ever questioned why there is a need to come out and be in people's face about your status, this is why. There's always a young person out there feeling alone

FIGURE 3   *Undocumented, Unafraid, Unapologetic. Image by Julio Salgado.*

and thinking that this [suicide] is the only way out. When anti-migrant bills all over the country exist, this shitty government is giving permission for others to hate and for some to feel dehumanized."[8] Coming out provides support to youths across the country by demonstrating they are not alone. Just as important for this DREAMer, it affirms the humanity of undocumented youths by countering the dehumanizing discourses of the government and public.

FIGURE 4 *I Exist! Image by Julio Salgado.*

The theme of coming out and being unafraid provided the movement with added momentum and energy. "But I think across the board, everybody saw that people also have the right to be undocumented and unafraid, and you shouldn't take that away from anybody. And it's an empowering identity, something that's grown, something that has fueled our momentum."[9] Another DREAMer remarked that this theme inspired youths across the country to come out and join the struggle:

Last year, with this coming out, events started happening all over, students were coming out for the first time in public about their status, and they were not afraid. It was very empowering to see students in Georgia and Arizona coming out, and this whole hostile anti-immigrant space, and like "wow, they're doing it, so why can't I do it?" We were able to empower each other through this very meaningful, inspiring wave of events that were happening and occurring all over.[10]

One youth who went on to become a leading DREAMer noted that the theme motivated him to join the campaign in 2010:

DREAMer: But when they had that coming out on Pershing Square [in downtown Los Angeles] and they had the "I Am Undocumented" shirts, I thought: okay, that's interesting. That's really good; people should know that we are undocumented. They started going around Pershing Square, talking to people and telling them that they were undocumented, and then having them sign a petition for the DREAM Act. That's when I was like "Okay, this is something good." It was pushing those boundaries, right? *They were undocumented and unafraid, and I thought, "Hell yeah, me too! And it's about time!"*

Interviewer: So, the message of undocumented and unafraid played a role in joining the movement?

DREAMer: Yeah, of being unafraid, of stepping out of our comfort zone, stepping out of the shadows and showing people who we really are. Before, when folks were fighting for the DREAM Act, I never heard something like that. It didn't seem like the message was coming from an organizing perspective, from the grassroots. It just seemed like a nonprofit was trying to pass a policy that was good but . . . I didn't really see us defining or pushing the campaign. When I saw this I was like "Okay, this is good."[11]

The "undocumented and unafraid" theme has complicated the simple and clean discourse of the past. Rather than undocumented youths presenting themselves as good and humble immigrants, the new discourse stresses that their undocumented status is a part of who they are as Americans. Indeed, they are Americans but also Americans who are undocumented. The combination of being both American and undocumented has complicated past depictions of the good immigrant, which stressed total conformity with national values and silencing of foreignness. The aim of dissident DREAMers was to collapse the boundary between the two and assert that one can be both simultaneously. In Jacques Rancière's terms, the dissident DREAMers were aggressively staking out a political subjectivity based on their "in-between" status.[12] This has presented a challenge and disruption to mainstream ideas of what it meant to be American and what it meant to be undocumented. Moreover, the assertion of being "unapologetic" presented a further challenge because it defies national ideas of acceptable behavior from immigrants. A good immigrant knows his or her place within the receiving context and seeks to humbly and silently fit in. The brash statements of the DREAMers challenge the established norms of Americanness and do so *unapologetically*.

Further complicating matters, DREAMers now talk about the "intersectional" character of their struggle. They are not only undocumented Americans; they are also Queer, minorities, women, and so on. They believe themselves to be positioned at the intersection of overlapping powers, with each power producing its own distinctive form of repression and injustice. The embrace of intersectionality as an overarching theme resulted from the positioning of student activists in multiple struggles, such as union organizing, feminism, LGBT, and so on. But it also reflects the growing influence of the poststructural political theory among this new generation of youth activists. The DREAMers have also stressed sexuality as a core part of their identities. Self-identified Queer youth have assumed a prominent role in the leadership of the movement. "I don't know if you picked up on this—also, a lot of key leaders or folks at the forefront of the DREAM Movement have been women and Queer people. And so for me, I also identify as queer."[13] This has encouraged strong affinity with the Lesbian Gay Bisexual Transgender Queer (LGBTQ) movement and resulted in the appropriation of core symbols, discourses, and rituals (for example, "coming out"). This perspective was expressed in the op-ed piece in *Dissent* magazine:

FIGURE 5 *Queer, Undocumented, and Unafraid.*
Image by Julio Salgado.

We have lived with fear since arrival and our exploitation runs rampant because we are also women, Queer and transgender people of color. For those of us undocumented youth who identify as Queer, coming out is a something we must do twice. We come out as Queers to our families and friends and then come out again as undocumented in this country. . . . We can no longer be afraid of revealing our status or identities. We must fiercely challenge privilege and oppression, whether located among allies or the opposition.[14]

The strong assertion of Queer identity has become a strong part of the general messaging strategy (see Figure 5 below).

The public expression of multiple identities (especially sexuality) is a departure from the earlier strategy of narrowly focusing on the attributes that made undocumented youth good, exceptional, and deserving immigrants. The old messaging strategy focused on one narrow aspect of their identities—Americanness, good students, and so forth—and silenced other aspects that would divert attention from the central message of a campaign. Presenting the Queer identity of a DREAMer in public was previously discouraged because it distracted from the central message. During earlier actions young gay couples were discouraged from public displays of affection by immigrant rights associations because such displays would complicate the central message. These acts of silencing by immigrant rights associations elicited resentment by many activists, especially those with identities that did not conform to the script. Many DREAMers have expressed deep satisfaction with recent changes: "When I first came into the movement, I used to have to engage in painful negotiations over whether to wear my undocumented hat or Queer hat. But because of the empowerment that happened last year, I could stop these negotiations and say who I was and not hide any aspect of myself."[15]

The traditional messaging strategy also aimed to cleanse undocumented youth of the stigma of "illegality." The talking point "no fault of their own" was used to stress the innocence of the undocumented, but it did so by attributing guilt to parents and others in the community.

> A key talking point created in the past was that we were brought here by "no fault of our own." This was created by policymakers and advocates, but most DREAMers disagreed with that statement. Now what we do is intentionally let people know that we don't agree with that statement. We no longer say "through no fault of our own." We now say we were brought here by our parents who are courageous and responsible and who would not let their children die and starve in another country.[16]

DREAM activists have reconstructed the "no fault" theme by stressing that family migration was a response to structural or political forces and not a matter of choice. Parents sought out a better life for their children rather than allow them to perish in another country. By shifting responsibility to structural causes rather than "choices," the message absolves both youths and parents from the guilt and stigma of "illegality." Rather than framing parents as guilty, they are now framed as responsible and courageous in their struggle to provide a better life for their children. Dream Team Los Angeles has worked with others to circulate this message to DREAMers in the broader movement (see Figure 6 below).

In a Facebook posting announcing the new messaging campaign, a DREAM activist posted the following commentary: "Our parents are still being blamed and criticized for our situation. Next time you hear someone blame the parents, tell them: MY PARENTS ARE COURAGEOUS AND RESPONSIBLE. THAT'S WHY I AM HERE! This next set of drawings is dedicated to my fellow DREAMers, risking their whole lives in the name of justice."[17] The illustration and commentary elicited more than one hundred responses from DREAMers across the country:

- STOP BLAMING OUR PARENTS FOR PURSUING A BETTER LIFE FOR US. THEY DESERVE OUR RESPECT. DOPE IMAGE.
- I think it's so appropriate considering the amount of blame put on our families.
- DON'T BLAME MY MOTHER FOR WORKING HARD ALL HER DAMN LIFE SO THAT SHE COULD BRING BREAD AT THE TABLE.
- Right on! the political game is so tired. Parents didn't have a choice-they were forced too.
- awwwwwwww! this is bad ass ! thanx!
- this is so great! it captures what i've been thinking about my own immigrant family. beautiful.
- love it!!! That's what I've been feeling!! That was the best choice my parents every made for me!! I wouldn't be in this fight and meet everybody because of that choice they made . . . A Better life for me.

The comments reflect the strong resonance of the new message. The California Dream Network, an organization that had tense relations with Dream Team Los Angeles and Orange County Dream Team because of

FIGURE 6 *Courageous and Responsible Parents. Image by Julio Salgado.*

conflicts in 2010, also adopted this new messaging. One DREAMer from the network notes, "So when we have big campaigns, like the DREAM Act campaign in California, we had this caravan across California, and we were meeting with members of the legislature. So every time we were going through—we were telling the students, 'When you tell your story, don't blame your parents.'"[18]

In exercising their autonomy, this new generation of DREAMers has sought to refashion and reconstruct traditional representations of themselves and their cause. In the past, the representations of undocumented youth were designed primarily to produce resonance with a hostile American public. This resulted in tight and narrow depictions of the good immigrant. They were exceptional Americans (and not foreign) and wholly innocent of the choice to migrate (and not guilty like their parents). This narrow depiction was successful in opening up opportunities where none had previously existed, but it also came at the cost of stigmatizing others in the immigrant community and silencing important parts of themselves. Now, dissident DREAMers maintain certain themes from the past (American values, talented students, and so on), but they have also crafted more complex, nuanced, and forceful representations of DREAMers.

The Dilemmas of Complex Discourses

The proliferation of different and sometimes discordant discourses within the same social movement has raised important dilemmas for DREAMers and allies alike. There has been growing concern over whether DREAMers are speaking too much to themselves and not enough to the general public. Like other identity movements, discourses that assert the right to recognition may satisfy the claimants' political-existential needs, but these same discourses may not be effective in gaining broad support for legal-juridical rights. One longtime DREAMer expressed this dilemma:

> I think they have produced messages that resonate a lot with DREAMers. It appears that the message is to the rest of the [DREAMers'] movement instead of messaging to the masses. The messaging itself has been like, "We're undocumented, unafraid, and unapologetic. We will not live in shadows, we will not live in chains, etc." It is very poetic in many ways, but it doesn't have that practical and concise, "what do you want, what are you doing" focus needed for an effective message.[19]

The new tone, themes, and rhetoric risk dulling the concise messaging needed to achieve the movement's most pressing goal: legalizing the status of undocumented immigrants in a country that remains largely hostile.

There has also been greater openness to using theoretical and philosophical discourse. DREAMers who master this language have been well received by other activists in the network. "I don't know if you checked out any of the work of [———]? [This DREAMer] is very much a Marx-ian, Foucauldian theorist. . . . She's a social media guru. Every time she writes something it gets spread out through the blogosphere. Her politi-cal message is very deconstructed, post-national and post-everything."[20] DREAMer intellectuals are influential discourse makers in their own right, with their ideas and language achieving great influence and reso-nance within the movement. "Some of these DREAMers are calling for a postnational world. They want to believe in it, they want to create it, and they want to belong to it. Not all these people are intellectuals in this way, but some are. Still, their influence has been important. The concept of "intersectionality" now roles off the tongue of the average DREAMer like water. *This is a good and fine concept, but you can't make an easy talking point with it.*"[21] Concepts like "intersectionality" inspire DREAMers intellectually and emotionally, but they do not lend them-selves to clear messaging. Moreover, discourses that reject assimilation and celebrate postnationalism are more likely to trigger hostility from a broad American public than support.

Many DREAMers have addressed the dilemma by trying to strike a balance between messages "for themselves" and the messages for the general public. United We Dream has been careful to craft a compel-ling message for public consumption, but it also fosters new discourses and identities for internal communications and events. "United We Dream—we're definitely into much of this new language. But when it comes to the press, it's very much like a mainstream message. NIYA [National Immigrant Youth Alliance] can do that game too when they want to. So it's like divided between the conversations that you have for community building within your activists and when you bring people together, and the message that you put out—your political message."[22] Rather than argue that there are good and bad discourses, this strategy suggests that there are many discourses, but some are more appropriate for broad audiences while others are better suited for DREAMers and their supportive allies. While many of the prominent DREAM organi-zations have employed this strategy, others have argued that discourses on intersectionality and "undocumented and afraid" are frontal critiques on discourses that stressed national identification and assimilation. These discourses cannot coexist within the same movement because one negates the other. This dilemma is captured in an exchange between DREAMers on Facebook:

Henry: Our audience is vast, and we need different messages to attract different people. There isn't "one" narrative . . .

Lisa: Henry, "attracting" different audience means playing on the oppressors' terms. I deal with elitist people all day long at my elitist private liberal arts school, and I've learned the importance of not doing activism for allies but for our people. This is exactly the same problem in national messaging by RIFA and FIRM this time around (and last). The worst thing is there are lots of undocumented people giving into documented people's thinking. Come on, we don't have to! Why resist the truth when you can hop on and join the fight? . . . Human rights for human rights. No need to be "American," no need to be aspiring, just human rights. I'm done here.[23]

Stitching together the different discourses, arguments, and messages has by no means been easy. Some DREAMers have sought to incorporate these various discourses and deploy them selectively for different audiences, but others continue to maintain that one (undocumented and afraid) negates the other (assimilationist, good American line). These disagreements over representations are associated with different factions and organizations of the broader youth movement. Whereas United We Dream has sought to incorporate these different discourses, the National Immigrant Youth Alliance has expressed a preference for a more radical line.

The new and more complex discourses haven't only resulted in important dilemmas. They have also created new opportunities. The employment of new and diverse discourses has helped to align the mobilizing frames of DREAMers with the frames of different rights movements in the United States.[24] This facilitates the abilities of people in other movements to see how the DREAMer's struggle links to their own movements and struggles. The strong incorporation of LGBT themes into the DREAM movement (for example, "coming out," "undocuqueer," and so on) has helped draw in support from outside activists. The appropriation of civil rights discourses has also facilitated activists to find similarities in the struggles of the civil rights movement. In one campus meeting, the organizer leads a lengthy discussion concerning similarities between African Americans fighting for equality in the 1960s and undocumented immigrants fighting for equality today. A participant observer described the meeting:

> He [lead organizer of the campus group] wants to show us a tape of the SNCC [Student Nonviolent Coordinating Committee]. He explains to the group that African Americans couldn't eat in diners back then and these students organized sit-ins, hunger strikes. They were beaten and arrested although they were nonviolent. He asks the group what similarities they see between the African Americans back then and the undocumented youth movement right now. The other lead organizer continues. He says that back then the mainstream organizers of the civil rights movement did not want to organize any real big campaigns. The young students wanted to push on and escalate the struggle. He says, "It is always the youth who feels what is right. They are the ones willing to fight for what is right. They are always bombarded with negative criticism. People are telling us not to fight and to just get a Latino Democrat into power. But we know we need to fight.[25]

They not only identify similarities between movements (fight for equality by oppressed people), but also use other movements to explain and give meaning to the dynamics found within their own struggles (the importance of youth in escalating struggles). These kinds of exercises permit DREAMers to create symbolic, analytic, and emotional bridges, providing the conceptual foundations to build alliances across race, class, and sexual differences.

Disciplining and its Limits

Striking a balance between what should and shouldn't be expressed in public has remained an important strategic concern of this new generation of DREAMers. DREAMers remain extremely vigilant about what is said in public and have worked hard to train their activists in recognizing the line between "acceptable" and "unacceptable" public speech. Before 2010, the process of making undocumented youths into disciplined deliverers of the DREAM message was largely directed from the top down. After 2010, the disciplining process has largely been managed

by the DREAMers themselves. Leading activists have assumed prominent roles in producing strategies, developing campaigns, and shaping
the discourse and messaging of the movement. They have also played
a very important role in ensuring discipline among the ranks of the
DREAMers.

Good public messaging has continued to be goal of this new generation of DREAMers. Constant trainings and workshops have remained
core techniques to ensure a high level of messaging discipline among the
activists. A leading member of Dream Team Los Angeles described one
such training session:

> We provide a lot of media training in things like how to talk to reporters
> and how to stick to our talking points. Training people to deliver a message
> is a distinct talent. We do a three-legged dog activity. Everything I ask a
> person, they have to respond with "three-legged dog." For example, I would
> ask, "How was your day?" and they would respond, "Oh fine, I went to the
> store and there was a three-legged dog." We then tell them that the three-
> legged dog is the DREAM Act talking points. So whatever a reporter is ask-
> ing, they have to go back to the three-legged dog, the DREAM Act talking
> points. We stress that you don't have to answer everything the media asks
> you, just be sure to consistently hit the talking points. *Whatever comes out on
> air is whatever comes out of your mouth.*[26]

Controlling what comes out of an activist's "mouth" has remained a strategic priority. These constant trainings help create a seamless channel
between the general message, the "mouth" of the activist, and the public
sphere.

Activists who have been trained by leading DREAMers go on to
employ the same techniques to train new recruits to their own organizations. One DREAMer describes the use of the same technique to train
new recruits in her campus organization:

> An exercise we usually do is the three-legged dog. You make people prac-
> tice by telling them, "Pretend you're being interviewed and every time
> the reporter asks you any kind of question you have to bring it back to
> the three-legged dog." So that forces them to make sure to stay on track,
> to not let the reporter throw them on a tangent, to not repeat anything

that the reporter might say that might be used in a snapshot of them, and it forces them to think that they need to stay on point for themselves. I need to be aware that the reporter is not necessarily there to support me; they're just there to get a story. So it's making sure that people think about those things. *You're not going to know if you're just thrown into that space [interview with reporter]. You're just going to say whatever comes out of your mouth.*[27]

The above DREAMer replicates not only the technique but also the rationale: new recruits don't know how to express themselves in public and often say "*whatever comes out of your mouth.*" Off-message utterances divert from the central message of a campaign, missing an opportunity to shape perceptions in the public debate and raising the risk of reinforcing negative stereotypes of the group. Undisciplined utterances are fine when expressed behind the scenes, but they work against the movement when expressed in public. This requires experienced DREAMers to mold the minds and mouths of new recruits.

Storytelling has remained an important technique in the movement's general messaging strategy. This new generation of DREAMers employs storytelling trainings mastered in the earlier stage of the movement. An activist from the San Fernando Valley Dream Team recounted her training:

So they [Dream Team Los Angeles] have taught us a lot how to structure our stories. The story has to have a character and it has to have a challenge, then a choice, then the outcome. That's kind of how you structure it. . . . You could have a thousand different versions of your story. . . . So, for example, I've told my story in many different ways because I've been practicing with myself how to make an impact on people. What they taught us also in the Dream Summer is also to have *vulnerability* when we tell our stories. *If your level of vulnerability is low then you're not going to have an impact on people; you have to have that emotional connect with people that don't understand the movement or don't understand the struggle.* So, through this workshop I learnt how to tell my story from a point of view that it's vulnerable for me. . . . So I kind of bring that emotional connect to people, like, who hasn't felt that way in their lives? So "I overcame my insecurities; I overcame the fears. I'm still fighting for having dignity and individually, but now as a collective, the organizing has empowered my life and rescued me to become who I am today." That's what we do at stories.[28]

This DREAMer highlights three important points about storytelling: it is a process that is taught to activists through formal training sessions, but it is also something that DREAMers work on by themselves. The DREAMer notes that we can tell our stories in many ways, but not all stories will have the same level of impact on the public. This requires a process of self-disciplining (retelling stories to themselves many times) in which tangential utterances (noises) are silenced and a compelling message is carefully honed to maximize its resonance in the public sphere (voice). The aim is not to say "whatever comes out of your mouth" (noise) but only those things that that cohere with the message and discourse of the movement (voice). Moreover, creating resonance in the public sphere is enhanced when one uses emotions to create a connection between one's self and the general public.[29] The construction of an effective discourse not only depends on the right choice of words but also on the themes, intonations, and gestures intended to maximize the emotional impact of those words. Lastly, the process of storytelling is instrumental in forging the identity and subjectivity of individual activists. Refining one's story repeatedly to oneself and to different publics ultimately results in a fusion of public and private selves. The above DREAMer recounted her story: "I overcame my insecurities; I overcame the fears. I'm still fighting for having dignity and individually, but now as a collective, the organizing has empowered my life and rescued me to become who I am today." This is a story that is crafted for public consumption, but also one she believes and uses to structure her interpretation of herself and her life in the United States. The DREAMers' internalization of the story—through recurrent tellings to different audiences and to one's own self—covers the gaps between the movement discourse, the "mouth" of the activist, and the public sphere.

The workshops and trainings provided by DREAM organizations continue to be extremely important in harnessing emotional energies among the new generation of DREAMers. These have become crucial spaces where youths can come out and share their experiences with one another. The process of talking oftentimes creates a powerful level of emotional energy that opens up the "soul" of youths and allows for public stories to enter and shape the internal subjectivities of the undocumented youths. The emotional and trusting environments allow DREAMers to talk about themselves and align visions of their selves with the visions of the movement. "Yeah. I think, to be quite honest, the training at most retreats [is] geared towards storytelling because I feel when we do go to these trainings a lot of it is therapy session for a lot of people. Yeah, so, it's a big part in the training. I feel like those who have done it every time, I think it's kind of like medicine to them. It gives them support and new ideas. *It allows them to open up and think things through more clearly.*"[30]

The result of disciplining is that DREAMers come to know at an implicit level the line separating "acceptable" from "unacceptable" public speech. An activist with Dream Team Los Angeles emphasized the divide between what's stated in public and what's stated behind the scenes:

DREAMer: Everybody knows that is what we do, that's what we are. I understand that's how we're going to present ourselves, because we can't be out there promoting ourselves as coming from South Central and that we're *cholos* or whatever.[31]

Interviewer: So the poster-child strategy is largely intact?

DREAMer: Well, we might deviate from group to group, but it's up to everybody's discretion about what you want to promote. *But it's almost unspoken. You don't even need to think about it. Everybody knows you promote a positive image.*

Interviewer: So what about the *chola* illustration you talked about earlier?[32]

DREAMer: That was just more for us, within ourselves.[33]

Well-trained activists implicitly know that what comes out of their "mouths" must cohere with the "positive" image of the DREAMer. They also know the difference between what is expressed to the public and what is expressed to DREAMers in private (front-stage versus back-stage messaging). While certain identities (Queer, undocumented and unafraid) are now readily embraced and expressed in public, other identities associated with inner-city culture (South Central, "cholos") continue to be suppressed by the movement. These suppressed identities can be circulated and sometimes celebrated behind the scenes, but an "unspoken" rule restricts most well-trained DREAMers from expressing such stigmatized identities, images, and utterances in public. This new generation of DREAMers has therefore celebrated the new discourses and messages within the movement, but they have continued to exert control over how they craft representations of themselves in the public sphere, carefully choosing to highlight certain attributes of this complex group while actively silencing others.

The high degree of disciplining exercised by the DREAMers has exacerbated tensions and disagreements over how DREAMers should represent themselves in public. In fall 2011, two DREAMers affiliated with NIYA (both from Los Angeles) arranged for their own arrest by Immigration and Customs Enforcement agents in Alabama. Their intention was to infiltrate the detention center, support migrants in the process of removal proceedings, and gather information on the detention center and the conditions of the detainees. They also filmed their own arrest and posted it to the Internet. While many celebrated this action, the activists were also criticized by some leading DREAMers for the lack of preparation and undisciplined messaging. There was concern by some leading DREAMers that these actions could produce negative blowback for the movement. Frustrated with these criticisms, one of the arrestees posted the following response on his Facebook wall:

> Posting: The only thing that upset me is people criticizing the way I *talked* to border patrol [captured in the film clip posted to the Internet]. *They said I should have been more formal and articulate because I needed to represent dreamers.* Those people are obviously idiots. 1. why should i try to impress homeland security. I'm trying to get detained not a fucking scholarship. 2. why should I change the way I speak. I'm from [a Latin American country] raised in the [. . .] projects in East LA.[34] *I'm hood and proud of it.* 3. i was undercover. my action's success was contingent on the fact that they thought i was a regular undocumented person, not an organizer who had a specific goal to accomplish . . . 4. *I do not believe that i should be the "good Immigrant" [. . .]to get respect and dignity.* we need to be college graduates with no criminal records and be "american."[35]

His posting elicited ninety-two Facebook "likes" and twenty-six comments. Some of the comments included:

- YES YES YES YES!!! Those people are obviously too dumb to get the point! ♥
- hmmm, assimilation or fearlessness?—thanks for leading!
- I'll give you a scholarship just for being a no nonsense sin pelos en la lengua[36] from east los![37] thanks for standing up for your beliefs!
- And I bet those people saying that would not have the courage to do what you guys did. *Tired of people telling me I have to be a model citizen to prove I'm a dreamer. I'm not trying to kiss ass to get my way into american citizenship. . . .*
- *You can't please everyone. I remember when there was that video of me rappin' in the car going around, and all these folks were talkin' 'bout, "This is ok, but . . . why does he have to curse? He's representing all of us." All you can do is represent yourself and keep it as real as you can.* Personally, I thought you didn't say enough. =)
- ♥ *i used to organize with the dream team as a youth and i experienced the same. Also the projects represent!*

This exchange reveals several important aspects concerning the self-disciplined DREAMer: crafting a compelling and disciplined public representation of the DREAMer remains a top priority. This has resulted in continued efforts to highlight attributes that make them "good" Americans and *selectively* silencing conduct, utterances, and images that reflect stigmatized attributes. The above arrestee was criticized because his conduct and speech represented an undocumented youth that was too working class, too inner city, too foreign, too unschooled, too criminal, and so on. The new generation of DREAMers permits new themes to be expressed in the public sphere (Queer, unafraid) but ensures that certain stigmatized attributes remain out of public sight. Policing the boundaries of acceptable and unacceptable conduct and speech continues to be a central concern of the new generation of DREAMers. The process of silencing problem utterances, conduct, and images involves intensive self-disciplining. This occurs in the micromanagement of conduct and speech during trainings, but it also occurs through online and offline communication between DREAMers. The criticisms of the arrestee's behavior were communicated to him directly by other DREAMers and through chatter in online communication spaces (blogs, Facebook, and so on). Several responses to the posting confirm similar experiences by other youth activists. In these instances, it was not immigrant rights associations governing the public speech and conduct of the DREAMers (top down) but the DREAMers who were governing themselves (bottom up). Many DREAMers had internalized the rationale of presenting a good public image, and they assumed an active role in guarding the image of the group and movement. A rather intense effort has therefore been made to minimize instances in which stray and deviant DREAMers just say whatever comes out of their mouths.

The self-disciplining process introduces important levels of resentment, disagreement, and conflicts within the ranks of the DREAMers. The arrestee expressed anger for criticism directed at his speech and viewed it as a way to silence an important part of his cultural identity. He argued that he should not be ashamed of where he came from and asserted pride for being Latin American and raised in Los Angeles's inner city ("why should I change the way I speak. . . . I'm hood and proud of it"). He went on to argue that rights, respect, and dignity should be granted because he is human and not because he presented himself as a "good immigrant" or a culturally assimilated "American" ("I do not believe that i should be the 'good Immigrant' [. . .]to get respect and dignity"). This argument resonated with several commenters ("Tired of people telling me I have to be a model citizen to prove I'm a dreamer. I'm not trying to kiss ass to get my way into american citizenship.").

In the past, when frustrations arose in response to disciplining, DREAMers directed their criticisms at national rights associations. These associations were accused of silencing the DREAMers and limiting their abilities to speak in public. The "rules of the game" continue to require a disciplined message, but now the DREAMers are in charge of the disciplining process. The grievances and resistances that inevitably result from disciplining have now been directed at fellow DREAMers and not the "social justice elite" or the "nonprofit industrial complex." In spite of changes in the leadership, the representational cleavages that emerged in the earlier rounds of mobilization have therefore resurfaced in this new round, once again planting seeds of conflict and disagreement. The necessity of producing effective and compelling representations in the public sphere is a process that requires constant monitoring and silencing of deviant conduct and utterances within the ranks. Who leads may aggravate such conflicts, but the leadership itself may not be the root cause, as the new leaders of the DREAM movement are finding out.

In 2010 and 2011, undocumented youths began to express their own voice, largely in response to conflicts with their traditional representatives in the immigrant rights movement. They have tried to strike a balance between a discourse that is both compelling to a hostile and conservative public and that also stresses the need for recognition as complex human beings. This has marked an important departure from the previous phase of the immigrant rights movement. Most mainstream immigrant rights associations viewed these campaigns as struggles to win legal-juridical rights of undocumented immigrants. Thus conceived, representing immigrants in ways that cohered most closely with the core national values was for them the most effective way to achieve this goal. By contrast, the new generation of activists came to believe that the struggle was indeed about gaining legal-juridical rights, but it was also about gaining recognition as political equals. The conflict between mainstream associations and undocumented youths helped generate different visions and discourses on rights and citizenship within the same movement. The struggle for this new generation of youth activists has been to reconcile these different and sometimes conflicting discourses.

While DREAMers have achieved autonomy, they continue to be saddled with the contradictions of the past in spite of the change in leadership. DREAMers are aware that winning support and legitimacy requires a compelling message that resonates with a xenophobic public. This encourages arguments that stress the exceptional qualities that make youths especially deserving of legality. But producing a discourse of the "good immigrant" requires silencing the more stigmatized parts of themselves. This process of silencing reinforces feelings of stigma associated with these "other" parts of their selves (that is, working-class habitus, inner city, and so on). Those who experience this silencing feel compelled to revive the radical critiques that have already been circulating in the movement's networks. They seize upon these lines of argument and express them with intense emotional energy in their own networks. They argue that equality should not be granted because of conformity to dominant national norms. Equal rights should be granted only on the basis that immigrants are human beings with inalienable rights. There is a consensus that a legitimate "voice" requires a positive image, but the consensus reaches its limits when the process of producing this voice results in silencing deviant identities, utterances, and conduct. The contradictory process of voice making (producing a public voice necessitates silencing multiple forms of otherness) therefore results in constantly resuscitating dissenting discourses within the same movement. While such a process results in bad blood and destructive factionalism, it also revives alternative ideas of equality and rights and holds the movement accountable to its own exclusionary tendencies.

6

DREAMers and the Immigrant Rights Movement

At the meeting marking the DREAM Act's defeat on December 21, 2010, the DREAMers and their allies sketched a political path forward in the face of diminishing political opportunities. While the immediate goal was to pass the DREAM Act, youths in the room believed their struggle should not stop at the DREAM Act. They expressed the need to work with allied organizations to struggle against federal and local enforcement measures and for the rights of all undocumented immigrants. DREAMers would continue their own campaign *and* work with their allies as equals in other campaigns. They also embraced a new strategy for going forward. Rather than only focus on attaining a single big law from Congress, they shifted their attention to smaller and more winnable struggles in a wide variety of political arenas. Congress was now viewed as one front in a multifront war. They would target the executive branch of the federal government, state legislatures, and local (county and municipal) governments as well. Moreover, they would work alongside their allies to build political power in localities and states across the country. Once territorial strongholds were established in certain cities and states, they could use these as bases to strengthen their negotiating hand with the federal government and assist the struggles of immigrants in hostile localities, notably Arizona and southern states. The "top-down" and centralized strategy of the RIFA years was thus surpassed by a "bottom-up" and decentralized strategy that focused on establishing political control over cities, counties, and states. The director of MAL-DEF outlined the strategy in his speech to the attendees of the meeting:

> California is going to become the anti-Arizona. We will get the California DREAM Act, and we will make California the good model in contrast to Arizona. California can then put pressure on the Federal government. . . . We have to recognize the opportunity we have in California. We need to make the life of all people in the state easier, regardless of their status. *Together we will make this a Dream state on our way to making it a Dream nation.*[1]

The rights of immigrants would be fought in the local trenches, building up territorial strongholds in places like California and other friendly states and using these strongholds to enhance their mobilization capacities in a range of big and small campaigns.

Two factors have accelerated the decentralization of the immigrant rights movement: on the one hand, the localization of federal immigration policy hastened a return to the grassroots. The localization of policy helped make states, counties, and municipalities into political spaces where immigration battles needed to be fought. In jurisdictions with friendly political officials, rights advocates could push for inclusive measures and make these jurisdictions into territorial platforms for launching broader struggles. In jurisdictions with antagonistic officials, restrictive enforcement has triggered resistance among rapidly growing immigrant populations and their supporters (Arizona, for example). On the other hand, leading activists had now developed a clear strategic vision. In the past, small and piecemeal mobilizations dominated the advocacy work of the rights community, but this had never been formulated into an explicit strategy. Incrementalism was a practical response to narrow windows of opportunity and not a full-blown strategy. Now, DREAMers, MALDEF, NDLON, and others drew upon this past approach to develop a formal, bottom-up, and piecemeal strategy. Thus, these institutional and strategic factors have converged to mark a turn away from the top-down and centralized strategy of the late 2000s and toward a new incremental, bottom-up, and decentralized strategy of the 2010s.

Localizing Enforcement, Localizing Immigration Struggles

Before 1996, local and state-level officials had been discouraged from producing their own immigration policies. Courts had long protected federal authority to design and implement immigration policy.[2] Localities certainly passed "backdoor" measures to address immigrants within their jurisdictions, but they were forbidden from developing policies that explicitly dealt with the issue or to use immigration status as a criterion to limit eligibility for local services. While local residents may have directed their ire about "immigrant floods" to local and state-level representatives, constitutional restrictions barred localities from acting on the issue in an explicit way.

The passage of federal immigration laws and policies in 1996 provided greater opportunities for local involvement. These and subsequent measures aimed to recruit state and local officials into new enforcement efforts.[3] The passage of PROWARA in 1996 required state and local officials to employ immigration status as a condition for determining eligibility for important welfare services. This was the first time in the legal history of the United States that states and local governments were given the power to discriminate on the basis of immigration status. IIRIRA, passed in 1996, introduced contracts for local law enforcement agencies to work in partnership with the federal government to detect and deport undocumented people from their jurisdictions (287[g] agreements). This program was succeeded by the Secure Communities program, which was introduced as a pilot program in 2008 by the Bush administration. The Secure Communities program required local police agencies to detain "criminal aliens" for Immigration and Customs Enforcement, which would then prioritize them for deportation. Lastly, PROWARA mandated that if states chose to provide services denied by federal law, they had to finance these provisions with state revenue, rather than federal grants, and pass state legislation expressing the intention to do so.

Thousands of local officials were now confronted with a population that had been outside their jurisdiction in the past. Local officials charged with welfare and policing functions used their discretion to define this population, assess its potential risks and contributions to localities, and design the most appropriate methods to intervene within the framework of the federal law. Whereas some officials and civil servants drew upon a zero-tolerance and "punitive" vision to address the undocumented population in their jurisdictions, others have taken a more "rational" view of this population as permanently settled parts of their communities. The local application of 287(g) partnerships and Secure Communities programs has been particularly uneven.[4] Some local police agencies have conceived all undocumented immigrants as purely "illegal" and all as existential threats to their community and country. In accordance with this position, they have used their new authority to detect and remove these populations from their jurisdictions.[5] By contrast, officials in other localities have accepted large populations of undocumented immigrants as the new reality and developed measures to mitigate the risks associated with the population. The police have resisted cooperation with federal programs because they undermine the trust in undocumented communities. Having been drawn into the federal government's enforcement net, local officials use their discretion to develop their own definitions and prescriptions to treat the problem of "illegality" in their jurisdictions. This has resulted in a patchwork of different measures that vary widely from one place and jurisdiction to another.

State and local officials also saw an opportunity to develop and pass their own laws and ordinances that directly addressed immigration issues. Local and state officials felt justified on the grounds that they were complementing federal, constitutional law, rather than supplementing it, which would be viewed as unconstitutional. The passage of local ordinances and state laws had the effect of localizing how categories of illegality were constructed and enforced in different parts of the country. Certain cities and counties enacted measures that were quite inclusive and called on local civil servants to resist the enactment of the new federal rules and programs. This marked the proliferation of "sanctuary cities." Moreover, PROWARA introduced a stipulation that made it possible to provide services and provisions to undocumented populations only under the condition that state legislatures pass them. This encouraged pro-immigrant lawmakers and activists in several states (including California, Texas, Massachusetts, New York, and so on) to devise legislation regarding in-state tuition for undocumented college students, drivers' licenses, identification, and so forth that explicitly favored undocumented immigrants.

Other states and localities drew upon more restrictive understandings of illegality and passed measures to render the existence of undocumented immigrants in their jurisdictions physically impossible, often using the principle of "attrition through enforcement" or self-deportation. Many local ordinances limited the abilities of undocumented immigrants to find employment, rent housing, make financial transactions, and seek employment in public spaces. Municipalities and counties came to serve as policy laboratories for restrictive and enforcement-oriented measures. This renaissance in restrictive local measures inspired a series of statewide laws beginning with the passage of Arizona's S.B. 1070 in 2010. The law made it a crime for immigrants to be without proof of legal residency, required police agencies to determine an individual's immigration status during a "lawful stop, detention or arrest" when there was "suspicion" that the person is "illegal," barred local officials and civil servants from restricting enforcement of federal immigration laws, and barred hiring, sheltering, and transporting undocumented immigrants. The intellectual architect of S.B. 1070 was Kris Kobach, who is an anti-immigration legal scholar, the secretary of state of Kansas, and Republican presidential candidate Mitt Romney's advisor on immigration.[6] The Arizona law served as a template for anti-immigration measures introduced in Alabama, Georgia, South Carolina, and Indiana.

Passing restrictive state laws and local ordinances has also helped draw local residents into public and political debates over how undocumented residents should be treated in their communities. A growing number of locals (businesses, landlords, contractors, managers of hardware stores, police, welfare officers, and so on) have been expected to play roles in enforcing national and local immigration measures. Thousands of locals have been expected to block undocumented immigrants from accessing jobs, public services, housing, public space, and whatever other sources needed to live a decent life. As entire communities assumed a role in this increasingly refined enforcement net, people have been forced to confront immigration as an issue with real moral, economic, and political implications. Many people drawn into the enforcement net were not entirely happy to comply with new rules, thus triggering public debate over the meaning of "illegality," where to draw the line between "legal" and "illegal" immigrants, how to detect one from the other, and what measures could be employed to seek out the removal of undocumented immigrants. In this way, the localization of immigration policies has served to politicize immigration in profoundly new ways.

The case of Long Island, New York, provides an interesting illustration. In 2003 the County of Suffolk passed an ordinance that banned day-labor hiring sites and contractors employing undocumented workers. It would later place a ban on renting housing to undocumented immigrants. A county executive explained his support of these measures: "The aim is to protect honest contractors against unfair competition from companies that exploit illegal workers by underpaying them. This bill will level the playing field. If you want a contract with Suffolk County, you have to play by the rules."[7] He went on to say that he hoped that the Suffolk model would be employed and adapted by local officials across the country. "My goal is to help stem the flow of illegal immigrants. The concept will spread like wildfire and have a major impact from California to Maine." The enactment of this measure turned contractors into enforcers of immigration law, which in turn sparked a political conflict with local officials. A year after this measure's enactment, a member of a local contractors' association expressed his frustration with the law: "The average contractor is not competent to determine if a green card is real or not. This makes our job much harder."[8] The head of the Long Island Farm Bureau echoed this frustration, "They [contractors] should not be obliged to be more vigilant about screening out illegal immigrants than any other employers, but they are. *The situation is getting to be a real problem in terms of policing who is legal and who is not.*"[9] As contractors and then also landlords were compelled to comply with their new roles as enforcers of immigration law, longtime Latino residents faced increased scrutiny, surveillance, and discrimination by employers. A frustrated Latino resident of Long Island noted, "We are not all illegal. I'm not illegal. My daughters are not illegal. You can't say that about all of us!"[10] Finally, after repeated reports of racial profiling and harassment of Latinos, local immigrant associations and the Catholic Church filed a formal complaint with the Justice Department for violations of the Civil Rights Act.

Local immigration measures in this instance triggered a *political chain reaction* that activated the involvement of broad segments of the local population as enforces or suspects. In requiring local civil servants and citizens, including contractors, landlords, managers of hardware stores, and so on, to enforce exclusionary laws, many locals did so with some resistance. However, in fulfilling their new responsibilities, these citizens used their "common sense" knowledge (ethnic markers and stereotypes) to identify potential "illegals." All immigrant residents with or without documents came under the watchful eyes of an array of newly deputized albeit somewhat ambivalent border enforcers: the police, civil servants, contractors, landlords, hardware store owners and managers, among others. As all immigrants, but especially Latinos, came under the increasingly watchful eyes of their neighbors, they experienced different forms of discrimination in their daily lives. They expressed their grievances among themselves and to the associations and churches they belonged to. Their grievances gave rise to complaints, mobilizations, and lawsuits, which drew in the federal government. The case of Long Island illustrates how the localization of immigration policy contributed to localizing political debate about rights, immigration, and illegalities. Rather than sharpening the line separating legal from illegal residents, localizing enforcement has made the issue of immigration very public and political, triggering heated battles over where and how to draw the lines between different members of these communities.[11]

Localizing immigration policy and the resulting political flux have made localities and states into important sites of mobilization for immigrant rights advocates and foes alike. Bringing these issues to the local level has also lowered the cost of entering these battles, making it possible for activists with lower levels of economic, political, and cultural capital to enter the political game. When battles centered on the federal government, only those organizations with sufficient resources could become major players in the field of immigration politics. Localization has lowered the threshold for entry, allowing hundreds if not thousands of smaller groups and organizations an opportunity to shape immigration policy. The great confusion and opportunities induced by the localization of immigration policies has therefore provided activists on both sides of the debate a unique opportunity to bypass the federal government and impose their own immigration policies, from the bottom up.

Though much of the focus of large immigrant rights associations (for example, RIFA) in the late 2000s centered on Congress, the major tectonic shifts in the field of immigration politics favored localities and states. Meanwhile, RIFA struggled to keep the national immigrant rights movement focused on congressional battles at the federal level. Their struggles were reminiscent of the little Dutch boy who used his finger to plug the hole of the overflowing and irreparable dyke.

Back to the Trenches

After the defeat of the DREAM Act in December 2010, most DREAMers turned their focus away from passing a measure in Congress. The aim now was to push for various measures that would increase opportunities for DREAMers and reduce the constant threat of deportation. DREAMers participated in many campaigns that targeted state legislatures, courts, and executive branch of the federal government. They hoped to cobble together a package of rights and privileges (in-state tuition, deferred action, and so on) that would amount to de facto legality and bring them closer to full permanent status. The DREAMers now moved into the trenches, fighting continuous battles to expand their legality and the legality of others with one small win at a time.

In California, DREAM activists in Dream Team Los Angeles and the California Dream Network took up leading roles in seeking out the passage of a California DREAM Act during summer 2011. The DREAM Act was composed of two smaller bills, A.B. 130 and A.B. 131. The bill A.B. 540 that had passed in 2001 allowed undocumented youths in California to pay in-state fees for higher education. The law did not, however, address the ban on financial aid to undocumented students that blocked access to private and public grants. Undocumented youths were permitted to attend academic institutions but were not provided the financial means to do so. This became particularly problematic during the 2000s when fees for public higher education institutions tripled. A.B. 130 made undocumented youths eligible for private grants, and A.B. 131 made them eligible for financial aid programs administered by California. A.B. 131 would make it possible for undocumented students to apply for the state's Cal Grant program, the most important source of financial aid provided by the state. The measure's principal advocate was Assemblyman Gil Cedillo, a former labor leader from Los Angeles and supporter of this and other immigrant-specific measures.[12] Assemblyman Cedillo worked closely with CHIRLA, the California Dream Network, and Dream Team Los Angeles to mobilize support for A.B. 130 and A.B. 131. The different DREAMer groups organized public actions, media events, and sent delegations to the state Capitol to lobby for the bill. On the eve of a crucial vote, the California Dream Network and Dream Team Los Angeles ran phone banks to lobby critical state legislators. Labor unions associated with the UCLA Labor Center also contributed to the push by lobbying the Senate, Assembly, and governor to support the bills. While this was a statewide effort, the activist networks powering the campaign were firmly rooted in Los Angeles, with veteran youth, labor, and immigrant rights activists in the region assuming primary responsibility for driving the bills forward.

In addition to pushing for state-level legislation, United We Dream and its Los Angeles affiliates supported campaigns to push for "administrative relief" for "low-priority" immigrants, which would include DREAM-eligible youth. DREAMers effectively shifted their target to the executive branch of the federal government, demanding the president use his authority to provide relief for DREAM-eligible youths and other low-priority undocumented immigrants. Administrative relief would provide temporary legal status, a work permit, and limited access to rights and privileges. While this status would not place them on a path to citizenship and could be reversed at any time, it would provide temporary relief from the threat of deportation and thus provide a semblance of normal life. The Obama administration had already issued an Executive Memo on June 17, 2011, to Homeland Security stating that field officers should use their discretion for "low-priority immigrants," which included DREAM-eligible youths. But the memo was ambiguous, provided few criteria to prioritize cases, and was not enforceable. DREAMers launched a campaign to pressure the administration to take a stronger stance on the issue.

In fall 2011, DREAM activists across the country launched a wave of coordinated civil disobedience actions aimed at the offices of Homeland Security and Immigration and Customs Enforcement. The campaign aimed to pressure President Obama by drawing the attention of Latino voters to his record on deportations and his poor treatment of DREAM-eligible youths. They wanted Obama to know that "'as a whole, the [Latino] community was behind us.'"[13] The DREAMers involved in the campaign demonstrated great skill and knowledge in preparing for the protest action. They invested extensive amounts of time scouting government offices for the occupation, selecting undocumented youths best prepared to undertake the occupation, choreographing the action, and creating an effective messaging machine. All DREAMers and allies participating in the action were also trained to use the following talking points: "We are asking Obama to stop the deportations of all DREAMers and to give administrative relief to all DREAM-eligible youth, giving them a work permit, and protected status against deportation. If Obama does not want to lose the Latino vote, he should give an Executive Order and grant all DREAM eligible youth administrative relief."[14] The field notes describe one of the training sessions: "The participants all read the talking points out loud, one by one. Maria asks the group if we understand what it means. John explains parts of it and Maria explains even more. Whenever we are interviewed by the media and we cannot forward the journalist to the media spokesperson, we always need to bring the question/interviews back to our talking point."[15]

The DREAMers also worked with close allies (for example, Labor Center, NDLON, IDEPSCA) for additional support, such as access to facilities, electronic equipment, PA system, megaphones, and so on. Most importantly for an action of this kind, they developed a powerful legal support team. The DREAMers met with a team of seven attorneys at the UCLA Labor Center to discuss the legal implications of their actions, logistical issues, relations with the police and security guards, the legal options facing arrestees, and defense strategies once the arrests had been undertaken.[16] The October 12 occupation of the Immigration and Customs Enforcement office in downtown Los Angeles went according to plan and resulted in the arrest of four DREAMers. It was experienced as another moment of intense emotional energy that helped to reinforce the bonds between the DREAMers. The participant observer described the arrests:

> We are told that they will be taken away any moment now. Some people start to cry softly. We can see the police officers inside the building and we see glimpses of Alex and Nelly. The whole crowd starts to roar. Cheering, yelling, whistling, chanting. I see more and more people crying, especially the women. I feel emotionally touched myself. Nelly's mother is crying; the women I have been chanting with all day are crying. I feel tears well up. Then we see Alex, cuffed and escorted by the police, smiling. We all cheer as loud as we can. I am completely emotionally high. We cheer as loud as we can. Everyone is really crying now.[17]

The Obama administration didn't immediately respond to this and other similar actions. But when other antienforcement activists escalated actions, the administration granted noncriminal offenders "low-priority" status, stressed the specific situation of DREAM eligible youths, provided field officers with clear criteria to evaluate the cases of undocumented immigrants, and created training programs that would allow field officers to implement the new procedures and guidelines. In effect, the White House responded by introducing ways to enforce the Executive Memo of June 17, 2011.

In spring 2012, DREAMers launched another wave of actions aimed at occupying several of President Obama's campaign offices. These actions were designed to increase pressure on the White House before the November elections. DREAMers were sensitive to the president's reliance on the Latino vote to secure his reelection. These actions would again emphasize his poor record on immigration in the Spanish-speaking media. They used this as leverage to pressure the administration to grant deferred action status to DREAM-eligible immigrants. Soon after these occupations, President Obama signed a memo calling for deferred action for undocumented immigrants who had come to the country as children. This measure, Deferred Action for Childhood Arrivals (DACA), granted temporary status and work authorization to eligible immigrants. It nevertheless denied eligibility for many services and privileges including the Affordable Care Act. The measure also did not provide a path to citizenship and could be revoked at any time by the sitting president. Youths needed to meet the following eligibility criteria: less than thirty-one years old, arrival before sixteen years old, continuous residence in the United States since 2007, proof of education, no serious misdemeanors (or 'multiple misdemeanors) or felonies, and so on. An estimated 1.2 million undocumented immigrants could benefit from the measure. However, by October 2012 only 100,000 youths applied, below expectations. Many had not applied because if the Republican presidential candidate had won and revoked DACA, they feared that their personal information would be used against them. High costs (application and lawyer fees) and excessive documentation requirements impeded other applications. Early estimates also revealed a high rejection rate due to incomplete documentation and applications. In spite of these significant problems, DACA has been viewed as a strategic "stepping stone" that will help facilitate the passage of favorable immigration legislation in a friendlier Congress further down the road.

In addition to pushing for DREAM-specific measures outside Congress, DREAMers have also become leading voices in antienforcement campaigns. These campaigns criticized the Obama administration's record on deportation, called for the end of the Secure Communities program, and fought local and state-level restrictions on undocumented communities.[18] The localization of enforcement has meant that while national rights associations have become involved in these efforts (including RIFA-affiliated organizations), local and regional coalitions have arisen to fight against enforcement measures in their jurisdictions. Areas of the country with established concentrations of immigrant rights activists, for example, Los Angeles, Washington, DC, Chicago, and so on, have become particularly powerful hubs in this national network of local antienforcement coalitions.

The engagement of DREAMers in these local antienforcement coalitions has resulted in interesting networking dynamics. Los Angeles DREAMers became active in a new antienforcement coalition spearheaded by NDLON. Participation in the coalition has contributed to strengthening ties with other activists in the city.[19] This coalition was made up of different Los Angeles-based immigrant rights associations, community organizations, and labor organizations.[20] Dream Team Los Angeles participated actively because members believed in the coalition's goals. Just as important, Dream Team Los Angeles was firmly embedded in what James Coleman has called systems of rotating credit. Its abilities to draw "credits," such as resources, support, expertise, and political backing, for its own campaigns required ongoing contributions to the campaigns of others. Maintaining a reputation as a trustworthy ally (namely, a "good credit score" in Coleman's terms) required the organization to demonstrate its capabilities to reciprocate for past support.[21] If Dream Team Los Angeles failed to fulfill its obligations to a past supporter like NDLON (a creditor), it would lose its reputation as a trustworthy ally, making it difficult to gain support for its own present and future campaigns. A bad reputation would, in other words, lead to sanctions not only by past supporters but by all the other organizations in the activist milieu. This system of rotating credit has bound the fate of Dream Team Los Angeles to that of the broader collectivity. Dream Team Los Angeles is compelled to contribute to the actions of others, nurture a good reputation as a trustworthy ally, and work to strengthen bonds across the activist milieu. The continued abilities of Dream Team Los Angeles to draw on support from its environment have depended on its abilities to demonstrate support for NDLON and its anti-Secure Communities coalition.

DREAMers had also been criticized by some leaders of the immigrant rights movement for being selfish and short-sighted. They were seen as focusing solely on DREAM-specific campaigns that benefited a small fraction of the undocumented population. By participating in the antienforcement coalition, DREAMers demonstrated their solidarity to the general immigrant rights movement. During a Dream Team Los Angeles meeting discussing participation in antienforcement campaigns, a leading member of the group reminded the others:

> *We know that we are part of communities and families and we will have to ask for their solidarity.* We also know that we have been supporting our communities with anti-S-Com [Secure Communities] work and that we have put a lot of our time and energy into that. In response to these critiques, we should mention our involvement in these actions and *should respond to the selfishness argument by claiming that we're doing anything that pushes the pro-immigrant agenda.*[22]

This DREAMer expressed keen awareness of the strategic importance of one's reputation for gaining the support of close and distant allies. The reputation of the DREAMers had been sullied by assertions that they were selfish. Participation in antienforcement campaigns not only reinforced the reputation of DREAMers as a stand-up and trustworthy ally among friends (NDLON, MALDEF, Labor Center, IDEPSCA, and so on), but also helped reinforce their good reputation in the general immigrant rights movement.

In addition to strengthening ties with allies, participation in the antienforcement coalition provided an opportunity for DREAMers to extend their networks and come into contact with new organizations and ideas in the Los Angeles activist environment. The antienforcement coalition placed it into contact with organizations beyond its close allies in the local immigrant rights community. Organizations not directly linked to immigration like the homeless associations Los Angeles Community Action Network (LACAN) and the community organization Labor/Community Strategy Center were also involved in NDLON's antienforcement coalition. These organizations were not immigrant rights organizations, but many of their constituents were undocumented immigrants and targets of enforcement measures. As their constituents expressed greater fear about being transferred to Immigration and Customs Enforcement by local law enforcement agencies, representatives of these organizations felt compelled to join the antienforcement coalition. The localization of enforcement policies made immigration an important political issue that needed to be dealt with more directly by these organizations. NDLON's coalition provided them with an opportunity to do so.

Participants in this coalition needed to develop new discursive frames to provide a common ground for their participation. Correct framing is important for building internal solidarity and attracting broad public support.[23] At a practical level, an effective frame allows organizers to justify their contributions in new areas (immigration enforcement) to their funders and members. Organizations (for example, homeless or youth advocacy) are required to demonstrate how such activities are relevant to their traditional goals and values. In the case of the antienforcement coalition, the frame that assumed increased prominence was "criminalization." New laws and policies have transformed marginalized communities, such as the homeless, the poor, immigrants, and inner-city youth, into criminal populations. This frame captured commonalities that transcended the differences of organizations and the communities they traditionally worked with. Developing the frame was a matter of negotiations between the actors involved. One DREAMer who partook in these discussions remembered:

> It has been a broad coalition. We had a conversation about what the focus of this coalition should be and we agreed that it should be broad, and should focus on criminalization and not just immigration. . . . *That would allow all of those organizations* [nonimmigrant rights organizations] *to contribute to this work and put that in their grants.* It would also open up the coalition and really bring in the social justice work that's going on, in terms of youth, homeless, and those other perspectives. NDLON supported this but didn't want to water down the 287(g) and Secure Communities point of the coalition either. IDEPSCA and the normal orgs were at the same table: *we can target 287(g) and Secure Communities but do it through a critique of criminalization. It's part of getting to that bigger picture.*[24]

The process of stitching together a common mobilizing frame was a negotiated one, with the different partners at the table working together to develop common principles, ideas, and language that adequately addressed the different needs and goals of their organizations.

DREAM activists and their close allies used intersectionality discourse to make the criminalization frame meaningful. During an anti-enforcement demonstration in September 2011, a member of Dream Team Los Angeles ("citizen ally") described criminalization of multiple communities in an emotionally compelling way:

> On Tuesday I learn of another youth in my neighborhood who was badly injured and received fifteen stitches after running away from police out of fear.
> On Wednesday I learn that a fellow DREAMer undocumented youth leader is facing deportation and wearing an electric shackle on his leg.
> Today is Thursday, and everyday is like this. . . .
> Every day I drive in constant fear to encounter police. I'm a US citizen,

I don't have deportation to fear, yet the sight of police, sheriffs, ICE, makes my heart pound, my stomach hurt. Because my heart, mind, and body know and witness the violence these authorities impose on a daily basis. I fear my womanhood, my youth, my queerness, my color, my arab, my Mexican, my immigrant background, I fear for my identity, my family, and the many communities we each represent. This is not Normal! Do not normalize violence in our lives, in our families, and our communities.[25]

Intersectionality has encouraged DREAMers to explore the ways in which different communities have experienced similar forms of injustice in spite of their differences in these multiactor coalitions. Their openness to thinking in intersectional terms facilitates their abilities to find similarities and solidarities across different struggles.

The process of creating the antienforcement coalition helped extend the immigrant rights movement beyond its traditional base. It connected a diverse group of organizations working with immigrants but that were not necessarily immigrant rights organizations. While nonimmigrant rights organizations may have sympathized with past struggles to win immigration reforms like Comprehensive Immigration Reform or even the DREAM Act, they were reluctant to contribute their own resources to these campaigns because their goals were narrow—immigration reform—and targeted a distant political world—Congress. By contrast, enforcement affected their constituents in a very direct and tangible way and the targets of the campaign were both local (city and county) as well as distant (state and federal government). Moreover, the process of negotiating a common frame with diverse activists has encouraged local activist organizations to recognize their own complementary positions in a broader struggle for social justice. Immigrant rights activists (like DREAMers) have come to recognize that there are multiple movements for social justice and that their efforts constitute one part of the general struggle to create a more just world. As one of the DREAMers put it, "It's part of getting to that bigger picture."

Extending Power up from the Grassroots

The antienforcement coalition headed up by NDLON launched a two-prong battle against Secure Communities: it has called on the

Obama administration to cancel the program, but it has also called on local and state officials to resist complying with the program. The coalition has developed a strong network of supportive allies primarily based in the Los Angeles area including the extremely powerful County Federation of Labor, Los Angeles Mayor Antonio Villaraigosa, the city council, the Catholic Archdiocese of Los Angeles, and influential members of the state Assembly and Senate. This strong base of locally grounded political support has allowed the coalition to wage battles directed at municipalities, counties, the state, and the federal government. Within this new and more geographically complex landscape, states have been viewed as strategic targets for making immigrant rights claims. In the face of congressional intransigence, states with relatively friendly legislators and governors provide openings where rights can be extended, enforcement reduced, and broader demands made on the federal government. States are also viewed as laboratories for exploring policy possibilities for immigrants. One longtime veteran of the immigrant rights movement remarked on the strategic importance of states:

> But I think right now, there's a sense that we're not going to get anything [from the Congress] in the next two years. . . . And because nothing is happening in Congress, a lot of the fights are going to be at the state level. We continue to push Obama to stop deportations . . . stop deporting the DREAMers, and suspend the Secure Communities. *But our leverage is increased when we get states to push the Feds.* Now, some people don't agree with this strategy . . . and say, "No, you've got to focus only on the Feds and Congress in particular." But we've done that for ten years and the Feds are not moving but the States are—against us. So we have no choice, we have to push back in unfriendly states and take wins in those states where we can get them.[26]

This reflects what seems to be the prevailing strategy of the movement: targeting local, state, and federal institutions over a range of issues and using wins in certain arenas to push for concessions in others.

Others have advocated pushing this logic further and using the advantages acquired in friendly states to create a de facto legal status for undocumented immigrants. For advocates of this approach, strategic advances of anti-immigration advances at the state level serve as the model for how to move forward. Well-developed rights movements in friendly states like California can pressure the legislature to pass a series of measures to advance access to services and privileges (for example, DREAM Act, driver's license, suspension of towing cars of unlicensed drivers, and so on) and resist federal enforcement measures (for example, noncompliance with Secure Communities, 287[g], E-Verify, and so on). One prominent immigrant rights activist notes:

> The right is doing this. They are putting together bundles of different ideas together and then passing them as a state law. . . . That really is like a collection of this and that, and it all adds up into one bundle. Why can't we do that? Rather than pass these things altogether in a single law, we do it in bits and pieces which will eventually get us there. In the State of California, there's no reason why you shouldn't be able to do that. At the end, this is our only option. We really believe that there's not going to be immigration reform. I hope I'm wrong, but we just feel the current political climate won't allow that.[27]

Just as certain states have created inhospitable environments favoring "self-deportation," this strategy would do the opposite: it would create states that would allow undocumented immigrants to live relatively stable and secure lives short of full legal status. One common mobilizing slogan has been to make California the "anti-Arizona."

Some activists have raised concern about this strategy because it would privilege states with in-built political advantages and ignore those states facing greater barriers. On the evening of the DREAM Act's defeat in December 2011, a DREAMer from North Carolina questioned MALDEF's state-oriented strategy of making California into the anti-Arizona. This DREAMer believed that undocumented immigrants didn't have the political space or power to mobilize in southern states: "It's easy for Californians to say I'm undocumented and to mobilize. Here [California] it's much easier than in a place like North Carolina. People in California, in a place where people have [activist] skills, need to go out and help others organize themselves. MALDEF needs to develop a national organizing strategy, to take what you have here and change things in other states."[28] Leading immigrant rights associations have indeed been following the suggestion of this DREAMer. They have sought to scale out by building horizontal networks among activists in strong and weaker states.

Developments in Arizona provide an illustration of how these horizontal and interstate networks have developed and worked. In the mid-2000s, the sheriff of Maricopa County, Arizona, obtained a 287(g) contract with the federal government, which granted him the authority to detain undocumented immigrants and transfer them to Immigration and Customs Enforcement for deportation. His aggressive use of this new authority prompted immediate resistance by local associations, activists, churches, and citizens. While the initial coalition was able to challenge the sheriff, it had difficulty sustaining this challenge and elevating it beyond a local issue. NDLON based in Los Angeles had ties with organizers in Arizona through their previous work on day-labor advocacy. NDLON worked with these local organizations to create a more stable coalition, draw in outside resources from national funders, and develop a messaging campaign. They also helped create Alto Arizona, which would become the principal coalition spearheading the anti-enforcement and anti-S.B. 1070 campaigns in the state.

NDLON's strategy in Arizona was twofold: first, it sought to build up local mobilization capacities amongst core activists in the state. This entailed professionalizing organizers who had largely been engaged in local actions and had little experience in mounting large campaigns with an extralocal reach. They worked to provide community-based immigrant organizers with activist skills and encourage these organizations to train their own members and constituents to become activists as well. Coming from Paolo Freire's popular education tradition, organizers from NDLON believed in the importance of using organizing to enhance political capacities and consciousness of marginalized people. The aim was to build grassroots organizational capacity but also to provide poor undocumented people with the tools to speak for and organize themselves. Second, while there was a heavy emphasis on building local capacity, NDLON had experience in using local enforcement issues (that is, bans on day-labor sites) for broad political and legal advantages. Their aim was not only to criticize the application of 287(g) and Secure Communities in Maricopa, County, but also to use this local case to demonstrate to the national public, federal government, and national courts how these enforcement programs resulted in egregious and alarming human rights violations. By transforming Maricopa County's sheriff into the "poster boy" of federal enforcement programs, they made this local affair into a national civil rights scandal and an indictment of enforcement programs. This was a conscious adaptation of the Southern Christian Leadership Conference's strategy in 1963 to draw national attention to the injustices of the South by highlighting the abuses of Alabama's Eugene "Bull" Connors.[29]

Their campaign against 287(g) and the sheriff of Maricopa County provided Arizona organizers with the organizational infrastructure and capacity to escalate their struggle when S.B. 1070 was passed in 2010. Diverse local associations and organizers had already established a strong coalition and built up neighborhood-level structures to alert immigrants of police raids ("Barrio Defense Committees"). This local infrastructure was effective because it provided associations with a vehicle to pool their different resources for different antienforcement campaigns and it provided organizers access to the everyday worlds of thousands of immigrants. NDLON also brokered relations between local activists and the outside world. Their connections to national funders were used to funnel important resources into the local movement infrastructure. Their connections to media and entertainment personalities allowed them to bring the case of Arizona to national attention. Lastly, their legal capacities allowed them—in partnership with other national associations—to push the Obama administration to legally challenge S.B. 1070.

The campaign that ensued after the passage of S.B. 1070 was impressive because of its breadth and complexity. In addition to mass demonstrations and media messaging, the campaign employed boycotts in a way that helped to extend the issue of immigration and enforcement beyond the traditional immigrant rights community. In calling for a boycott of the state, they called upon influential allies (not necessarily activists) to cease activities in Arizona. Thousands of politicians, businesses, entertainers, academics, and many others became directly involved in the antienforcement campaign through their direct participation of the boycott. The boycott impacted Arizona's economy and reputation, which had particularly negative effects on the state's powerful tourist industry. While the industry had already expressed concerns about employers' sanctions, the boycott aggravated existing grievances, drawing it directly into the campaign against S.B. 1070 and other enforcement measures.

One of the particular advantages of this antienforcement campaign was that it provided rights activists with an opportunity to politicize immigration and draw a broad array of individuals and organizations directly into the movement. While they have not convinced the Arizona legislature and governor to repeal the law, the campaign has pressured the Justice Department to challenge S.B. 1070 and indict the sheriff of Maricopa County for civil rights violations. It has also contributed to ousting Arizona Senate Majority Leader Russell Pearce, who was the principal sponsor and advocate of S.B. 1070, in a special runoff election. In addition to raising the political costs of these measures, the Arizona campaign has reinforced a statewide immigrant rights infrastructure that can be deployed for other campaigns.

Arizona's S.B. 1070 was used as a template for state laws in Alabama, Georgia, South Carolina, and Indiana. NDLON has responded in a similar way to the Arizona case but with greater difficulty. In Georgia, it has sought to locate community allies in the state, to reinforce the local social movement infrastructure and thus enhance its mobilization capacities, and to connect these local movements to the outside world. Much of the focus has been on local capacity building and training immigrants to defend themselves against local and national law enforcement agencies. In a discussion of its work in Georgia, the director of NDLON relates a story about training immigrants to carry out the fight for themselves:

> I was at a neighborhood workshop we held in Georgia and a guy pulled out a flier, and it's one of our fliers saying, "These are your rights. . . . " And then the guy says, "You know what? This is what happened. I found this flier and I went and made 500 copies and I distributed them in my neighborhood. I think I can do things like that but I really don't know how. That's why I'm here [at the NDLON workshop]." So our workshop was designed for people exactly like him. The idea was to give him and others the tools to do more things like that in their neighborhoods. And at the end of our workshop, the same guy stood up—and he was a very humble guy who probably never finished elementary school— and he walked in the middle of the circle with his head down, and he says, "When I came in, I came in like *this* [head down], literally, and now I'm going back like this [head upright.]" To me, that guy

is not only going to make 500 copies, he's going to make 1,000 copies from his own money. Three days later we get a call and he says, "I recruited thirty people for my committee already." You know, wow, that is really cool! The bottom line is this: I am not going to be there, our lawyers or any national organizations either, when ICE knocks on their doors. People must protect themselves on their own and need to be trained to do so in their communities. To me that is when things start to change, because that guy who learned things in our workshop is going to go and tell others in his neighborhood what they can do.[30]

While NDLON has sought to build up grassroots capacities of communities through trainings and workshops, their abilities to do so in new immigrant destinations like Georgia has been difficult because there have been few immigrant-based community organizations or immigrant rights associations in place. Such organizations existed in Arizona and they provided the building blocks for a local social movement infrastructure. In new immigrant destinations, similar organizations are weak or nonexistent, presenting NDLON and its allies a major strategic challenge. This, however, has prompted efforts to turn to organizations associated with the historical civil rights movement, especially African American churches. The effort to build bridges beyond the traditional immigrant rights movement has resulted in attempts to adopt new discursive frames that enable African Americans to recognize similarities between their struggles and those of undocumented immigrants.

The immigrant rights movement is therefore "scaling out," which has meant that immigrant rights activists have moved "horizontally" from strong territories (Los Angeles, California) to weaker territories (Arizona, Georgia, and so on), building up infrastructure and mobilization capacities in localities and states across the country. Their effort has been to transfer resources, skills, and knowledge to new localities and build activist clusters with the capacities to sustain aggressive immigrant rights campaigns. Potentially, this presents opportunities to expand the geographic reach of the immigrant rights movement and provide an important vehicle to incorporate a wide range of different actors, including immigrants, minorities, progressives, and businesses, in campaigns to defend and eventually extend the rights of immigrants.

This particular phase of the immigrant rights movement has a geography and strategy that contrasts sharply with the top-down and centralized strategy of the past. Just as important, the general tendency toward localizing immigration policy has drawn the attention of most activists to state and local-level battles, without forgetting about the continued importance of the federal government and courts. Moreover, activists in this latest phase have focused more on fostering and harnessing local mobilization capacities as a way to pass measures at local, state, and national scales. While the strategic and geographic characteristics of the movement have become more complex than before, the movement has by no means become chaotic. Most advocates of the new strategy have embraced a common vision that rests on building mobilization capacities in communities and cities (that is, local capacity building), mobilizing through whatever windows of opportunity are available to them at whatever scale of government (that is, incrementalism), and employing concrete wins in these political arenas as leverage for making broader demands further down the road (stepping stones).

In March 2006, immigrants, activists, and allies in Los Angeles mobilized more than *one million* people for a demonstration *against* the Sensenbrenner Bill and *for* the Comprehensive Immigration Reform Act.[31] Massive demonstrations across the country took place on the same day. Such actions reflected the potential of the immigrant movement rights movement to concentrate its power and exert its influence in the national political arena. This was the beginning of national efforts to centralize the immigrant rights movement. Five years later in Los Angeles, the annual immigrant rights demonstration on May 1 was smaller than the massive 2006 event and also fragmented. There were four to five different demonstrations held in the downtown area on the same day. While the size of demonstrations provides only surface indications of a social movement, a quick comparison of these two would lead most observers to question the health of the immigrant rights movement in 2012.

The strategy of centralization was a response to the combination of unique threats and opportunities. Many believed the 2006 and 2007 reform bills failed because of the movement's internal fragmentation.

Funders and national immigrant rights associations believed that the only remedy would be the further centralization of the movement and the creation of RIFA. This strategy was designed with the assumption that there were political opportunities in Congress. The architects of the strategy had all the reason in the world to believe that political opportunities were available in 2008–10. Candidate Barack Obama promised to make immigration reform a top priority in his first year in office, progressive Democrats controlled the House, and Democrats possessed a supermajority in the Senate.

The strategy of top-down centralization was an appropriate and sophisticated effort to maximize advantages within the particular context. However, the strategy had two major drawbacks: first the act of maintaining discipline over a diverse movement aggravated powerful conflicts within it. While DREAMers and antienforcement activists were drawn into other battles, RIFA placed great pressure on them to focus all their attention on the passage of comprehensive reform. Rather than corraling these dissenters, RIFA's actions only accelerated their separation. Second, when political opportunities did not materialize, the centralization strategy proved to be inflexible. RIFA could not pivot to different goals (the DREAM Act, for example) or different political arenas (local and state) once it became clear that the White House would not support the Comprehensive Immigration Reform bill in 2010. Instead of shifting to different fronts, RIFA doubled-down and committed itself to a costly strategy that was bearing no fruits. This strengthened the hand of critics and dissidents, which precipitated the decline of RIFA and its strategy of movement centralization.

The bottom-up and decentralized strategy that followed has proven to be effective in winning small but important battles, encouraging the involvement of new actors beyond its traditional base of supporters, building up local mobilization capacities, and leveraging local and state-level wins to pressure the White House to pursue changes in national immigration policy. The new strategy is also extremely flexible and can shift from one opportunity to the next and use each struggle as building blocks for larger battles. When windows of opportunity close in one place, activists do not feel compelled to double-down and try to seek out a win. They can close operations and move on to more opportune targets.[32] This strategy also encourages greater involvement of grassroots immigrants as leaders in local struggles. Activists in this new model function more as autonomous guerrilla armies than as the disciplined foot soldiers of the RIFA generals. This provides more channels for new recruits to become grassroots leaders, helping to empower them and become important voices in the movement. Lastly, the strategy seeks to extend the struggle beyond the traditional base of immigrant rights supporters. By localizing struggles, gaining rights for immigrants becomes a direct interest of local businesses, community organizations, activists, political officials, public servants, and so on. Localization transforms all those people who are in touch with immigrants to take a direct stake in the politics of immigration in their communities and country.

In spite of the positive qualities of this new strategy, there are important risks as well. The movement loses its capacities to develop a strong, coherent, and disciplined message that resonates with the American public. As the movement becomes dominated by smaller campaigns and coalitions and gives greater opportunities for more marginal groups to express themselves, it has greater difficulty in maintaining messaging consistency and discipline. Many voices are now emerging: some are designed to cohere with American values, while others ignore them, and still others consciously reject them. At best, this can water down the central message of the movement. At worst, timorous natives may move to reject all immigrant claims as "noise" from a foreign and threatening mob. The strategy and organizational structure of the movement also encourages factionalism as different groups and actors in the movement develop their own particular frames, goals, and ideologies. This factionalism was reflected in the May 1 demonstration. If opportunities were to open up in Congress for large comprehensive reform, factionalism could undermine the abilities of the different forces to pull their resources in a more concerted action. A divided movement provides it with flexibility to respond to many small openings, but it may also hinder its abilities to unify when real opportunities open up in the center of political power, Congress.

Conclusion

Dreaming Through the Nation-state

"We Are All Human!" This prominent slogan captures the essence of the immigrant rights movement. At its core, this is a struggle over who should be considered fully "human" and how those deemed "less-than-humans" should be treated by the government and members of the national community.

Anti-immigrant forces justify stripping undocumented immigrants of basic rights on the grounds that they are less than truly human beings. They produce discourses and arguments that deprive immigrants of the "humanity" needed to be considered eligible for basic rights in the country. For example, Hector Tobar of the *Los Angeles Times* highlighted some of the comments made by readers of his op-ed columns on immigration. One reader argues, "'Illegals are like fleas on a dog. . . . By definition they are a class of criminals and you [Tobar] romanticize them. Perhaps we can starve them out with no benefits.'"[1] This rhetoric reveals a logic common of anti-immigrant reasoning: undocumented immigrants are a criminal and parasitic population, and because of this, they *need* to be denied basic rights and starved out of the country. Failure to do this because of "romantic" feelings places the national host at risk of being devoured by this outside force. Reducing immigrants to this less-than-human threat makes them ineligible for rights and subject to *inhuman* and despotic forms of repression ("starve them out"). If weak and romantic immigrant sympathizers reject these arguments, the default response of anti-immigrant advocates is some variation on "What part of illegal don't you understand?" This retort denies recognition of basic human rights to undocumented immigrants because of their status. They cannot speak, make claims, or argue for rights in public because of their "illegality."

These sentiments have helped shape government polices over the last twenty years. The federal government has introduced countless measures to militarize borders, monitor "illegals," restrict access to basic rights and fundamental services, roll out infrastructure to deport hundreds and thousands of people on a yearly basis, and recruit frontline service providers to assist in enforcement measures. National and local restrictions have been designed for the purposes of creating an uninhabitable environment that would "starve" undocumented immigrants out of the country (that is, "attrition through enforcement"). As rights are systematically stripped away, undocumented immigrants in certain parts of the country are left with no protections from the arbitrary powers of the state and the tyrannical will of the majority. In states like Arizona, Georgia, and Alabama, they are reduced to "bare life," with most legal protections suspended for this population.[2] These outsiders are forced to rely on the "civility and ethical sense" of individuals to provide protection from a majoritarian and a revanchist state.

When undocumented immigrants face this level of hostility, they do not necessarily accept their fate as less-than-human subjects. We have learned, through the case of the DREAMers, how they struggle against remarkable odds to reconquer basic rights that have been stripped away over the years. As dehumanizing discourses ("flees on a dog," "illegal") have provided a pretext to justify the rollback of rights, immigrant rights activists have needed to demonstrate their humanity as the basis to assert their claims for fundamental rights. If stripping rights from immigrants is made possible by denying their humanity, acquiring rights becomes possible by demonstrating that the immigrant is in fact human. Achieving legitimacy for rights claims has therefore depended on gaining recognition for immigrants as truly *human* beings.

Demonstrating common humanness has not driven these stigmatized immigrants to embrace universal discourses, principles, and attributes. Their chances of gaining recognition as humans improved when they demonstrated identification with *national* values and norms. Revealing one's belonging and identification with the nation is one of the only ways in which stigmatized immigrants can reveal their humanity. For the DREAMers, this was demonstrated by the themes repeatedly stressed in their public claims. They have been framed as "de facto" Americans who cannot be held legally responsible for the act of crossing the border. They are just as American as any other, and *because of this*, they are rights-deserving human beings. The battle of the immigrant rights movement is about gaining recognition for undocumented immigrants as human beings, but the way in which people gain this recognition is by demonstrating belonging, identification, and contributions to the national community. The human being as a figure imbued with inalienable rights therefore continues to be mediated by the nation-state.[3]

The National Limits of Human Rights

There has been a proliferation of theoretical writings on human rights, social justice, and equality.[4] Intellectuals have long sought to theorize unambiguous and transcendent definitions of equality and justice, devise criteria to distribute rights equally, and design institutions to ensure equality and justice over extended periods of time. These theories are designed to function as beacons of light that guide activists through the fog of everyday struggles. Without the guiding light of high theory, activists would be derailed by particularistic concerns, short-term interests, and co-optation by the powers that be. Theoretical schemas of "equality" and "justice" are therefore supposed to infuse particular battles with broader meanings and direction.

These kinds of theoretical writings provide nice reminders of what *could* be done, but they serve as poor guides for producing just worlds because they ignore the limits imposed by the persistence of national political communities. This study reveals that rights are constituted, managed, and distributed by the nation-state.[5] By definition, such political communities are closed, employ insider-outsider categories to distribute rights, and exclude outsiders as a necessary means to ensure their reproduction.[6] The essence of this political community pivots on maintaining the lines separating members from interlopers.[7] The nation-state may proclaim equality for all, but equality of rights is reserved only for its core members. The exclusionary nature of the nation-state, therefore, makes it an entity that is by definition unequal and unjust. Theories of rights and equality are certainly thought provoking, but they serve little purpose as political guides when they fail to take into account the real politics of the nation-state.

Undocumented immigrants and their allies are certainly motivated by a strong sense of justice. Principles of equality and justice drive these outsiders to call for an extension of rights. However, rights advocates mobilize in a context in which equality, justice, and rights are shaped by a national political community. They certainly express their claims and arguments through a discourse of equality and justice, but these concepts are grounded in national values and norms. The "wrong" they are calling attention to is based on the national community's definition of justice, not universal principles. For outsiders to gain recognition from "established" members, they must articulate a message of injustice that coheres with the national community's particularistic vision of equality, fairness, and justice. They must celebrate a nation's particular notions of justice and fairness and then assert that the exclusion of a certain group is morally wrong because it violates core national principles. The situation of undocumented youths was a wrong because the youths played according to the "rules of the game" and they were still punished for decisions that were "no fault of their own." These are strongly American assertions of justice and fairness. Demonstrating that an injustice has been done results from acts, struggles, and statements that ultimately celebrate exclusionary national moralities. This helps to reinforce the normative bonds of the nation rather than unravel them.[8]

In addition to reinforcing national norms and moralities, the struggle for equal rights produces new inequalities and injustices that are typically not anticipated by rights activists or their supporters. The established political community is by definition closed, and access to it depends on whether an outsider can sufficiently demonstrate identification with its values and norms. This means that those people with the finest cultural and social attributes (good, productive, and "normal" people) are best placed to make an argument that a wrong has been done. *Outsiders are subsequently stratified from most to least deserving of "equal" rights on the basis of their social and cultural attributes.* Those considered most deserving face the greatest likelihood of gaining recognition as equal human beings while those who are considered least deserving face the greatest likelihood of being brutally repressed by the state and spurned by natives. No matter how brilliant their theories of equality or committed they are to a just world, equal rights advocates produce new hierarchies, inequalities, and closures because of the limits on the distribution of rights imposed by the nation-state.

In the case of the immigrant rights movement in the United States, the DREAMers assumed the most prominent position in the undocumented immigrant community because of their abilities to publicly demonstrate their fit in the national community. Their ability to demonstrate such a fit has convinced important segments of the public that an injustice has been committed against this particular group. Moreover, the ways in which they developed an argument that a wrong had been done speaks to a specifically American notion of justice. While this has not yet resulted in the passage of the DREAM Act, it has led the White House to introduce a new and exceptional measure to grant this group administrative relief from deportations. At the other end of the spectrum, undocumented immigrants who have criminal records are placed at the bottom of the immigrant hierarchy, with few activists willing to argue that they deserve full recognition as rights-deserving human beings. Progressive antienforcement organizations have argued against Secure Communities not because it violates the rights of all undocumented immigrants (criminals and innocents), but because it targets innocent immigrants along with "truly dangerous" criminals. They argue that Secure Communities is a blunt instrument and cannot sufficiently distinguish between "true" criminals and "good" law-abiding immigrants. The default assumption is that criminals may be less deserving of full rights. This particular struggle for equal rights has resulted in the production of new inequalities and injustices, with undocumented immigrants ranked hierarchically according to their cultural and social attributes.

Feelings of justice are important drivers of these struggles. Activists are moved to struggle because they believe that the existing system produces inequalities and that such inequalities are fundamentally wrong.

However, the exclusionary nature of national communities sets up real limits on what can actually be done while simultaneously producing new inequalities that had not been anticipated before. When faced with these new inequalities, equal rights advocates may adjust their strategies to become more inclusive (for example, the most recent cycle of DREAMers' mobilization), but many may also recognize the creation of new inequalities (such as the banishment of criminal immigrants) as an unfortunate but necessary compromise. In spite of the extremely good intentions of activists and their commitment to equal and just societies, the reality of fighting for equality in exclusionary nation-states necessarily results in the reproduction of certain existing injustices and the creation of new, unanticipated ones.

This does not mean that the struggle for equality and justice *should* be abandoned. Rather, by pointing out the contradictions involved in the struggle for more just and equal societies, we reveal that social justice is a *dynamic process* rather than a *static end state*. Equal rights activists can never achieve the end state of social justice as posited by political theorists and philosophers. Every movement within the confines of the nation-state results in triggering new boundaries, exclusions, and inequalities. However, the promise of equality coupled with the proliferation of exclusions encourages outsiders to continually mobilize to have equality extended to them. As these outsiders engage in their struggles, they eventually produce their own hierarchies, closures, and exclusions. New lines of struggle are introduced and new rounds of activism ensue. In this way, each struggle produces new closures and categories of exclusion, with those on the outside prompted to develop new strategies and discourses to demand equality for their excluded group.

Abstract theories of rights, justice, and equality suggest that these activists should orient themselves toward an end game, a state where a transcendent ideal of social justice prevails and where institutions are designed to sustain these permanently just systems. However, when we analyze real struggles for equality, such prescriptions appear more "utopian" than "realistic."[9] A realistic analysis of these movements suggests the impossibility of defining an end state (either norms or institutions) because the struggle for equality constantly produces new inequalities and new lines of struggle. Rather than conceiving social justice as an end state, we can only conceive of it as an ever-extending, self-negating, and multiplying *process*.

The Sociology of Global Immigration in National Times

Ulrich Beck argued that the nation-state has strongly shaped the ways in which social scientists have come to see and know the world.[10] Sociologists have assumed that modern society is equivalent with the nation-state, and they rarely question the historically specific nature of this sociopolitical structure. "Methodological nationalism" assumes the nation-state as permanent, natural, and fixed container of social relations. This has led sociologists to develop models of society that never considered the constructed and permeable qualities of their unit of analysis. For immigration scholars, "methodological nationalism" has closed off sociologists to the possibilities of examining how transnational forces and ties have always made up our modern worlds. "What we discover is how transnational the modern world has always been, even in the high days when the nation-state bounded and bundled most social processes. Rather than a recent offspring of globalizations, transnationalism appears as a constant of modern life, hidden from a view that was captured by methodological nationalism."[11]

Though one must largely agree with this assessment, we must also recognize the importance of the nation-state and nationalism that results from globalization. While Beck develops a powerful critique of "methodological nationalism" with one hand, he reminds us that globalization also causes the resurgence of nationalism. "What has to be understood, above all, is the *ethnic globalization paradox*. At a time when the world is growing closer together and becoming more cosmopolitan, in which, therefore, the borders and barriers between nations and ethnic groups are being lifted, ethnic identities and divisions are becoming stronger once again."[12] Globalization has contributed in important ways to thickening transnational networks and cultures, but this same process has sharpened the national sensitivities of natives. Poor immigrants from the global south have been the principal targets of these newly reinvigorated national states, with countless measures having been created to rollback rights, punish immigrants, and extract them from national territories.

Immigration scholars must not only seek to uncover "hidden" transnational connections. They must also reexamine the centrality of nation-states in structuring the worlds of different immigrant groups. Globalization has not caused the nation-state to recede from the lives of immigrants but quite the contrary: it has reasserted the centrality of the nation-state as a principal structure for shaping the lives and futures of immigrants.[13] Students of immigration must pay more (not less) attention to how national borders are being physically maintained, how symbolic categories of inclusion-exclusion result in real policies and institutions, how categories and borders penetrate the life worlds of immigrants, how immigrants build identities and meanings within these nationalizing "cages," and how immigrants assert their rights and humanity in political arenas defined by national belonging.

Immigration researchers should pay more attention to the complex roles of the nation-state, but they should also develop new theoretical tools to do so. The literature addressing the nation-state continues to be inspired by the "national models" approach fashioned by Rogers Brubaker twenty years ago.[14] While this theoretical approach has helped identify the institutional and discursive forces that structure immigration politics, it overemphasizes differences between national models and underemphasizes the common processes across a range of cases.[15] Additionally, the theory of "national models" overemphasizes path-dependent mechanisms and underemphasizes the internal contradictions that drive dynamic changes within any given citizenship regime.[16] Lastly, while this theory provides tools to identify some political and cultural rules, it provides few insights into how these "structural rules" penetrate the life worlds of actual immigrants, how civil organizations (associations, rights organizations, churches, and so on) play an important role in this process, how these rules shape subjectivities and identities, and how immigrants' actions contribute and resist the reproduction of the nation-state. In other words, we are not provided the theoretical tools to understand how immigrants internalize the nation-state and how this process affects their own contributions to national reproduction. Thus, while sociologists of immigration should interrogate the nation-state more, they should also draw on theoretical tools that would allow them to examine how macrostructures connect and shape the microworlds of immigrants. This book has aimed to contribute one small step in this direction.

Immigrant Rights, a Global Struggle

The discussion in this book centered on the case of the United States. However, the struggle to gain recognition of undocumented immigrants as rights-deserving human beings has unfolded in many receiving countries of the global north.[17] In countries as diverse as France, the Netherlands, the United Kingdom, Belgium, Spain, and the United States, undocumented immigrants have launched high-profile campaigns for greater rights, less repression, and the legalization of their status. In spite of growing hostility in all these countries, undocumented immigrants have opted to make the public sphere the key arena to express claims to basic rights.

In looking across these different cases, we begin to note that the process of making rights claims in these different countries largely coheres to the process identified in the United States: niche openings provided small windows of opportunities for particularly well-placed immigrants; these immigrants produced strong representations and arguments of themselves as "exceptional" and deserving immigrants; they tapped into a range of support networks to craft representations and articulate them in the public sphere; they developed methods to discipline the message and the messengers; and the process of producing a legitimate argument ultimately introduced internal conflicts and disagreements that helped change how they conceived of rights and equality in the nation-state. While there are certainly important differences resulting from the institutional and cultural particularities of different countries, we can nevertheless identify a common and generic process. The regularities of immigrant rights movements indicate that a common set of rules structure the field of immigration politics. High levels of discursive and institutional hostility toward undocumented immigrants have contributed to niche openings for certain groups but not most. This common structure requires immigrants to respond to whatever openings available to them and to demonstrate that they indeed deserve recognition as rights-deserving human beings in these countries.

For example, an early and prominent immigrant rights movement occurred in France during the 1990s. Responding to a highly restrictive set of laws passed in 1993 (called Loi Pasqua), undocumented immigrants mobilized across the country to demand the reinstatement of basic rights and the extension of permanent residency status to this population.[18] While many undocumented immigrants mobilized, a niche opening was provided to the undocumented parents of French-born citizens. The situation of these immigrants tapped into the moral ambiguities of the French population, and lawyers argued that the government was obliged by international law to recognize the rights of families to live together. Facing this niche, immigrants and prominent rights associations quickly framed the immigrant "family" in a way that cohered with French values of the family. While the family may be a universal institution, anti-immigrant advocates in France had long highlighted the polluting and threatening qualities of the *immigrant* family (large, welfare dependent, freeloading, oppressive, communitarian, sexist, and so on).[19] In making a public argument, immigrant activists and their supporters produced a counterframe of the immigrant family that stressed attributes that the French nationals would recognize as a good and virtuous. They stressed a family unit that was hardworking, nuclear, and free of all the typical dysfunctions attributed to foreign families. This made it unjust to deport these good and hardworking parents from the country. This representation of immigrants and their cause was expressed by the immigrants themselves but also by the leading human rights organizations. As this mobilization unfolded and gained greater resonance in the public sphere, political officials legalized those immigrants with the most compelling cases (parents of French children). Those left out of this agreement (single and recently arrived men in particular) found weaker grounds to make their own rights, prompting them to embrace the more radical line of "regularizing" all undocumented immigrants, not just those with families.

In the Netherlands, a series of mobilizations have arisen since 2010 around the "special" cases of adolescents who had spent considerable time in the country under temporary protected status. As protected minors moved into adulthood, they lost their protected status and were slated for removal. Advocates have stressed their identification with the national culture and norms. Particular attention has been paid to the cultural dispositions of these youths, with advocates stressing regional accents ("speaks with a Limburg accent"), tastes for national foods and fashion, and "modern" behavior and dispositions. These representations are aimed at demonstrating identification and belonging to the national community. In addition to stressing national belonging, advocates have used images of dangerous foreign countries to assert that these "modern" youths would be at peril if returned to their homelands. In a very paradoxical way, advocates have sought to gain acceptance for this group of well-placed immigrants by drawing on Dutch fears of foreigners and foreign lands (dangerous cultures that violently reject Dutch "progressive" values). Although these mobilizations have largely been supported and led by progressive activists, they have raised sharp criticisms by intellectuals who have noted that such arguments simply reinforce the importance of national culture for obtaining basic rights.[20]

In spite of important variations in their citizenship regimes, immigrant rights mobilizations in the United States, France, and the Netherlands (among others) have unfolded in remarkably similar ways.[21] The process identified in the book appears generalizable.[22] There remain important differences between the cases in terms of the issues stressed, the construction of mobilizing frames and arguments, and the structure of alliances. Nevertheless, the existence of strong similarities between these cases indicates commonalities in the rules of the game governing immigration politics. Further comparative study would allow us to better understand these fields, the mobilizations within them, and the kinds of differences that arise from national particularities.

Undocumented immigrants face an enormous political barrier: their "illegality" makes it impossible for many nationals to see them as bearers of inalienable human rights. Many nationals do not believe that undocumented immigrants have the right to speak and make demands in the country. Highly repressive measures to detect and deport immigrants have also become banal, with many nationals believing that these are the normal instruments needed to protect the nation against a threatening immigration flood.[23] Unlike other minority groups demanding full citizenship rights, undocumented immigrants begin their struggle without recognition of having the right to have any rights in the country. The stigma of "illegality" has made it difficult for undocumented people to form into political groups as "undocumented immigrants" and to make demands for basic rights on the basis of this particular political identity. While undocumented immigrants mobilized under the more legitimate banner of the labor movement, mobilizations under the explicit banner of "undocumented immigrants" were difficult and rare in the United States.[24] In spite of the enormous barriers facing them, undocumented immigrants have recently mobilized for rights, and some have gained great legitimacy and become central actors in national political debates.

We could follow the lead of some scholars by arguing that transnational immigration and globalization have presented important challenges to nation-centered accounts of citizenship.[25] The national state is no longer the sole institution responsible for distributing rights. International courts and multilateral institutions have assumed great authority in this domain.[26] These institutions have played crucial roles in pressuring national states to recognize the rights of immigrants, not on the basis of their national membership but on the basis of being humans. Supported by international institutions and universal norms, undocumented immigrants and rights advocates have greater institutional and cultural opportunities to assert their "right to have rights" in what had been closed citizenship regimes. These favorable political and cultural conditions provide possibilities for undocumented immigrants to be considered political actors with legitimate rights claims. The success of one group of undocumented immigrants creates legal and cultural momentum in this direction, with each small win contributing to opening the pathway for postnational citizenship.

We could also address the issue by going to the opposite theoretical direction. Rather than globalization and transnational immigration creating new openings, we could say that these twin forces have sharpened the national sensibilities of natives.[27] Years ago Hannah Arendt argued that political philosophers talked about universal rights, but national states had become the principal vehicles through which rights were realized and distributed. Membership in national communities became a central criterion for determining access to "universal" and inalienable rights, with those dispossessed of a nation-state (that is, refugees, immigrants, "gypsies," ethnic minorities, and so on) considered ineligible for basic rights. Over the course of the twentieth century national citizens enjoyed an increasing range of rights that protected them from the arbitrary powers of the state and the tyrannical impulses of the majority, but "stateless" peoples didn't. Rapid economic change and globalization have only sharpened national sensitivities,[28] pushing stateless peoples further to the margins and making them subject to the despotic rule of the nation.[29] Rather than globalization opening spaces for undocumented immigrants, it has closed down these spaces, with citizens accepting the use of the state's exceptional powers to extract these populations from national territories.

Taken together, these positions suggest that immigrants face an uneven set of opportunities and barriers, but they provide little insight into how undocumented immigrants respond and embark on the long process of transforming themselves into a potent group with a legitimate political voice. The case of the DREAMers and the immigrant rights movements reveals that in spite of growing anti-immigrant hostility in the 1990s and 2000s, legal, political, and moral ambiguities produced "niche openings" for some undocumented youths because of their favorable attributes (for example, culturally integrated, having morally compelling stories). Early in their struggle, these well-positioned immigrants still faced intense hostility from adversaries. They had to separate themselves from the negative stigmas attributed to the general immigrant population (that is, foreign, illegal, welfare cheats, lazy). They showed that they were not criminals and "illegals" who threatened the moral fabric of the national community. They had the same aspirations and values as nationals and they stood to make an important contribution to the country. These representations of undocumented youth as exceptionally good immigrants enhanced support for their cause and opened the door to a national debate on granting them an exemption from normal exclusionary rules.

The struggle to demonstrate identification with national values improved chances for those groups of undocumented immigrants in possession of certain positive attributes (children, well-integrated, educated), but it also accentuated the stigmas attributed to other immigrant groups. Poor men and women, the homeless, the unemployed, the unassimilated, criminals, and so on all possess attributes said to pollute and threaten the national community. Not only are these immigrants unable to cleanse themselves of their stigmatized attributes, but the success of better positioned immigrants ("the good immigrant") only serves to magnify the attributes that make them irreducibly different. The well-placed undocumented youth had to respond to whatever niche openings became available to them, but the strategy of responding (national identification) reinforced the centrality of *national belonging* as a criterion for gaining basic human rights.

This has raised a central paradox in the immigrant rights movement: gaining rights for some undocumented immigrants contributes to reproducing the national basis of citizenship. These struggles for rights are therefore not a harbinger of postnational citizenship. They are constrained by rules of the game that continue to center on the nation-state. Gaining rights encourages activists to fashion arguments, discourses, and performances that demonstrate national belonging as a means of gaining recognition of the right to have basic human rights. The paradox of these struggles introduces countless disagreements and conflicts in the broader immigrant rights movement, which opens up new visions and paths to express rights within a national context. These disagreements have certainly helped to radicalize and universalize the rights claims of activists. But in spite of this, the existing rules of the game continue to favor those discourses that resonate with national norms and values over these more radical alternatives.

There are possibilities for other undocumented immigrants to become a potent political group with a legitimate voice, but the process of achieving this kind of power unfolds within the narrow confines of the nation-state. The trends toward universalizing human rights have been offset by the growing importance of the nation-state in determining the meanings, distributions, and struggles for rights in today's global world.[30] The great challenge for rights activists in the coming years is to develop ways to push for maximum equality in national contexts that are necessarily exclusionary and unequal.

Appendix

Principal Immigration Rights Organizations

American Federation of Labor and Congress of Industrial Organizations (AFL-CIO)

Americans for Immigration Control (AIC)

America's Voice

California Dream Network

California Dream Team Alliance

Center for Community Change (CCC)

Center for Humane Immigrant Rights of Los Angeles (CHIRLA)

Central American Resource Center (CARECEN)

Deferred Action for Childhood Arrivals (DACA)

Dream Team Los Angeles (DTLA)

Dream Is Coming

Dreamers Adrift

Dream Activist

Federation for American Immigration Reform (FAIR)

Fair Immigration Reform Movement (FIRM)

Instituto de Educacion Popular del Sur de California (IDEPSCA)

Immigration and Naturalization Service (INS)

Immigration and Customs Enforcement (ICE)

Improving Dream, Equality, Access, and Success (IDEAS UCLA)

Los Angeles Community Action Network (LACAN)

Mexican American Legal Defense and Educational Fund (MALDEF)

National Council of La Raza (NCLR)

National Day Labor Organizing Network (NDLON)

National Immigrant Youth Alliance (NIYA)

National Immigration Forum
National Immigration Law Center (NILC)
Numbers USA
Orange Country Dream Team
Reform Immigration for America (RIFA)
Southern California Immigrant Rights Coalition (SCIRC)
United We Dream
UCLA Labor Center
Wise-Up

Principal Immigration Laws and Measures

Border Protection, Anti-terrorism and Illegal Immigration Control Act
("Sensenbrenner Bill," H.R. 4437)
California Dream Act of 2011 (A.B. 130 and A.B. 131)
California Immigrant Higher Education Act (A.B. 540)
Comprehensive Immigration Reform Act (S. 2611)
Deferred Action for Childhood Arrivals (DACA)
Development, Relief and Education for Alien Minors Act (DREAM
Act)
Illegal Immigration Reform and Immigrant Responsibility Act (IIRIRA)
Personal Responsibility and Work Opportunity Reconciliation Act
(PROWARA)
Nicaraguan Adjustment Central American Responsibility Act
(NACARA)
Secure America and Orderly Immigration Act ("McCain-Kennedy Bill,"
S. 1033)
Support Our Law Enforcement and Safe Neighborhoods Act (S.B. 1070)

Researching the DREAMer: A Note on Methods

The case of the DREAMers is used to show how immigrant rights
activists and advocates have identified niches, crafted compelling representation, formed alliances, and disciplined their messages and messengers. It also shows how gaining recognition for undocumented
immigrants through these means resulted in disagreements between

the different groups making up the immigrant rights movement. The DREAMers' mobilization helps reveal the dynamic and contradictory process of creating a legitimate voice for highly stigmatized groups. The case is therefore strategic because it has arguably been the most success-ful mobilization of the immigrant rights movement over the last twenty years. This provides us with a unique window into how immigrants transform themselves from a stigmatized and illegitimate other into a political group with a legitimate public voice.

The primary focus is on the process that has unfolded over an eleven-year period (2000 to 2011). This sequence of time marks several important phases of the evolution of the general immigrant rights move-ment: (1) a period of small-scale, decentralized, and niche mobilizations (pre-2000 to 2005); (2) a period in which political openings helped accelerate consolidation and the push for Comprehensive Immigration Reform (2006 to 2007); (3) a period in which the movement achieved a degree of centralization (2008 to 2010); and (4) a period marked by the emergence of a more decentralized strategy and organizational structure (2010 to 2011). The mobilization of the DREAMers was directly shaped by and contributed to these different phases of the movement's develop-ment. The early DREAMer campaign reflected other nichelike mobi-lizations that characterized the movement during its early years (that is, refugees, agricultural workers). Once the general immigrant rights movement moved toward consolidation and centralization (2006 to 2010), the DREAMers and their campaign became a part of the "com-mon" struggle for the Comprehensive Immigration Reform Act. This process resulted in important conflicts between DREAMers and some of the leading forces of the general movement. These conflicts triggered the move toward a more decentralized and pluralistic immigrant rights movement. By examining the process over this period of time, this book serves to reveal how the DREAMers emerged from the immigrant rights movement but also contributed directly to driving its dynamic evolution.

Social movements are conceived here as contentious political strug-gles that are carried out through the public sphere.[1] The public sphere is understood broadly and extends beyond protest events.[2] It consists of the physical and discursive arenas where a broad range of stakeholders (activ-ists, advocates, sympathizers, adversaries, politicians) make claims for a particular cause. By conceiving of social movements as broad struggles that engage in contentious struggles through this public sphere, the book avoids some of the pitfalls stemming from a narrow focus on protest events.[3] As one group of scholars have noted, "But what does protest event analysis do? It measures only protest, nothing else. How can protest event analysis capture the importance of social movements' embeddedness in multi-organizational fields if it a priori excludes many of the relevant contextual acts and actors from the analysis?"[4] This book aims to capture the complex field through which the DREAMers formed and mobilized over this period of time.

One of the principal aims of the book is to reveal how a legitimate political voice was constructed for this group of undocumented youths. It spends just as much time on the process of crafting representations as it does analyzing the outputs (that is, statements, arguments, messages) in the public sphere. The book conceives of the public sphere as made up of discursive (media, Internet) and physical arenas (colleges, schools, churches, community centers, markets) where claims and counterclaims are made. In terms of discursive arenas, particular attention is paid to the statements made in the media. I analyze claims and counterclaims captured through the *New York Times* from 2000 to 2010. Key words (immigration policy, immigrant rights, DREAM Act) were introduced into the *New York Times* search engine, and the results were arranged by year, statements, stakeholders making statements, and contextual issues involved in the story. The database has been used to identify the principal actors involved in the struggle for and against immigrant rights, the political contexts facing immigrant rights advocates, and the principal themes employed by advocates and adversaries to assert their different claims in the public sphere.

Newspaper statements constitute only one part of the "discursive arena"; the Internet has provided undocumented youths with another important arena to produce representations of themselves and their struggles. Web sites, blogs, and Facebook are important sites for experimenting with arguments and discourses, circulating mobilizing frames and talking points across a national social movement network, and encouraging public discussions and debates over how to push the movement forward. Information from Internet sources was particularly useful for understanding the latter part of the struggle (2010 to 2011). I identified several prominent blog sites and closely followed discussions that unfolded within them. Additionally, I became Facebook "friends" with several prominent members of the DREAMers movement. This provided access to an important discursive arena for youth activists. For both the blogs and Facebook, I developed an "observation journal," which accounted for the themes of different discussions, statements made, and reactions.

The public sphere of DREAM activists is also constituted by physical arenas (demonstrations, high schools, churches, public markets, associations, cafes, unions, college campuses) where activists come out, represent themselves, and argue why they deserve recognition as rights-bearing subjects. DREAMers carry their "stories" and arguments into a wide array of concrete spaces where they seek to disseminate information to other undocumented youths, reinforce support by sympathetic audiences, convince less friendly audiences, and counter the arguments of their adversaries. The microspaces constituting the public sphere are important for carrying out representational battles for rights. Through one speech, presentation, and argument at a time, activists reach out to new recruits, bolster support, and convince skeptics of the just nature of their cause. Moreover, in performing and articulating arguments in these diverse spaces, activists hone their arguments, become powerful debaters, and learn how to modify arguments for different audiences (supporters, politicians, reporters, adversaries, and so on). These are therefore crucial spaces in which activists learn how to craft arguments for the right to have rights in the country.

Information on how arguments have been crafted and expressed in these arenas has been obtained through semistructured interviews and participant observations. Most of the interviews were with undocumented youth activists, but a number of interviews were also conducted with rights advocates and other supporters. The interview questions addressed three major issues: (1) political context and mobilization strategies; (2) messaging strategies and training; and (3) alliances between the different activists and organizations making up the campaign and the rights movement. The interviews with veteran immigrant rights associations were particularly useful in assessing the political context and strategy and the interviews with youth activists were helpful in assessing the production and use of mobilization frames. As is standard practice, the interview materials used in the book do not use the names of respondents in order to protect identities. Most interviews were performed with Los Angeles-based activists and advocates because the city has become an important center of the DREAM and immigrant rights movement. In addition to interviews, a participant observation was performed from September 2011 to January 2012 by two of my graduate students, Tara Fiorito and Dirk Eiseman. They embedded themselves in one of the most prominent DREAMer associations in the country, Dream Team Los Angeles. They wrote detailed field notes and communicated regularly with me about their observations and activities in the field.

The interviews and observations focused on how representations were produced but also how they carried their message into various local public arenas. Activists used connections with high school counselors to take their message to their old schools; they worked with college administrators, teachers, and student associations to develop their own campus-based support groups and engage in campus debates; they used their connections to pastors and local immigrant associations to gain access to immigrant audiences; they developed strategies with supportive allies to create high-profile protest events; they went to public markets to hand out information and argue their case directly to skeptical audiences; and they developed connections to reporters and producers to transmit their arguments to the broader media. Thus, the methods employed here reveal how DREAMers got their voice out there by engaging in painstaking microlevel struggles through the diverse arenas of the "public sphere."

In addition to examining actual engagements in the public sphere, the book also focuses on the actual process of *crafting* public representations. The focus, in other words, is not only "what is said" but also the processes of actually producing representations, arguments, and messages for public consumption. Choices are made over what arguments to stress and what arguments to silence, how to assemble arguments and symbols into structured representations, and how to train activists to stick to "talking points" and deliver messages in emotionally compelling ways. Moreover, the process of actually producing discourses and representations involves many different actors, including professional rights associations, unions, intellectuals, and activists. These different actors form a division of labor concerning the production and dissemination of representations.

By focusing on how representations are produced and disseminated, the book marks a break from standard discourse analyses of social movements.[5] Standard accounts focus almost exclusively on public statements (what is said), rather than the complicated processes involved in *producing* these statements. *This book asserts that the production process is just as important as the output because the process of producing representations and discourses shapes the nature of relations between the different actors making up actual social movements.* Producing representations brings together different actors into new alliances and partnerships, but it also introduces disagreements over how representations of immigrants and their cause should be expressed in the public sphere. In this way, public representations are both necessary for gaining recognition and access to legal rights and also become a driving force of networking dynamics that underlie immigrant rights movement. The semistructured interviews and participants observations are well suited to gain insights into the process of producing public representations.

The research and theorizing of the book is inspired by Michael Burawoy's "extended case method."[6] He argues that researchers should use "general theories" to inform how we interpret the many facts and issues we find in our cases, but we should also use the lessons derived from these cases to extend outward and propose corrections to general theories. The theory underlying the study of the DREAMers draws as much from the European literature as it does from the American literature.[7] By engaging in this dialogue between the particular case of the DREAMers in the United States and the struggle of undocumented immigrants in many different countries, the book aims to contribute to our general understandings of how highly stigmatized groups create legitimacy for themselves and their struggles in inhospitable environments. By using this case, the book aims to inform more general discussions and theories of how highly stigmatized and marginalized groups exert their rights in harsh political and discursive environments.

Notes

Introduction

1. Arendt 1973; Benhabib 2004.

2. Abrego 2006, 2008, 2011; Abrego and Gonzalez 2010; Gonzalez 2011; Gonzalez and Chavez 2012.

3. The Supreme Court ruling of *Plyler v. Doe* (1982) struck down a Texas law denying education to undocumented children. The Court asserted the Equal Protection Clause of the Fourteenth Amendment protected children from municipalities and states seeking to discriminate on the basis of immigration status (Varsanyi 2008, 887).

4. Organizer 2, Dream Team Los Angeles, personal interview.

5. Gonzalez and Chavez 2012.

6. Abrego 2008.

7. Organizer 8, Dream Team Los Angeles.

8. Email correspondence sent by DREAM organizer to Dream Team Los Angeles, September 21, 2011, emphasis added.

9. Berezin 2009; Raissiguier 2010.

10. Arendt 1973; Benhabib 2004.

11. Agamben 1998, 75, emphasis added.

12. Agamben 1998; De Genova 2007; Rancière 2007.

13. For the French case, Raissiguier employs the concept of "impossibility" in the following way: "I use the concept of impossibility to conjure up the complex mechanisms (both material and discursive) that establish impossible subject positions within the French nation. These mechanisms include discursive practices that turn certain immigrants into unthinkable members of the national body as well as material/legal practices that locate them in spaces of impossibility" (2010, 4).

14. Rancière 1999; Dikeç 2004.

15. Siméant 1998; Cissè 1999; Blin 2005; Iskander 2007; Laubenthal 2007; Cordero-Guzmán et al. 2008; Benjamin-Alvarado, De Sipio, and Montoya 2009; Anderson 2010; Voss and Bloemraad 2011; Nicholls 2012.

16. Hirschman 1970.

17. Cordero-Guzmán et al. 2008; Benjamin-Alvarado, De Sipio, and Montoya 2009; Pallares and Flores-González 2010; Voss and Bloemraad 2011.

18. Calavita 1996.

19. M. Coleman 2007; De Genova 2007; Chavez 2008; Raissiguier 2010; Massey and Pren 2012.

20. De Genova 2007; Massey and Pren 2012.

21. Freeman 1995; Coutin 1998; Joppke 1999; Bosniak 2006; Honig 2006; Menjívar 2006.

22. Van der Leun 2006; Coutin 1998, 2003; Bosniak 2006; Menjívar 2006.

23. Freeman 1995; Money 1999; Schain 1999.

24. Passeron and Grignon 1989; Fassin 2012.

25. De Genova 2013.

26. Coutin 1998, 2001.

27. Coutin 1998, 906.

28. Elias 1994; Alexander 2006.

29. Honig 2006.

30. Bourdieu 1994; Wacquant 2005.

31. Fine 1995; Jasper 1998; Polletta 1998.

32. Milkman 2006; Cordero-Guzmán et al. 2008; Voss and Bloemraad 2011; Nicholls 2012.

33. Rancière 1999; Dikeç 2004.

34. Foucault 1980, 1982; Ong 1996, 1999; Cruikshank 1999.

35. Their arguments mirrored Hannah Arendt's discussions of the importance of politics and public life for human existence (see Arendt 1958).

36. Mouffe 1992; Rancière 1999.

37. Landa 2006.

Chapter 1

1. http://www.youtube.com/watch?v=lLIzzs2HHgY.

2. http://www.splcenter.org/get-informed/intelligence-files/ideology/anti-immigrant/the-anti-immigrant-movement.

3. Huntington 2004, 1.

4. After they regrouped in late 2007 and early 2008, "279 votes" became a rallying cry for immigrant rights leaders.

5. Calavita 1996; Nevins 2002; De Genova 2005, 2007; Menjívar 2006; Fernandez-Kelly and Massey 2007; Chavez 2008; Varsanyi 2008; Massey and Pren 2012.

6. Diamond 1996; Money 1999; also see http://www.splcenter.org/get-informed/intelligence-files/ideology/anti-immigrant/the-anti-immigrant-movement.

7. Diamond 1996; Money 1999.

8. Chavez 2008.

9. Kennedy, in Chavez 2008, 33.

10. Seif 2004.

11. Chavez 2008; Massey and Pren 2012.

12. Brader et al. 2008; Chavez 2008.

13. Massey and Pren 2012, 8.

14. Hopkins 2010, 41.

15. The main elements of the law were local law enforcement agencies were required to turn over people with questionable legal status to Immigration and Naturalization Service (INS); civil servants were required to inform enforcement officials concerning the questionable status of residents; all public social services and health care were denied to undocumented immigrants; the denial of educational access to undocumented children; school officials were required to verify legal status of children and parents; the Attorney General of California was required to create a common data base of immigrants who had been denied an education; among other things.

16. Calavita 1996, 298; Diamond 1996.

17. Nevins 2002.

18. Nevins 2002; Durand and Massey 2003.

19. Durand and Massey 2003.

20. Durand and Massey 2003; Fernandez-Kelly and Massey 2007; Massey and Pren 2012.

21. Fernandez-Kelly and Massey 2007, 113.

22. Gonzalez 2011; Passel and Cohen 2009.

23. Passel and Cohen 2009.

24. Gonzalez 2011.

25. Bosniak 2006; M. Coleman 2007; De Genova 2007; Varsanyi 2008.

26. M. Coleman 2007.

27. Varsanyi 2008; Olivas 2010.

28. "Crucially, PRWORA gives states the unprecedented ability to discriminate against noncitizens in deciding eligibility for their programs, *an act that prior to 1996 was considered an unconstitutional encroachment into federal powers over membership policy*" (Varsanyi 2008, 887, emphasis added).

29. Varsanyi 2008, 889, emphasis added.

30. Walker and Leitner 2011, 157.

31. Arizona Senate Bill 1070 made it a misdemeanor crime for immigrants in Arizona to not show proof of legal residency during a lawful stop. The law gave authority to police to stop people for reasonable suspicion of being an "illegal" immigrant. The law also introduced sanctions on renting to and hiring undocumented immigrants. While the first of its kind, the law has inspired similar measures in Georgia, South Carolina, Alabama, and other states.

32. Fernandez-Kelly and Massey 2007; Massey and Pren 2012.

33. Abrego 2011; Gonzalez 2011.

34. Gonzalez 2011.

35. Coutin 1998, 2003; Menjívar 2006.

36. Menjívar 2006.

37. Director of CARECEN, personal interview.

38. Coutin 1998, 2003.

39. Holley 2000.

40. The Immigration and Naturalization Service and then subsequent Immigration and Customs Enforcement agency.

41. Wadhia 2010, 254–55.

42. Project director, UCLA Labor Center, personal interview.

43. Ari Fleischer, quoted in "No Agreement Yet With Mexico On Immigration," *NY Times*, August 31, 2001.

44. Director, NDLON, personal interview.

45. De Genova 2007; M. Coleman 2007.

46. Dan Stein, quoted in "Changes Called Likely In Policy on Immigration," *NY Times*, September 24, 2001, emphasis added.

47. Condoleezza Rice, quoted in "Rice and Mexican Official Hint at Thaw in Relations," *NY Times*, March 11, 2005.

48. Grover Norquist, quoted in "Frist Opposes Amendments on Immigrants," *NY Times*, April 13, 2005.

49. USA Patriot Act (2001), National Intelligence Reform and Terrorism Protection Act (2004), and the Real ID Act (2005).

50. Operation Endgame (2003), Operation Frontline (2004), Arizona Border Control Initiative (2004), Operation Stonegarden (2004), Secure Borders Initiative (2005), Operation Streamline (2005). Massey and Pren 2012, 10–11.

51. Especially important were increasingly lowered thresholds for deportable offenses, restrictions on judicial discretion and appeals during deportation proceedings, cooperation with local law enforcement agencies, and expanded resources for border security.

52. Massey and Pren 2012, 16.

53. Wadhia 2010.

54. Judd Gregg, quoted in "DeLay Says Bush Promises Better Effort on Immigration Law," *NY Times*, April 13, 2005.

55. Tom Delay, quoted in "DeLay Says Bush Promises Better Effort on Immigration Law," *NY Times*, June 9, 2005, emphasis added.

56. Erin Healey, quoted in "DeLay Says Bush Promises Better Effort on Immigration Law," *NY Times*, June 9, 2005.

57. George W. Bush, quoted in "Across the U.S., Debate over the President's Plan," *NY Times*, November 29, 2005, emphasis added.

58. Michael Chertoff, quoted in "Bush Renews Push for Immigrant-Worker Plan," *NY Times*, October 19, 2005.

59. Fernandez-Kelly and Massey 2007, 108.

60. James Sensenbrenner, quoted in "Tough Border Security Bill Nears Passage in the House," *NY Times*, December 14, 2005, emphasis added.

61. John Culberson, quoted in "Tough Border Security Bill Nears Passage in the House," *NY Times*, December 14, 2005, emphasis added.

62. George W. Bush, quoted in "Bush Turns to House in Immigration Debate," *NY Times*, June 7, 2006.

63. George W. Bush, quoted in "Bush Suggests Immigrants Learn English," *NY Times*, June 9, 2006, emphasis added.

64. Ibid., emphasis added.

65. Dennis Hastert, quoted in "House G.O.P. Planning Recess Hearings," *NY Times*, July 28, 2006.

66. The Secure Fence Act, H.R. 6061.

67. Edward Kennedy, quoted in "Kennedy, Eager for Republican Support, Shifts Tactics on an Immigration Measure," *NY Times*, March 13, 2007.

68. Arlen Specter, quoted in "Bush Renews Call for Sweeping Immigration Reform," *NY Times*, April 9, 2007.

69. Barack Obama, quoted in '08 Candidates Weighing Consequences as They Take Sides on Immigration Plan," *NY Times*, May 19, 2007.

70. Roy Beck, quoted in "Defeat Worries Employers Who Rely on Immigrants," *NY Times*, June 29, 2007, emphasis added.

71. Edward Kennedy, quoted in "Defeat Worries Employers Who Rely on Immigrants," *NY Times*, June 29, 2007.

72. Frank Sharry, quoted in "Plenty of Apples, but Possibly a Shortage of Immigrant Pickers," *NY Times*, August 31, 2007.

73. The National Council of Agricultural Employers, quoted in "U.S. Seeks Rules to Allow Increase in Guest Workers," *NY Times*, October 10, 2007.

74. David James, Labor Department spokesman, quoted in "U.S. Seeks Rules to Allow Increase in Guest Workers," *NY Times*, October 10, 2007.

75. Voss and Bloemraad 2011.

76. LaMarche 2010.

77. A.B. 540 (California Immigrant Higher Education Act) refers to the California law passed in 2001 that allowed undocumented residents to pay in-state tuition fees in public universities. While A.B. 540 made it easier for undocumented immigrants to access universities, the law did not give these students access to most forms of financial aid. The student support groups played an important role in providing emotional support for these students but also information on grants and other sources of support.

Chapter 2

1. Abrego 2006, 2011; Gonzalez 2011; Gonzalez and Chavez 2012.

2. This largely reflects what sociologist Norbert Elias 1996 called a "national habitus."

3. Gonzalez 2011.

4. Organizer 1, UCLA IDEAS, personal interview.

5. Abrego 2011; Gonzalez and Chavez 2012.

6. Seif 2004.

7. Foucault 1980; Ong 1996, 1999; Cruikshank 1999.

8. Chavez 2008.

9. Benford and Hunt 1992; Benford and Snow 2000.

10. Organizer 1, California Dream Network, personal interview.

11. Organizer 1, Dream Team Los Angeles, personal interview.

12. The subject made explicit use of inverted commas to say good American.

13. Organizer 1, San Gabriel Valley Dream Team, personal interview.

14. Organizer 1, California Dream Network, personal interview, emphasis added.

15. Elias 1996.

16. Partha Banerjee, quoted in "Immigrants Lost in the Din: Security vs. the Dream," *NY Times*, September 20, 2004.

17. Former director, California Dream Network, personal interview.

18. Harry Reid, quoted in "Reid Trying Again on Immigration Bill," *NY Times*, November 17, 2010.

19. Anonymous DREAM activist, quoted in "Debates Persist Over Subsidies for Immigrant College Students," *NY Times*, December 12, 2007.

20. Anonymous Congressperson, quoted in "Measure Would Offer Legal Status to Illegal Immigrant Students," *NY Times*, September 20, 2007.

21. Janet Napolitano, quoted in "Napolitano Backs Immigration Bill," *NY Times*, December 2, 2010.

22. Harry Reid, quoted in "Reid Trying Again on Immigration Bill," *NY Times*, November 17, 2010.

23. Michael Crow, quoted in "Measure Would Offer Legal Status to Illegal Immigrant Students," *NY Times*, September 20, 2010, emphasis added.

24. Organizer 5, Dream Team Los Angeles, personal interview.

25. Polletta 2006.

26. Goffman 1959.

27. Organizer 1, United We Dream, personal interview.

28. Barack Obama, quoted in "'We Are Not Doomed to Endless Gridlock,'" *NY Times*, December 22, 2010, emphasis added.

29. Jasper 1997.

30. Michael Huckabee, quoted in "Debates Persist over Subsidies for Immigrant College Students," *NY Times*, December 12, 2007.

31. Roy Beck, quoted in "Illegal Immigrant Students Publicly Take up a Cause," *NY Times*, December 10, 2009.

32. Rick Perry, presidential candidate, CBS News, September 22, 2011, emphasis added.

33. Anonymous DREAM activist, quoted in "In Increments, Senate Revisits Immigration Bill," *NY Times*, August 3, 2007.

34. Carlos Saavedra, quoted in "Illegal Immigrant Students Publicly Take up a Cause," *NY Times*, December 10, 2009.

35. Demetrios Giannaros, quoted in "UConn to Assess a Policy On Illegal Immigrants," *NY Times*, March 7, 2004.

36. Richard Durbin, quoted in "In Increments, Senate Revisits Immigration Bill," *NY Times*, August 3, 2007.

37. Congressional aide, quoted in "Measure Would Offer Legal Status to Illegal Immigrant Students," *NY Times*, September 20, 2007.

38. durbin.senate.gov/public/index.cfm?p=dreamers-stories.

39. Laurence Downes, quoted in "Don't Deport Benita Veliz," *NY Times*, March 28, 2009, emphasis added.

40. Richard Durbin, quoted in "Behind Top Student's Heartbreak, Illegal Immigrants' Nightmare," *NY Times*, September 1, 2004.

41. Janet Napolitano, quoted in "Napolitano Backs Immigration Bill," *NY Times*, December 2, 2010.

42. Former director, California Dream Network, personal interview.

43. Organizer 1, Dream Team Los Angeles, personal interview.

44. Organizer 2, California Dream Network, personal interview.

45. Former director, California Dream Network, personal interview.

46. Organizer 2, California Dream Network, personal interview.

47. Former director, California Dream Network, personal interview.

48. Dikeç 2004, 2005.

49. Former organizer, United We Dream, personal interview.

50. Former director, California Dream Network, personal interview.

51. Organizer 2, Dream Team Los Angeles, personal interview.

52. Former organizer, United We Dream, personal interview.

53. Polletta 2006.

54. Coutin 1998, 2003.

55. Organizer 2, California Dream Network, personal interview.

56. Organizer 1, California Dream Network, personal interview.

57. Organizer 2, California Dream Network, personal interview.

58. Organizer 1, Orange Country Dream Team, personal interview.

59. Organizer 3, California Dream Network, personal interview.

60. Organizer 2, California Dream Network, personal interview.

61. Organizer 1, UCLA IDEAS, personal interview.

62. Collins 2004.

63. Organizer 4, California Dream Network, personal interview.

64. Organizer 2, California Dream Network, personal interview.

65. Organizer 6, California Dream Network, personal interview.

66. http://www.dreamactivist.org/resources/.

67. Organizer 2, California Dream Network, personal interview.

68. Jasper 1998.

69. Organizer 5, California Dream Network, personal interview.

70. Gonzalez 2011.

71. Organizer 2, California Dream Network, personal interview.

72. Organizer 2, UCLA IDEAS, personal interview.

Chapter 3

1. Perez et al. 2010.

2. Arendt 1958, 1973; Benhabib 2004.

3. Former organizer, United We Dream, personal interview.

4. Organizer 2, Dream Team Los Angeles, personal interview.

5. Organizer 2, Dream Team Los Angeles, personal interview.

6. Former organizer, United We Dream, personal interview.

7. Director, NDLON, personal interview.

8. Director, NDLON, personal interview.

9. Walker and Leitner 2011.

10. Project director, UCLA Labor Center, personal interview.

11. Ibid.

12. Former organizer, United We Dream, personal interview.

13. Organizer 5, Dream Team Los Angeles, personal interview.

14. Organizer 2, Dream Team Los Angeles, personal interview.

15. Instituto de Educacion Popular del Sur de California.

16. Former organizer, United We Dream, personal interview.

17. Project director, UCLA Labor Center, personal interview.

18. Organizer 3, Dream Team Los Angeles, personal interview.

19. Director, NDLON, personal interview.

20. Director, UCLA Labor Center, personal interview.

21. Project director, UCLA Labor Center, personal interview.

22. Organizer 5, Dream Team Los Angeles, personal interview.

23. Project director, UCLA Labor Center, personal interview.

24. Director, NDLON, personal interview.

25. Organizer 2, Dream Team Los Angeles, personal interview.

26. Project director, UCLA Labor Center, personal interview.

27. Organizer 2, Dream Team Los Angeles, personal interview.

28. Former organizer, United We Dream, personal interview.

29. Organizer 3, DREAM Team Los Angeles, personal interview.

30. Carlos Saavedra, quoted in "Students Spared Amid an Increase in Deportation," *NY Times*, August 8, 2010.

31. Organizer 3, DREAM Team Los Angeles, personal interview.

32. Organizer 4, Dream Team Los Angeles, personal interview.

33. Organizer 5, Dream Team Los Angeles, personal interview.

34. Former director, California Dream Network, personal interview.

35. Organizer 2, California Dream Network, personal interview.

36. Former director, California Dream Network, personal interview.

37. Editorial Board, "Courage in Arizona," *NY Times*, May, 19, 2010.

38. Andy Fischer, spokesperson for Richard Lugar, quoted in "Illegal Immigrant Students Protest at McCain Office," *NY Times*, May 17, 2010.

39. Former organizer, United We Dream, personal interview.

40. Organizer 3, Dream Team Los Angeles, personal interview.

41. Editorial Board, "A Rallying Cry in Support of an Immigration Bill," *NY Times*, November 29, 2010.

42. Organizer 1, Orange County DREAM Team, personal interview.

43. Carlos Saavedra, quoted in "Immigration Vote Leaves Obama's Policy in Disarray," *NY Times*, December 18, 2010.

44. Project director, UCLA Labor Center, personal interview.

45. Arendt 1973; Benhabib 2004.

46. Perez et al. 2010.

47. Ibid.

48. Anonymous DREAMer, quoted in "Illegal Immigrant Students Protest at McCain Office," *NY Times*, May 17, 2010.

49. Artist, Dreamers Adrift, personal interview.

50. Perez et al. 2010, emphasis added.

51. http://www.DREAMactivist.org/blog/2010/10/13/neidi-jonathan-jorge-nancy-re spond-sally-kohn/.

52. http://vivirlatino.com/2010/06/16/the-non-profit-industrial-complex-eats-reform -and-shits-on-DREAMs.php.

53. http://dreamdeployed.blogspot.com/2010/10/insults-aside-issues-emerge.html, emphasis in the original.

54. http://DREAMdeployed.blogspot.com/2010/10/insults-aside-issues-emerge.html, emphasis added.

55. Organizer 1, UCLA IDEAS, personal interview.

56. Gramsci 1971.

57. Arendt 1973.

Chapter 4

1. Field notes, December 21, 2010.

2. Ibid.

3. Bourdieu 1994; Wacquant 2005.

4. Pérez 2009; Abrego 2006, 2008, 2011; Abrego and Gonzalez 2010; Gonzalez 2011.

5. Abrego and Gonzalez 2010; Pérez 2009; Gonzalez 2011.

6. Artist, Dreamers Adrift, personal interview.

7. Gonzalez 2011.

8. Abrego and Gonzalez 2010; Pérez 2009.

9. Julio Salgado, personal interview.

10. Diani and Bison 2004; Nicholls 2008.

11. J. Coleman 1988.

12. Field notes, September 22, 2011.

13. Organizer 5, Dream Team Los Angeles, personal interview.

14. Organizer 1, Dream Team Los Angeles, personal interview.

15. Routledge 2003; Hardt and Negri 2009; Nicholls 2009.

16. These would include the campus groups of UC Berkeley, UCLA, UC Santa Cruz, CSU Long Beach, and CSU Fullerton, among others.

17. Organizer 1, UCLA IDEAS, personal interview.

18. Organizer 1, Orange County Dream Team, personal interview.

19. Hondegneu-Sotelo 1994; Valenzuela 2003; Milkman 2006.

20. Organizer 2, UCLA IDEAS, personal interview, emphasis added.

21. Director, Labor Center, personal interview.

22. Organizer 1, San Gabriel Valley Dream Team, personal interview.

23. Organizer 3, Dream Team Los Angeles, personal interview.

24. Organizer 1, Orange Country Dream Team, personal interview.

25. Organizer 1, Inland Empire Dream Team, personal interview.

26. Former organizer, United We Dream, personal interview.

27. Former organizer, United We Dream, personal interview.

28. Former organizer, United We Dream, personal interview.

29. Organizer 5, Dream Team Los Angeles, personal interview.

30. By radical I mean more willing to engage in high-risk forms of direct action, less willing to engage with national rights associations, and more critical of the traditional DREAMer discourse.

31. Former organizer, United We Dream, personal interview.

32. Former organizer, United We Dream, personal interview.

33. Uitermark and Nicholls 2012.

Chapter 5

1. http://DREAMdeployed.blogspot.com/2010/10/insults-aside-issues-emerge.html.

2. Organizer 1, Dream Team Los Angeles, personal interview.

3. Organizer 1, Orange County Dream Team, personal interview.

4. Organizer 1, Dream Team Los Angeles, personal interview.

5. Organizer 1, Dream Team Los Angeles, personal interview.

6. The slogan "I Exist!" is a poignant claim and reflects Hannah Arendt's discussion of the condition of the slave during Roman antiquity. For Arendt, the tragedy of the slave was not only the denial of freedom but also being condemned to the shadows of the private sphere and deprived of the need to express or reveal one's existence in public (Arendt 1958, 50).

7. Artist, Dreamers Adrift, personal interview.

8. Facebook posting, November 2011.

9. Organizer 1, IDEAS UCLA, personal interview.

10. Organizer 1, Orange Country Dream Team, personal interview.

11. Organizer 1, San Gabriel Dream Team, personal interview.

12. Jacques Rancière discusses the in-between status of an emergent political subjectivity in the following way: "Let me rephrase this: a subject is an outsider or, more, an in-between. Proletarian was the name given to people who are together inasmuch as they are between: between several names, statuses, and identities; between humanity and inhumanity, citizenship and its denial; between the status of a man of tools and the status of a speaking and thinking being. Political subjectivization is the enactment of equality-or the handling of a wrong-by people who are together to the extent that they are between. It is a crossing of identities, relying on a crossing of names: names that link the name of a group or class to the name of no group or no class, a being to a nonbeing or a not-yet-being" (1992, 61).

13. Organizer 1, Orange Country Dream Team, personal interview.

14. Perez et al. 2010.

15. Organizer 1, Orange County Dream Team, personal interview.

16. Organizer 1, Dream Team Los Angeles, personal interview.

17. Facebook posting, June 2011.

18. Organizer 5, California Dream Network, personal interview.

19. Former organizer, United We Dream, personal interview.

20. Former organizer, United We Dream, personal interview.

21. Former organizer 1, United We Dream personal interview.

22. Former organizer 1, United We Dream personal interview.

23. Facebook posting, December 2012.

24. McAdam, Tarrow, and Tilly 2001.

25. Observation, field notes, October 16, 2012.

26. Organizer 1, Dream Team Los Angeles, personal interview, emphasis added.

27. Organizer 1, UCLA IDEAS, personal interview, emphasis added.

28. Organizer 1, San Fernando Valley Dream Team, personal interview.

29. Jasper 1998.

30. Organizer 1, Inland Empire Dream Team, personal interview.

31. This is a low-income and stigmatized area of Los Angeles.

32. In an earlier part of the interview, the DREAMer referred to a powerful illustration of a Latina street youth (that is, *Chola*). He noted, "I brought up something like that, a poster that a friend made of like a Chola stereotype, with big hair and eyebrows, but in her hands she has two books. She has *Borderlands* [Gloria Anzaldúa's classic of postnational theory] and in the other hand it's blank and it says 'Support the DREAM Act'" Organizer 5, Dream Team Los Angeles, personal interview.

33. Organizer 5, Dream Team Los Angeles, personal interview.

34. East LA is East Los Angeles, which is the historical Latino barrio of Los Angeles.

35. Facebook posting, November 2011, emphasis added.

36. Literal translation: no hair in the tongue.

37. "East Los" is an idiomatic way to say East Los Angeles.

Chapter 6

1. Field notes, December 21, 2010.

2. Varsanyi 2008.

3. M. Coleman 1997; Varsanyi 2008.

4. Walker and Leitner 2011.

5. The case of sheriff Joe Arpaio of Arizona's Maricopa County stands out as the most celebrated example of this more punitive line.

6. The Republican presidential candidate of 2012.

7. Steve Levy, quoted in "In Island's Wealthiest Area, Backlash Against the Poorest," *NY Times*, August 17, 2003.

8. Local contractor, quoted in "A Change of Scene?" *NY Times*, January 18, 2004.

9. Long Island Farm Bureau, quoted in "The Changing Face of the Island's Labor Force," *NY Times*, November 14, 2004, emphasis added.

10. Long Island resident, quoted in "The Changing Face of the Island's Labor Force," *NY Times,* November 14, 2004.

11. To address this paradox, we can draw on Michel Foucault's (1976, 1978) discussions on illegality and interdictions. For Foucault, enforcing a rule to ban certain practices contributes to the proliferation of discourses and technologies about those same "illegal" practices. Laws banning nonprivate property ownership (1976, 167) and deviant sexualities (1978, 38) contributed to discursive explosions about variations of illegal and banned practices, measurements concerning how far they deviated from legal practices and norms, and widely varying methods to intervene and correct banned practices. The proliferating discourses on banned practices often harnessed and intensified them rather than achieved their repression and disappearance. The enforcement of interdictions contributes to the explosion of talk, ideas, controls, and practices of illegality rather than their repression.

12. Cedillo was a longtime advocate of a bill that would allow undocumented immigrants a license (repeatedly vetoed by Governor Arnold Schwarzenegger) and another bill that ended the towing of cars of unlicensed drivers (signed by Governor Jerry Brown in 2011).

13. Anonymous organizer, Dream Team Los Angeles, field notes, September 22, 2011.

14. Ibid.

15. Participant observer, field notes, September 22, 2011.

16. Field notes, October 6, 2011.

17. Participant observer, field notes, October 12, 2011.

18. According to ICE, deportation rates under the Obama administration achieved record high levels, with approximately 1.2 million undocumented immigrants being removed during this period of time. This places the Obama administration deportation rate at twice that of its predecessor.

19. Granovetter 1973, 1983; J. Coleman 1988; Portes and Sensenbrenner 1993; Nicholls 2008.

20. In addition to NDLON and DTLA, some of the other associations in the coalition were Southern California Institute for Popular Education (IDEPSCA), Coalition for Humane Immigrant Rights of Los Angeles (CHIRLA), Central American Resource Center (CARECEN), Mexican American Legal Defense and Educational Fund (MALDEF), Labor/Community Strategy Center, Southern California Immigration Coalition (SCIC), and Los Angeles Community Action Network (LA CAN), among others.

21. J. Coleman 1988, 102.

22. Anonymous organizer, Dream Team Los Angeles, field notes, September 22, 2011.

23. Benford and Snow 2000.

24. Organizer 4, Dream Team Los Angeles, personal interview.

25. Anonymous organizer (citizen ally), Dream Team Los Angeles, field notes, September 21, 2011.

26. Director, CARECEN, personal interview.

27. Director, Southern California Immigrant Rights Coalition, personal interview.

28. Anonymous DREAMer, field notes, December 21, 2010.

29. McAdam 1999.

30. Director, NDLON, personal interview.

31. Voss and Bloemraad 2011.

32. The concept of "flexible specialization" is a common term used in economic analysis of post-Fordism (Amin and Thrift 1992; Storper 1997). The concept suggests that small clusters of networked firms (as opposed to large, vertically integrated, and bureaucratic firms) are better able to respond to the rapidly shifting market opportunities of the new global economy. This same concept can be used to understand how the organizational structures of social movements (horizontal versus vertical) affect their abilities to respond to rapidly shifting opportunities.

Conclusion

1. http://www.latimes.com/news/local/la-me-0601–tobar-20120601,0,1233407.column. The rhetoric is extreme, but it is also the standard rhetoric used by those responding to Tobar's op-ed essays. It is also interesting to consider these readers are likely from California, a rather hospitable state with respect to immigrants.

2. Agamben 1998; M. Coleman 1997.

3. Arendt 1973; Agamben 1998; Benhabib 2004.

4. Blau and Moncada 2008; Fainstein 2010; Soja 2010; Wright 2010; among many others.

5. Weber 1958; Arendt 1973; Mann 1993.

6. Weber 1958; Mann 1986; Elias 1994; Isin 2000; Berezin 2009.

7. "The fundamental categorial pair of Western politics is not that of friend/enemy but that of bare life/political existence, *zoë/bios,* exclusion/inclusion" (Agamben 1998, 12).

8. Alexander 2006.

9. Wright 2010.

10. Beck 2000.

11. Wimmer and Glick Schiller 2002, 302.

12. Beck 2002, 37.

13. Durand and Massey 2003; Fernandez-Kelly and Massey 2007; Joppke 2007.

14. Brubaker 1992; Castles 1995; Koopmans et al. 2005; Bloemraad 2006.

15. Joppke 2007; Favell 2009.

16. Bader 2007.

17. Siméant 1998; Cissè 1999; Blin 2005; Iskander 2007; Laubenthal 2007; Benjamin-Alvarado, De Sipio, and Montoya 2009; Anderson 2010.

18. Siméant 1998; Blin 2005; Nicholls 2012.

19. In 1991 Jacques Chirac (at that time, former prime minister, sitting mayor of Paris, future president) characterized the typical "foreign" family unit in the following way: "How do you want a French worker who works with his wife, who earns together about 15,000 francs and who sees next to his social housing apartment, a piled-up family with a father, three or four spouses and twenty children earning 50,000 FF via welfare benefits, naturally without working. . . . If you add to that the noise and the smell, well the French worker, he goes crazy. And it is not racist to say this. We no longer have the means of honoring the family reunification policy, and we need to finally start the essential debate in this country, as to whether it is moral and normal that foreigners should profit to the same extent as French people, from a national solidarity to which they don't participate, as they pay no income taxes" (Chirac, in Nicholls 2012, 7). For Chirac, the qualities of the "typical" immigrant family violated threatened the national community and its system of solidarity, making it impossible for the state to grant immigrants equal rights.

20. Duyvendak 2012.

21. Koopmans et al. 2005.

22. Burawoy 1998.

23. Arendt 1977 [1963].

24. Milkman 2006.

25. Beck 2002.

26. Soysal 1994, 2000; Kaldor 1999; Wimmer and Glick Schiller 2002; Smith 2003; Blau and Moncada 2008.

27. Joppke 2007; Chavez 2008; Berezin 2009; Favell 2009; Raissiguier 2010.

28. Elias 1996.

29. Agamben 1998.

30. Blau and Moncada 1998; Beck 2002; Blau and Frezzo 2011.

Appendix

1. Koopmans and Statham 1999; McAdam et al. 2003; Koopmans et al. 2005.

2. Fraser 1991.

3. Gamson 1988; Koopmans and Statham 1999.

4. Koopmans and Statham 1999.

5. Koopmans et al. 2005; Giugni and Passy 2006.

6. Burawoy 1998, 2001.

7. Ireland 1994; Siméant 1998; Joppke 1999; Van der Leun 2003; Giugni and Passy 2004; Blin 2005; Koopmans et al. 2005; Anderson 2010; Nicholls 2012.

References

Abrego, Leisy. 2011. "Legal Consciousness of Undocumented Latinos: Fear and Stigma as Barriers to Claims-Making for First- and 1.5-Generation Immigrants." *Law and Society* 45 (2): 337–69.

———. 2008. "Legitimacy, Social Identity, and the Mobilization of Law: The Effects of Assembly Bill 540 on Undocumented Students in California." *Law and Social Inquiry* 33 (3): 709–34.

———. 2006. "'I Can't Go to College Because I Don't Have Papers': Incorporation Patterns of Latino Undocumented Youth." *Latino Studies* 4: 212–31.

Abrego, Leisy, and Roberto Gonzales. 2010. "Blocked Paths, Uncertain Futures: The Postsecondary Education and Labor Market Prospects of Undocumented Latino Youth." *Journal of Education of Students Placed at Risk* 15 (1): 144–57.

Agamben, Giorgio. 1998. *Homo Sacer: Sovereign Power and Bare Life.* Stanford: Stanford University Press.

Alexander, Jeffrey. 2006. *The Civil Sphere.* Oxford: Oxford University Press.

Amin, Ash, and Nigel Thrift. 1992. "Neo-Marshallian Nodes in Global Networks." *International Journal of Urban and Regional Research* 16 (4): 571–87.

Anderson, Bridget. 2010. "Mobilizing Migrants, Making Citizens: Migrant Domestic Workers as Political Agents." *Ethnic and Racial Studies* 33 (1) 60–74.

Arendt, Hannah. 1977 [1963]. *Eichmann in Jerusalem: A Report on the Banality of Evil.* London: Penguin Books.

———. 1973. *On the Origins of Totalitarianism.* New York: Harcourt, Brace, Jovanovich.

———. 1958. *The Human Condition.* Chicago: University of Chicago Press.

Bader, Veit. 2007. "The Governance of Islam in Europe: The Perils of Modeling." *Journal of Ethnic and Migration Studies* 33 (6): 871–86.

Beck, Ulrich. 2002. "The Cosmopolitan Society and its Enemies." *Culture and Society* 19 (1–2): 17–44.

———. 2000. "The Cosmopolitan Perspective: Sociology of the Second Age of Modernity." *British Journal of Sociology* 51: 79–105.

Benford, Robert, and Scott Hunt. 1992. "Dramaturgy and Social Movements: The Social Construction and Communication of Power." *Sociological Inquiry* 62: 36–55.

Benford, Robert, and David Snow. 2000. "Framing Processes and Social Movements: An Overview and Assessment." *Annual Review of Sociology* 26: 611–39.

Benhabib, Seyla. 2004. *The Rights of Others: Aliens, Residents, and Citizens.* Cambridge: Cambridge University Press.

Benjamin-Alvarado, Jonathon, Louis De Sipio, and Celeste Montoya. 2009. "Latino Mobilization in New Immigrant Destinations: The Anti—H.R. 4437 Protest." *Urban Affairs Review* 44: 718–35.

Berezin, Mabel. 2009. *Illiberal Politics in Neoliberal Times: Culture, Security and Populism in the New Europe.* Cambridge: Cambridge University Press.

Blau, Judith, and Mark Frezzo. 2011. *Sociology and Human Rights: A Bill of Rights for the Twenty-First Century.* Thousand Oaks, CA: Pine Forge Press.

Blau, Judith, and Alberto Moncada. 2008. "Sociological Theory and Human Rights: One World." In *Blackwell Companion to Social Theory*, edited by Bryan Turner, 496–512. Oxford: Blackwell.

Blin, Thierry. 2005. *Les Sans-papiers de Saint-Bernard. Mouvement social et action organisée.* Paris: L'Harmattan.

Bloemraad, Irene. 2006. *Becoming a Citizen: Incorporating Immigrants and Refugees in the United States and Canada.* Berkeley: University of California Press.

Bosniak, Linda. 2006. *The Citizen and the Alien.* Princeton, NJ: Princeton University Press.

Bourdieu, Pierre. 1999. *Acts of Resistance: Against the Tyranny of the Market.* New York: New Press.

———. 1994. *Language and Symbolic Power.* Cambridge, MA: Harvard University Press.

Brader, Ted, Nicholas Valentino, and Elizabeth Suhay. 2010. "What Triggers Public Opposition to Immigration? Anxiety, Group Cues, and Immigration." *American Journal of Political Science* 52 (4): 959–78.

Brubaker, Rogers. 1992. *Citizenship and Nationhood in France and Germany.* Cambridge, MA: Harvard University Press.

Burawoy, Michael. 1998. "The Extended Case Method." *Sociological Theory* 16 (1): 4–33.

Butler, Judith. 1988. "Performative Acts and Gender Constitution: An Essay in Phenomenology and Feminist Theory." *Theatre Journal* 40 (4): 519–31.

Calavita, Kitty. 1996. "The New Politics of Immigration: 'Balanced-Budget Conservativism' and the Symbolism of Proposition 187." *Social Problems* 43 (3): 284–305.

Castles, Stephen. 1995. "How Nation-states Respond to Immigration and Ethnic Diversity." *New Community* 21 (3): 293–308.

Chavez, Leo. 2008. *The Latino Threat: Constructing Immigrants, Citizens, and the Nation.* Stanford: Stanford University Press.

Cissè, Madjigène. 1999. *Parole De Sans-Papiers.* Paris: La Dispute.

Coleman, James. 1988. "Social Capital in the Creation of Human Capital." *The American Journal of Sociology* 94: 95–120.

Coleman, Matthew. 2007. "Immigration Geopolitics Beyond the Mexico-US Border." *Antipode* 38 (1): 54–76.

Collins, Randall. 2009. *Violence: A Micro-sociological Theory.* Princeton, NJ: Princeton University Press.

———. 2004. *Interaction Ritual Chains.* Princeton, NJ: Princeton University Press.

———. 2000. "Social Movements and the Focus of Emotional Attention." In *Passionate Politics: Emotions and Social Movements,* edited by Jeff Goodwin, James Jasper, and Francesca Polletta, 27–44. Chicago: University of Chicago Press.

Cordero-Guzmán, Hector, Nina Martin, Victoria Quiroz-Becerra, and Nik Theodore. 2008. "Voting with Their Feet: Nonprofit Organizations and Immigrant Mobilization." *American Behavioral Scientist* 52: 598–617.

Coutin, Susan. 2003. *Legalizing Moves: Salvadoran Immigrants' Struggle for U.S. Residency.* Ann Arbor: University of Michigan Press.

———. 1998. "From Refugees to Immigrants: The Legalization Strategies of Salvadoran Immigrants and Activists." *International Migration Review* 32 (4): 901–25.

Cruikshank, Barbara. 1999. *The Will to Empower: Democratic Citizens and Other Subjects.* Ithaca, NY: Cornell University Press.

De Genova, Nicholas. 2013. "Immigration 'Reform' and the Production of Migrant 'Illegality.'" In *Constructing "Illegality": Immigrant Experiences, Critiques, and Resistance,* edited by C. Menjívar and D. Kanstroom. Cambridge: Cambridge University Press, forthcoming.

———. 2007. "The Production of Culprits: From Deportability to Detainability in the Aftermath of 'Homeland Security.'" *Citizenship Studies* 11: 421–48.

———. 2005. *Working the Boundaries: Race, Space, and "Illegality" in Mexican Chicago.* Chapel Hill, NC: Duke University Press.

Diamond, Sara. 1996. "Right-Wing Politics and the Anti-Immigration Cause." *Social Justice* 23 (3): 154–68.

Diani, Mario. 2004. "Social Movements, Contentious Actions, and Social Networks: From Metaphor to Substance." In *Social Movements and Networks: Relational Approaches to Collective Action,* edited by Mario Diani and Douglas McAdam, 1–19. Oxford: Oxford University Press.

Diani, Mario, and Ivan Bison. 2004. "Organizations, Coalitions and Movements." *Theory and Society* 33: 281–309.

Dikeç, Mustafa. 2005. "Space, Politics, and the Political." *Environment and Planning D* 23 (2): 171–88.

———. 2004. "Voices into Noises: Ideological Determination of Unarticulated Justice Movements." *Space and Polity* 8 (2): 191–208.

Durand, Jorge, and Douglas Massey. 2003. "The Cost of Contradiction: US Border Policy, 1996–2000." *Latino Studies* 1 (1): 233–52.

Duyvendak, Jan Willem. 2012. "Het kinderpardon roept veel vragen op." http://www.trouw.nl/tr/nl/6704/Sociale-Vraagstukken/article/detail/3118352/2012/01/12/Het-kinderpardon-roept-veel-vragen-op.dhtml.

————. 2011. *The Politics of Home: Belonging and Nostalgia in Europe and the United States*. Basingstoke, UK: Palgrave.

Elias, Norbert. 1996. *The Germans. Power Struggles and the Development of Habitus in the 19th and 20th Centuries*. Cambridge: Polity Press.

————. 1994. *The Established and the Outsider*. London: Sage.

Fainstein, Susan. 2010. *The Just City*. Ithaca, NY: Cornell University Press.

Fassin, Didier. 2012. *Humanitarian Reason: A Moral History of the Present*. Berkeley: University of California Press.

Favell, Adrian. 2009. "Immigration, Migration, and Free Movement in the Making of Europe." In *European Identity*, edited by Jeffrey Checkel and Peter Katzenstein, 167–92. Cambridge: Cambridge University Press.

————. 1998. "The Europeanisation of Immigrant Politics." *European Integration Online Papers* 2 (10): 1–19.

Fernandez-Kelly, Patricia, and Douglas Massey. 2007. "Borders for Whom? The Role of NAFTA in Mexico-U.S. Migration." *The Annals of the American Academy of Political and Social Science* 610: 98–118.

Fine, Gary. 1995. "Public Narration and Group Culture: Discerning Discourse in Social Movements." In *Social Movement and Cultures,* edited by Hank Johnston and Bert Klandermans, 127–43. Minneapolis: University of Minnesota Press.

Fraser, Nancy. 1991. "Rethinking the Public Sphere: A Contribution to the Critique of Actually Existing Democracy." In *Habermas and the Public Sphere*, edited by Craig Calhoun, 109–41. Cambridge, MA: MIT Press.

Freeman, Gary. 1995. "Modes of Immigration Politics in Liberal Democratic States." *International Migration Review* 29 (4): 881–902.

Foucault, Michel. 1982. "The Subject and Power." *Critical Inquiry* 8: 777–95.

————. 1980. *Power/Knowledge: Selected Interviews and Other Writings, 1972–1977*. Edited by Collin Gordon. New York: Pantheon Books.

————. 1978. *The History of Sexuality*, Volume I: *The Will to Knowledge*. London: Penguin.

————. 1976. *Discipline and Punish: The Birth of the Prison*. New York: Pantheon.

Gamson, William. 1988. "Political Discourse and Collective Action." In *International Social Movement Research: From Structure to Action*, edited by Bert Klandermans, Hanspeter Kriesi, and Sydney Tarrow, 219–44. Greenwich, CT: JAI Press.

Giugni, Marco, and Florence Passy. 2006. *La Citoyenneté en Débat: Mobilisations politiques en France et en Suisse.* Paris: L'Harmattan

————. 2004. "Migrant Mobilization Between Political Institutions and Citizenship Regimes: A Comparison of France and Switzerland." *European Journal of Political Research* 43: 51–82.

Goffman, Erving. 1959. *The Presentation of Self in Everyday Life*. New York: Doubleday.

Gonzalez, Roberto. 2011. "Learning to Be Illegal: Undocumented Youth and Shifting Legal Contexts in the Transition to Adulthood." *American Sociological Review* 76 (4): 602–19.

Gonzalez, Roberto, and Leo Chavez. 2012. "'Awakening to a Nightmare': Abjectivity and Illegality in the Lives of Undocumented 1.5–Generation Latino Immigrants in the United States." *Current Anthropology* 53 (3): 255–81.

Gould, Roger. 1995. *Activist Identities: Class, Community, and Protest in Paris from 1848 to the Commune.* Chicago: University of Chicago Press.

Gramsci, Antonio. 1971. *Prison Notebooks.* New York: International Publishers.

Granovetter Mark. 1983. "The Strength of Weak Ties: A Network Theory Revisited." *Sociological Theory* 1: 201–33.

———. 1973. "The Strength of Weak Ties." *The American Journal of Sociology* 78 (5): 1360–80.

Guarnizo, Luis, and Michael Peter Smith. 1998. *Transnationalism from Below.* New Brunswick, NJ: Transaction Publishers.

Hajer, Martin. 2005. "Coalitions, Practices and Meaning in Environmental Politics." In *Discourse Theory and European Politics,* edited by David Howarth and Jacob Torfing, 297–314. London: Palgrave.

Hardt, Michael, and Antonio Negri. 2009. *Commonwealth.* Cambridge, MA: Harvard University Press.

Hirschman, Alberto. 1970. *Exit, Voice, and Loyalty: Responses to Decline in Firms, Organizations, and States.* Cambridge, MA: Harvard University Press.

Holley, Michael. 2000. "Disadvantaged by Design: How the Law Inhibits Agricultural Guest Workers from Enforcing their Rights." *Hofstra Labor and Employment Law Journal:* 573—621.

Hondegneu-Sotelo, Pierette. 1994. "Regulating the Unregulated?: Domestic Workers' Social Networks." *Social Problems* 41 (1): 50–64.

Honig, Bonnie. 2006. *Democracy and the Foreigner.* Princeton, NJ: Princeton University Press.

Hopkins, Daniel. 2008. "Politicized Places: Explaining Where and When Immigrants Provoke Local Opposition." *American Political Science Review* 104 (1): 40–60.

Huntington, Samuel. 2004. "The Hispanic Challenge." *Foreign Policy* (March–April), http://www.foreignpolicy.com/articles/2004/03/01/the_hispanic_challenge.

"Illegal Border Crossings Dip, and Official Cites Security." *New York Times,* August 24, 2006.

Ireland, Patrick. 1994. *The Policy Challenge of Ethnic Diversity: Immigrant Politics in France and Switzerland.* Cambridge, MA: Harvard University Press.

Isin, Engin. 2000. *Democracy, Citizenship and the Global City.* New York: Routledge.

Iskander, Natasha. 2007. "Informal Work and Protest: Undocumented Immigrant Activism in France, 1996–2000." *British Journal of Industrial Relations* 45 (2): 309–34.

Jasper, James . 2010. "Strategic Marginalizations, Emotional Marginalities: The Dilemma of Stigmatized Identities." In *Surviving Against Odds,* edited by Debal Singha Roy, 29–37. New Delhi: Manohar Publishers and Distributors.

———. 1998. "The Emotions of Protest: Affective and Reactive Emotions in and Around Social Movements." *Sociological Forum* 13 (3): 397–424.

———. 1997. *The Art of Moral Protest.* Chicago: University of Chicago Press.

Joppke, Christian. 2007. "Beyond National Models: Civic Integration Policies for Immigrants in Western Europe." *West European Politics* 30 (1): 1–22.

———. 1999. *Immigration and the Nation-state: The United States, Germany, and Great Britain.* New York: Oxford University Press.

Kaldor, Mary. 1999. "Transnational Civil Society." In *Human Rights in Global Politics,* edited by Tim Dunne and Nicholas J. Wheeler, 195–213. Cambridge: Cambridge University Press.

Koopmans, Ruud, and Paul Statham. 1999. "Political Claims Analysis: Integrating Protest Event and Political Discourse Approaches." *Mobilization* 4 (1): 203–21.

Koopmans, Ruud, Paul Statham, Marco Giugni, and Florence Passy. 2005. *Contested Citizenship: Immigration and Cultural Diversity in Europe.* Minneapolis: University of Minneapolis Press.

LaMarche, Gara. 2010. "A Growing Drumbeat from Activists Energizes Drive for Urgent Immigration Reform." www.atlanticphilanthropies.org/.

Landa, Manuel. 2006. *New Philosophy of Society: Assemblage Theory and Social Complexity.* New York: Continuum Books.

Laubenthal, Barbara. 2007. "The Emergence of Pro-Regularization Movements in Western Europe." *International Migration* 45 (3): 101–33.

Lipsky, Martin. 1980. *Street-level Bureaucracy: Dilemmas of the Individual in Public Services.* New York: Russell Sage Foundation.

Mann, Michael. 1993. *Sources of Social Power,* Volume II: *The Rise of Classes and Nation-states, 1760–1914.* Cambridge: Cambridge University Press.

———. 1986. *The Resources of Social Power: A History of Power from the Beginning to A.D. 1760.* Vol. 1. Cambridge: Cambridge University Press.

Massey, Douglas, and Karen Pren. 2012. "Unintended Consequences of US Immigration Policy: Explaining the Post-1965 Surge from Latin America." *Population and Development Review* 38 (1): 1–29.

McAdam, Douglas. 1999. *Political Process and the Development of Black Insurgency, 1930–1970.* 2d ed. Chicago: University of Chicago Press.

McAdam, Douglas, Sydney Tarrow, and Charles Tilly. 2001. *Dynamics of Contention.* New York: Cambridge University Press.

Menjívar, Cecilia. 2006. "Liminal Legality: Salvadoran and Guatemalan Immigrants' Lives in the United States." *American Journal of Sociology* 111 (4): 999–1037.

———. 1997. "Immigrant Kinship Networks and the Impact of the Receiving Context: Salvadorans in San Francisco in the Early 1990s." *Social Problem* 44 (1) 104–23.

Milkman, Ruth. 2006. *L.A. Story: Immigrant Workers and the Future of the U.S. Labor Movement.* New York: Russell Sage Foundation.

Miller, Byron. 2000. *Geography and Social Movements: Comparing Antinuclear Activism in the Boston Area.* Minneapolis: University of Minnesota Press.

Money, Jeannette. 1999. *Fences and Neighbors: The Political Geography of Immigration Control.* Ithaca, NY: Cornell University Press.

Mouffe, Chantel. 1992. *Dimensions of Radical Democracy: Pluralism, Citizenship, Community.* London: Verso.

Nevins, Joel. 2002. *Operation Gatekeeper: The Rise of the "Illegal Alien" and the Making of the U.S.-Mexico Boundary.* New York: Routledge.

Ngai, Mae. 2004. *Impossible Subjects: Illegal Aliens and the Making of Modern America.* Princeton, NJ: Princeton University Press.

Nicholls, Walter. 2012. "Fragmenting Citizenship: Dynamics of Cooperation and Conflict in France's Immigrant Rights Movement." *Ethnic and Racial Studies.* http://dx.doi.org/10.1080/01419870.2011.626055.

———. 2009 "Place, Relations, Networks: The Geographical Foundations of Social Movements." *Transactions of the Institute of British Geographers* 34 (1): 78–93.

———. 2008. "The Urban Question Revisited: The Importance of Cities for Social Movements." *International Journal of Urban and Regional Research* 32 (4): 1468–2427.

Olivas, Michael. 2010. "The Political Economy of the DREAM Act and the Legislative Process: A Cases Study of Comprehensive Immigration Reform." *The Wayne Law Review* 55: 1757–1810.

Ong, Aihwa. 1999. *Flexible Citizenship: The Cultural Logics of Transnationality.* Durham, NC: Duke University Press.

———. 1996. "Cultural Citizenship as Subject Making: Immigrants Negotiate Racial and Cultural Boundaries in the United States." *Current Anthropology* 37 (5): 737–51.

Pallares, Amalia, and Nilda Flores-González, eds. 2010. *¡Marcha! Latino Chicago and the Immigrant Rights Movement.* Urbana: University of Illinois Press.

Passel, Jeffrey, and D'Vera Cohen. 2009. "A Portrait of Unauthorized Immigrants in the United States." Pew Research Center, Washington, DC.

Passeron, J. P., and C. Grignon. 1989. *Le Savant et le Populaire. Misérabilisme et populisme en sociologie et en littérature.* Paris: Seuil.

Péchu, Cecile. 2004. *Du Comité des Mal Logés au Droit au Logement, Sociologie d'une Mobilisation.* PhD diss., Institute d'Etudes Politiques de Paris.

Perez, Jonathan, Jorge Guitierrez, Nancy Meza, and Neidi Dominguez. 2010. "DREAM Movement: Challenges with the Social Justice Elite's Military Option Arguments and the Immigration Reform 'Leaders.'" *Dissent.* http://archive.truthout.org/dream-movement-challenges-with-social-justice-elites-military-option-arguments-and-immigration-refo.

Pérez, William. 2009. *We Are Americans: Undocumented Students Pursuing the American Dream.* Sterling, VA: Stylus Publishing.

Piven, Frances, and Richard Cloward. 1979. *Poor People's Movements.* New York: Vintage.

Polletta, Francesca. 2006. *It Was Like a Fever: Storytelling in Protest and Politics.* Chicago: University of Chicago Press.

———. 1998. "Contending Stories: Narrative in Social Movements." *Qualitative Methods* 21 (4): 419–46.

Portes, Alejandro, and James Sensenbrenner. 1993. "Embeddedness and Immigration: Notes on the Social Determination of Economic Action." *American Journal of Sociology* 98: 1320–50.

Raissiguier, Catherine. 2010. *Re-Inventing the Republic: Gender, Migration, and Citizenship in France.* Stanford: Stanford University Press.

Rancière, Jacques. 2007. "What Does it Mean to Be *Un?*" *Continuum: Journal of Media and Cultural* Studies 21 (4): 559–69.

———. 1999. *Dis-agreement: Politics and Philosophy.* Minneapolis: University of Minnesota Press.

———. 1993. "Early French Socialism: Ways to Construct Social Identity." *Labour History Review* 58 (3): 8–13.

———. 1992. "Politics, Identification, and Subjectivization." *October* 61: 58–64.

Routledge, Paul. 2003. "Convergence Space: Process Geographies of Grassroots Globalisation Networks." *Transactions of the Institute of British Geographers* 28 (3): 333–49.

Schain, Martin. 1999. "Minorities and Immigrant Incorporation in France: The State and the Dynamics of Multiculturalism." *Multicultural Questions* 26: 199–224.

Seif, Hinda. 2004. "'Wise Up!' Undocumented Latino Youth, Mexican-American Legislators, and the Struggle for Higher Education Access." *Latino Studies* 2: 210–30.

Siméant, Johanna. 1998. *La Cause des Sans-Papiers.* Paris: Presses Sciences-Po.

Sites, William, and Rebecca Vonderlack-Navarro. 2012. "Tipping the Scale: State Rescaling and the Strange Odyssey of Chicago's Mexican Hometown Associations." In *Remaking Urban Citizenship: Organizations, Institutions, and the Right to the City,* edited by Michael Peter Smith and Michael McQuarrie, 151–71. New Brunswick, NJ: Transactions Publishers.

Smith, Michael Peter. 2003. "Transnationalism, the State, and the Extraterritorial Citizen." *Politics and Society* 31 (4): 467–502.

Snow, David, and Robert Benford. 1988. "Ideology, Frame Resonance, and Participant Mobilization." In *International Social Movement Research: From Structure to Action,* edited by Bert Klandermans, Hanspeter Kriesi, and Sydney Tarrow, 197–217. Greenwich, CT: JAI Press.

Soja, Edward. 2010. *Seeking Spatial Justice.* Minneapolis: University of Minnesota Press.

Soysal, Yasemin. 2000. "Citizenship and Identity: Living Diasporas in Post-war Europe? *Ethnic and Racial Studies* 23 (1): 1–15.

———. 1994. *Limits of Citizenship: Migrants and Postnational Membership in Europe.* Chicago: University of Chicago Press.

Storper, Michael. 1997. *The Regional World: Territorial Development in a Global Economy.* New York and London: Guilford Press.

Tilly, Charles. 2005. *Trust and Rule.* Cambridge: Cambridge University Press.

———. 2004. *Social Movements, 1768–2004.* Boulder, CO: Paradigm Publishers.

Uitermark, Justus, and Walter Nicholls. 2012. "How Local Networks Shape a Global Movement: Comparing Occupy Mobilizations in Amsterdam and Los Angeles." *Social Movement Studies* 11 (3–4): 295–301.

Valenzuela, Abel. 2003. "Day-Labor Work." *Annual Review of Sociology* 29 (1): 307–33.

Van der Leun, Joanne. 2006. "Excluding Illegal Migrants in the Netherlands: Between National Politics and Local Implementation." *West European Politics* 29: 310–26.

Varsanyi, Monica. 2008. "Rescaling the 'Alien,' Rescaling Personhood: Neoliberalism, Immigration, and the State." *Annals of the Association of American Geographers* 98 (4): 877–89.

Voss, Kim, and Irene Bloemraad. 2011. *Rallying for Immigrants: The Fight for Inclusion in 21st Century America.* Berkeley: University of California Press.

Wacquant, Loic. 2005. "Symbolic Power in the Rule of the 'State Nobility.'" In *Pierre Bourdieu and Democratic Politics,* edited by Loic Wacquant, 133–50. London: Polity.

Wadhia, Shoba. 2010. "The Role of Prosecutorial Discretion in Immigration Law." *Connecticut Public Interest Law Journal* 9 (2): 243–99.

Wahnich, Sophie. 1997. *L'impossible citoyen. L'impossible citoyen l'étranger dans le discours de la révolution française.* Paris: Albin Michel.

Walker, Kyle, and Helga Leitner. 2011. "The Variegated Landscape of Local Immigration Policies in the United States." *Urban Geography* 32 (2): 156–78.

Waters, Malcolm. 1996. "Human Rights and the Universalisation of Interests." *Sociology* 30 (3): 593–600.

Weber, Max. 1958. *From Max Weber: Essays in Sociology.* Edited by H. H. Gerth and C. Wright Mills. New York: Knopf Press.

Wimmer, Andreas, and Nina Glick Schiller. 2002. "Methodological Nationalism and Beyond: Nation-state Building, Migration and Social Sciences." *Global Networks* 2 (4): 301–34.

Wright, Erik Olin. 2010. *Envisioning Real Utopias.* London: Verso.

Zolberg, Aristide. 1999. "Matters of State." In *The Handbook of International Migration: The American Experience,* edited by Charles Hirschman, Peter Kasinitz, and Josh De Wind, 71–93. New York: Russell Sage Foundation.

Interviews Conducted During Research

California Dream Network

Organizer 1

Organizer 2

Organizer 3

Organizer 4

Organizer 5

Organizer 6

Organizer 7

Organizer 8

Former Director (also at the Center for Humane Immigrant Rights of Los Angeles [CHIRLA])

Central American Resource Center
Director

Dream Team Los Angeles
Organizer 1
Organizer 2
Organizer 3
Organizer 4
Organizer 5
Organizer 6
Organizer 7
Organizer 8
Organizer 9
Organizer 10

Dreamers Adrift
Artist

Hermandad Mexicana Latinoamericana / Mexican American Political Association
Director

Improving Dream, Equality, Access, and Success, University of California Los Angeles (DREAMS UCLA)
Organizer 1
Organizer 2

Inland Empire Dream Team
Organizer 1

Instituto de Educacion Popular del Sur de California (IDEPSCA; Institute of Popular Education of Southern California)
Director

National Day Laborer Organizing Network (NDLON)
Director

Orange County Dream Team
Organizer 1

San Fernando Dream Team
Organizer 1

San Gabriel Valley Dream Team
Organizer 1

Southern California Immigrant Rights Coalition (SCIRC)
Director

United We Dream
Former Organizer

University of Los Angeles California, Labor Center
Director
Project Director

Index

A.B. 130, 150
A.B. 131, 150–51
A.B. 540, 150–51, 195n77
Activism, 4–5; RIFA response to, 86–88
Advocacy, 12–13
African Americans, 133, 164
AFL-CIO, 83–84
Alabama, 138–39, 147, 162, 163, 169, 193n31
Aliens: characterization as, 8
Alto Arizona, 161
Americans for Immigration Control, 23
American Southwest: reconquest, 24
Amnesty, opposition to, 38
Anchor babies, 24
Antienforcement campaigns, 154–56, 172, 203n20; in Arizona, 161–63; criminalization as frame for, 157–58; in Georgia, 163–64; NDLON, 158–59
Anti-immigrant advocacy, 11, 20, 21, 23, 40, 50; political, 25–26; rights and, 168–69
Anti-Secure Communities coalition, 155, 158–59
Arizona, 143, 169; antienforcement campaigns in, 161–63; border crossers in, 26–27; DREAMer activism, 1, 85, 90; S.B. 1070, 28, 44–45, 78–79, 147, 193n31
Arrests, 138–39, 152
Assimilation, 15, 20, 23–24, 50, 56
Asylum-seekers, 30–31

Atlantic Philanthropies, 43
Attrition through enforcement, 25, 147, 169
Autonomy, 84, 114, 141

Barrio Defense Committees, 162
Beck, Roy, 21
Bernstein, Joshua, 32, 44
Blogs, 68, 69
Border crossers: death rates, 26–27
Border Patrol, 26
Border Protection, Anti-terrorism and Illegal Immigration Control Act, 37, 165
Border security, 10, 25, 26, 34, 35, 45, 194nn50, 51; focus on, 36–38
Boycott: of Arizona, 79, 162
Bush, George W., 33, 145; border security, 36–37; immigration reform, 22, 36, 38–40, 42

Cal Grant program, 151
California, 20, 26, 160, 203n12; A.B. 540, 150–51, 195n77; demonstrations in, 49–50; DREAMers in, 18, 107, 144; Dream Teams in, 109–10, 112–14; in-state tuition, 146, 195n77; organizations, 61–62; Proposition 187, 25–26, 49–50, 193n15
California Dream Network, 52, 58, 82, 88–89, 107–8, 111, 151; on college campuses, 70, 71, 89; messages of,

Made in the USA
Lexington, KY
28 February 2015